Through My Gift

FRANCES SCHERVIER

THROUGH MY GIFT

The Life of
FRANCES SCHERVIER

By
THEODORE MAYNARD

"What is mine through Thy gift,
let it be Thine through my gift."

Written in FRANCES SCHERVIER'S NOTEBOOK, 1867

New York
P. J. KENEDY & SONS

Nihil Obstat: Rev. Thomas W. Smiddy, S.T.D. *Censor Librorum*
Imprimatur: ✠ THOMAS B. MOLLOY, S.T.D. *Bishop of Brooklyn*

Brooklyn, N.Y.
April 16, 1951

In conformity to the Decree of Pope Urban VIII, the author un-
reservedly submits all statements herein to the judgments of the
Holy See and the decisions of the Sacred Congregation of Rites.

To

KATHERINE D. SHEEHAN

Contents

Through My Gift

The Background

AACHEN, known to the French as Aix-la-Chapelle, the birthplace of Frances Schervier, is one of the oldest of German cities. If Cologne, Roman outpost on the Rhine originally named Colonia Agrippina for the odious Nero's equally detestable mother, soon overshadowed its neighbor to the west, Aachen came to achieve a kind of primacy as the city of Charlemagne, who was probably born there. Vitellius and Trajan were proclaimed Roman Emperors and Clovis the King of the Franks, but in Aachen no less than 37 emperors of the later Holy Roman Empire were crowned.

Charlemagne's highly uncomfortable throne may still be seen in the *dom*, or cathedral, he had built. Under this throne is an opening through which (so it is said) his vassals had to crawl on hands and knees as a token of submission. In the *dom* Charlemagne was buried in a sitting position. It was only in fairly recent times that his bones were discovered, and they are now preserved in the armoire of the cathedral, where hangs his candelabra. It was at Aachen, according to the *Song of Roland*, that Bramimunde, the Queen of the Saracens, was baptized after the battle of Roncesvalles under the new name of Juliana. This of course is pure fiction. The Saracens had no part in that battle, which involved only the cutting off and extermination of the rear guard of Charlemagne's army by the Basques, traditional enemies of the Franks. So also it is probably legendary that the Emperor was summoned in sleep to new wars by an angel, and groaned, "My life is hard indeed!" But if these legends give an added aura to Aachen, the ascertainable facts of history are wonderful enough. Though long before the early nineteenth century it had dwindled into somnolence, it was full of the kind of memories of the past that are a powerful stimulus to anyone with imagination.

The city was (and is) surrounded by an almost circular wall and lies in a cup of gently sloping, wooded hills. But it has long since spread out beyond its ancient fortifications which were partially damaged in the Second World War, though not by any means to the extent that Cologne has done so. It has some very old houses, though fewer than might be expected. Its principal architectural glory is the cathedral begun by Charlemagne and added to at various times (and in various styles) during the Middle Ages. The cathedral was relatively little damaged in the recent war, but the *Rathaus,* or town hall, on the site of Charlemagne's palace, which was a really magnificent specimen of what the fourteenth century was capable of erecting, was devastated.

The Schervier home, adjoining the Schervier needle factory, is illustrative in masonry of the city's history. Part of it had been a house used during the Middle Ages by a neighboring abbot when he had occasion to be in Aachen. Yet one would have to look hard for vestiges of antiquity, for the general impression presented is one of modernity in a utilitarian and rather unattractive mood. The compensation was that it was more comfortable than most of the surviving Gothic structures.

Cologne and Aachen had in many ways a common destiny. Cologne, which at first was hardly more than a kind of distant suburb of Aachen, grew in strength while Aachen slumbered. Cologne's cathedral, much more recently built than the *dom* of its neighbor — for it had been started in 1248 and was not quite completed until 1880 — is not only one of the grandest edifices of Christendom but has what purports to be the relics of the Magi. Similarly the Church of St. Gereon, heavily damaged in the war, boasts the bones of the martyred Theban Legion, while another church, St. Ursula's, claims the bones of its patroness and the 11,000 British virgins who are supposed to have been slaughtered with her. St. Ursula may repose there, but the number of her companions has been shown to be due to a copyist's error, or to a misreading of an early manuscript. On the other hand, since the relics at Aachen are more anciently bestowed, they are in all likelihood more authentic than some of those at Cologne. For they go back to Charlemagne, who received them from the Popes of his time, Hadrian I and Leo III, and from the Patriarchs of Jerusalem and Constantinople. They include the swaddling clothes with which Our Lord was wrapped in the manger and the loincloth He wore on the Cross, the robe of the Blessed Virgin, and the linen sheet on which the body of St. John the Baptist was laid after his beheading by Herod. Only once in seven years are they displayed, after which they are sewn into silken coverings and locked away in a silver-gilt casket until the time arrives for the next exposition. On that occasion a famous statue of Our Lady is carried in procession. Its antiquity (to judge from photographs) is not very great, but still inspires immense popular enthusiasm. This statue possesses nearly 40 dresses and is credited with being the medium of many miracles.

The diocese of Aachen was originally established in 1801, but was suppressed 20 years later, and not re-established until 1930; however, its cathedral was always referred to as the Aachenerdom, even while under the jurisdiction of Cologne. During the last hundred years the city had doubled its population and so was entitled to ecclesiastical autonomy. Whatever may be the situation today, at the beginning of the nineteenth century over 80 percent of its inhabitants were Catholics, a considerably higher proportion than Cologne could claim. Though the Catholics of Aachen, as will appear, were not all of them what they should have been, a strong Catholic tone prevailed. The vigor of the city's spiritual life is revealed by the remarkable fact that almost simultaneously three new religious congregations were founded there, all by young women who had been at school together. One of these, Frances Schervier, is the subject of this book.

Though not actually in the Rhine valley, Aachen partakes of the general character of the Rhineland. From Aachen to Cologne, about 50 miles away, stretch farmlands, and only further south do the celebrated vineyards begin. It was roughly from Düsseldorf in the north to Coblenz in the south — a strip of not much more than a hundred miles along the Rhine — that Frances found her field of action, until an apparent accident brought the United States into her orbit.

Vast ravages had been wrought both at Cologne and Aachen in the French Revolutionary Wars, and in 1801 the small feudal states west of the Rhine were annexed by France, which held the area until 1814–15, when most of the states were incorporated into Prussia. In 1819, when Frances * Schervier was born, though recovery had begun, Aachen still showed many scars. Yet Frances's father, John Henry Casper Schervier, was one of the most prosperous and respected of its citizens, the assistant burgomaster, and the owner of a flourishing factory. This factory indeed must have been regarded as one of the most interesting things to be seen in the city, from the industrial point of view, for when the Czar of Russia, the King of France, and the Emperor of Austria met at Aachen in conference at the end of 1818, the Emperor made it a special visit.

Francis II was the last emperor of the so-called Holy Roman Empire, which was formally dissolved after Napoleon routed the Austrians and the Russians in the battle of Austerlitz on December 2, 1805. He found it prudent to renounce

---

* In German, Franziska. The English forms of German baptismal names will be used throughout this book.

4

the old imperial title and be content to be known as Francis I, the Emperor of Austria, a title he had assumed in 1804. It was his young daughter Marie Louise whom Napoleon married after discarding Josephine, and she was the mother of the unfortunate King of Rome. By 1818 the world was of course free of the Corsican upstart, finally put under restraint at St. Helena, and Europe could now be remodelled, which meant restoring it, as far as possible, to its former shape. This was why the monarchs had met in Aachen in 1818. But as the spirit of the Confederation of the Rhine was still very much alive, there could be no question of Francis's resuming his old grandiose title.

Although the Emperor visited the Schervier factory, he probably did not have an overpowering interest in the manufacture of needles; he was intending, it may be supposed, to show a courtesy to a very ancient family, not one of aristocratic pretensions or immense wealth, but nevertheless a family of solid social standing. The research of Dr. Joseph Gerard Rey, the son of one of the cousins of our Frances, shows that the name Schervier,* though it has a somewhat French look, is actually of pure Germanic origin. Dr. Rey, in his sumptuously printed book, full of the most recondite sort of German scholarship, traces it back to a lawyer named William Schaldir, who died in 1150. He proves fairly conclusively that the Schervier coat of arms, which had once been taken to represent an eagle, really exhibits a dove with a twig in its claws. In 1292 the name is found in the official records of Aachen, by that time as Scherviel. This Scherviel, who died about 1304, had no direct descendants, but there is evidence that he was of the same family stock as Reimarus Schervier, brother of the Governor William Schervier who built Servielsburg, a manor in the territory of Aachen. During the fifteenth and sixteenth centuries various members of the family were tenants of the canons in the city. Although the family almost died out, it revived during the

* It is pronounced Sher-veer.

eighteenth century, when we find Scherviers conducting copperworks in Aachen, an industry so prominent at that time that in 1752 its guild numbered 162 members with 154 apprentices.

Frances's grandfather, John Gerard Schervier, had a copper factory on Pontstrasse, which he conducted with his father-in-law, Peter Thielen, until the latter died in 1796 in his eighty-fifth year. Four of this Schervier's 10 children were living in Frances's time, the last of them dying in 1856 at the age of eighty-eight. The factory he established at the corner of Templergraben and Eilfschornsteinstrasse was, so Dr. Rey tells us, still existing when he published his book in 1936. John Gerard seems to have specialized in the manufacture of brass lanterns which, suspended on chains running from side to side, were used in lighting the streets. That product alone gave him an assured income. His lanterns were also found in almost every house and were carried at night by such people as priests and doctors when they answered their calls. And his three-footed coffee pots, his warming pans, his ornate fireplaces, candlesticks, and candelabra, breadbaskets, bird cages, and ornamental door knockers — mostly figures of angels or lions' heads — were much in demand. Even his casserole dishes were well moulded, with simple designs. These articles may have been less profitable than his lanterns, but they provided him with an outlet for his ingenuity and therefore gave him satisfaction. He did well in spite of the invading French. But with their arrival he retired from the office of Councillor, and in 1807 from business. When, six years later, he and his wife Elizabeth celebrated their golden wedding anniversary, they were surrounded by a posterity that included 27 grandchildren and one great-grandchild. He died in 1826, at the age of eighty-three. It is evident that the Scherviers were a sturdy stock; whatever physical weakness came into Frances's immediate family was brought there by her mother.

One of John Gerard's sons, John Joseph, was a city councillor, and with his brother, the father of our Frances, entered into partnership with two French brothers named Migeon in establishing a needle factory at 664 (the present 15) Eilf-schornsteinstrasse. John Henry Casper Schervier, Frances's father, eventually became sole owner of this business. One of John Joseph's sons, Gerard (1821–1892), became a doctor. He was in close association with his cousin Frances when her life work began. Gerard was a man of such piety that he never failed to attend five o'clock Mass throughout the week, unless he was prevented by sick calls. He never married and lived more like a monk than a physician.

John Henry Casper Schervier, the younger son of John Gerard and his wife Elizabeth, was born on January 5, 1784, and on May 28, 1807, married Maria Gertrude Teresa Priem, a girl of 20 who died the following year, leaving him with a daughter, Maria Elizabeth, two months old. On March 13, 1811, he remarried, this time taking as his bride Marie Louise Victoire Migeon, a sister of the two Frenchmen with whom he and his brother had started their needle factory. She was born in 1781 at Charleville in the Ardennes. During the French Revolution the Migeons were imprisoned, and had Robespierre not fallen it is likely that all of them except this child would have been sent to the guillotine. It was in prison that Louise Victoire made her First Communion. Control of the prisoners was lax and haphazard; when the first Bishop of Vincennes, Indiana, the charming and eccentric Simon Bruté, was a boy during the Revolution, he used to accompany the priests who slipped into the prisons, ostensibly to sell bread but actually to administer the Eucharist under cover of the loud bargaining that went on. Perhaps it was under somewhat similar circumstances that Frances's mother for the first time received the Sacrament.

Maria Elizabeth, the only child of Herr Schervier's first marriage, was married on August 15, 1830, to Paul Christian Thywissen, and died 10 years later. Her husband lived until 1879, when he died at the age of seventy-four. Of their four children only one reached maturity, and this one, a daughter named Henrietta, had two grandchildren who were still alive in 1936, one of them a Religious of the Sacred Heart in Holland.

There are no living descendants from John Henry Casper Schervier's second marriage. Two daughters died young; two became nuns; the youngest son became a priest; the eldest, Henry, married twice and lived — the only one of his mother's children to do so — to a ripe old age (he died in 1896), but had no children by either wife. Though from the Schervier relatives of Frances's time there are a number of collateral descendants, the direct line became extinct.

So excellent a stepmother was the second Frau Schervier that Maria Elizabeth did not discover until her own marriage that Louise Victoire was not her real mother. The fact that her own children had not been informed about the relationship would seem to indicate something close-lipped and cautious about Frau Schervier, but this we may attribute to her husband's injunctions, because everything known of Louise Victoire indicates a lively and expansive temperament. Unfortunately she brought tuberculosis into the family, and the disease carried off herself and all of her children except Frances and Henry. Not much was known about the treatment of tuberculosis in those days.

What should be grasped at the outset is that Aachen was a very Catholic city, that the Schervier connections were numerous (and all pious), and that the most pious family of all was that into which Frances had been born. Frances's sister Pauline joined her congregation, and her brother Karl became a priest and served as a teacher of religion in the schools of Aachen, being therefore styled "Herr Professor." Even if all the Scherviers did not aspire to sanctity, they were at least good people, devout, loyal Catholics — solid, if also perhaps a little stolid. Here was a family group which did not seem likely to set the world on fire, but upon the fire, once started, it would throw a good many useful fagots.

At the time that the Emperor of Austria was visiting her husband's needle factory, Frau Schervier was expecting her fifth child. The Scherviers' social position was respectable, and the Migeons were aristocratic enough to embolden Louise Victoire to ask — possibly in reply to some gallant question of the Emperor's as to what he could do for her — that he should stand as godfather to her baby when it should be born. Here was an impulsive woman, possibly one who was a bit aghast at her own temerity. But that she could venture to make such a request at all indicates her social standing.

The request was promptly granted, though it might have met with an evasive answer or even a rebuff. The Emperor was a highly efficient person inclined to be pedantic and sometimes rather cruel. But he was, of course, very much of a gentleman, and on the occasion of his visit to the Schervier factory, he was in an affable mood. He promised to be the godfather of the unborn child, named Frances for him after she came into the world on January 3rd of the new year 1819.

By that time the potentates had long since departed. But the sponsorship of the child was provided for by proxy. In Aachen there lived a well-born and wealthy ecclesiastic to whom the Emperor assigned this office. He was Canon Anthony William Deboeur, who doubtless already knew the Scherviers, if only slightly, but who was to become their intimate friend as he fell more and more under the charm of the little girl as she grew up. He even thought to make her his heiress and to spend his declining years under her care.

This was not to be: neither her father's wealth (which turned out to be much less than was supposed) nor the Canon's ever came to the Emperor's goddaughter. Instead the Providence of God drew her into an eagerly embraced poverty and a career of charity much more illustrious than wealth and social position could have given. The most that can be said is that the circumstances narrated above probably helped to frame in her an audacity of mind that was to fit her for the work she was called upon to do.

The Pious Child

THE TITLE of this chapter is perhaps not very appealing. So I say at once that a pious child is not at all the same thing as a pietistic child, by which I understand one a little too studied, too artificial, and too conscious of himself. An adult of this sort is obnoxious, and even though a pietistic child may be pardoned, he can still be rather distressing. But a pietistic child is not to be confused with one of genuine piety, who shows it sometimes charmingly, sometimes quaintly, but also sometimes a bit painfully. Childish make-believe (for with the pietistic it is mainly that) is the very last quality to be found in the later life of those who show themselves broad in their sympathies, deep in their insight, heroic in their exercise of the virtues. Though it may be true that the most genuine sort of religious sentiment in the very young goes through its awkward age, that period soon passes. If these observations should seem at times to fit the childhood of Frances Schervier, let them be accepted patiently for the moment. Here was a little girl who matured spiritually with astonishing rapidity, and while not always escaping some childish errors, she showed herself, while still only a child, valiant in the love of God. Frances assumed a woman's responsibilities long before she was a woman. Should there be in her earliest years anything that even slightly disturbs us, there is no need to take it too seriously, for even as we look at it we shall find it fading away.

Yet it is evident that there was an interim stage during which her excessive conscientiousness and the tensions and feelings of frustration that she had to undergo put her into a somewhat over-sensitive condition, which will be considered later. That too was a passing thing, and as such should not be stressed too much, though it cannot be completely ignored. There may be a good deal of significance in the fact that she played with her dolls long after the time when these are ordinarily discarded. It means, perhaps, that, unable as yet to give human beings all the love in her heart, she lavished it on these toys. As such it may have helped her maintain her balance through difficult years. She was not merely a normal little girl playing at being a mother, for such a girl soon enough leaves her dolls and occupies her thoughts with other matters. If Frances was to be a great mother, it was not in the usual sense. She took all the poor and suffering for her children. As she could not do anything for them at that time, she comforted her maternal instincts with her dolls.

Her upbringing was strict, even for that age. And one imagines that on the continent of Europe, domestic discipline was more severe than it was in early nineteenth-century England, and still more so than it was in the United States. The household was rigidly pious; possibilities for mischief or amusement were few, and these were guarded against in the Schervier household because of the abundance of servants. One of them was always deputed to accompany the children when they went outside the house, even to church, and to keep an eye on them at play. Children who visited the little Scherviers from other households — even the most respectable — saw them only in the presence of their father and mother. Such a system would now seem very repressive. Frances, as it happened, was released from it while she was still a young girl, and that stimulated in her independence and what might be described as adventurousness. But prior to that she had derived the opposite benefit, that of a careful training.

For this, as might be supposed, Frances's mother was mainly responsible. The mode of life — at least for the girls of that household — was French rather than German. Frau Schervier was a Frenchwoman and Frances's nurse a Walloon. They used French when talking to the girls. Indeed at this time Frances knew French better than German so acted as her mother's interpreter in giving orders to the servants or talking with callers.

It must not for a moment be supposed, however, that this life was at all unhappy. No one misses what it has never occurred to him to have. The household was united in close-knit affection and spent its days in the solid German comfort in which kindliness had its part. There were many little special festivals — more so, perhaps, than with us. If Christmas did not then have its modern (but largely artificial and commercialized) importance, there was its equivalent on the eve of December 6th, the Feast of St. Nicholas of Bari — now transmogrified beyond recognition as Santa Claus. Then he arrived, not driving through the sky in a sleigh and climbing down a chimney, but riding on a donkey. Hay had to be spread out in front of the house to make that donkey stop; then the gifts Santa Claus brings now were laid out in a brightly lighted room for the children to find on the morrow.

When Frances was ready to go to school she attended, as a day student, St. Leonard's Institute, which must have had classes corresponding to our grades as well as courses that would belong to our high schools. As girls of the more well-to-do categories of society were, at that time, never expected to earn their own living, the curriculum was more "literary" and less practical than it is today.

The school was conducted, not by nuns, but by a Madame Nicolay and had as its chief ornament a rather remarkable teacher in the person of Louisa Hensel, a convert, daughter of a Lutheran minister. She had some reputation as a poet and a great faculty for imparting knowledge and impressing herself upon her charges.

As only the higher classes were taught by Fräulein Hensel and she left the school in 1832, it is not likely that she gave Frances much if any formal instruction. But her influence over Frances, as over the whole school, was strongly felt. She was not only a brilliant teacher, capable of making any subject come alive with interest, but also a woman of deep piety. About 20 of her pupils became nuns, and three of them — Clara Fey, Pauline von Mallinckrodt, and Frances Schervier herself — each founded a new religious congregation. Much must be credited to their mentor, but their vocations also reveal something of the tone of Catholic life in Aachen.

Louisa Hensel made a great point of awakening a love of poetry in her students. With this in mind, she obliged them to learn a poem a week, and inspired by her enthusiasm and fame, many of them were stimulated to write poetry themselves. Clara Fey, who was nearly four years older than Frances, emulated her teacher, with the result that many of the hymns she came to write are still sung in her Congregation, that of the Poor Child Jesus. Frances Schervier also wrote a good deal of verse in her spare moments. She might, of course, have done so without any prompting from Louisa Hensel, but it would seem safe to infer the influence of the teacher here.

Frances continued with this versifying until comparatively late in life. Then she stopped at the suggestion of her confessor, who might have thought all writing of verse to be a waste of time or who might have realized that Frances's versifying, while fluent and sensitive, showed no very high degree of creative power.

We do not hear of any very close association between Frances and her schoolmate, Pauline von Mallinckrodt, who founded a religious congregation whose distinctive work was for the blind. But we know that, especially as the disparity between her age and that of Clara lessened, Frances came to frequent the house of the Feys. There she came to be the friend of all five Fey children. Both Fey boys became priests, one a Redemptorist and the other the spiritual director of his sister's congregation; as such he was usually styled (German fashion) Director Doctor Fey. To their names must be added those of two cousins, who became Good Shepherd nuns under St. Euphrasia Pelletier at Angers, a refoundation of the work for fallen women begun in the seventeenth century by St. John Eudes. The Fey household, with its happy piety and its enthusiasm for every kind of good work, made a deep impression on Frances Schervier's mind. With all the Feys she had much to do during her later life.

What made the deepest impression on Frances, however, was a dream that came to her when she was nine, something that she records in her fragmentary autobiography but which, with her cool detached honesty, she would never so much as hint might have been a vision. In this dream she saw herself with other girls in the room of the headmistress, Madame Nicolay, when she was told by the portress that somebody was waiting to see her in the parlor. She wondered at this, for she had never had anyone call on her and was not expecting anyone to do so. Madame Nicolay told Frances to follow the portress, who led her down the corridor, opened the door of the parlor, and left her alone. There in the room stood Christ as a boy, beautiful and welcoming. She went up to Him without hesitation and they embraced, and as Frances leaned her face on His shoulder, weeping, with love and sorrow contending in her heart, she was filled with contrition for her sins. "My soul," she was to write, "was in a state of bitter sweetness and sweet bitterness; but strong as the sorrow was, the prevailing feeling was sweetness." Then the silence was broken by what sounded like dry leaves in the autumn wind. She knew somehow that these were her repented sins, swept away for ever. She has a reference to this dream in a poem, written long afterwards:

Deep within my heart I carry
Christ's dear image, strong impressed;
And the pangs of love it causes
Give my longing soul no rest.

In her autobiography she says she heard a Voice saying that through the love of Jesus all her sins were forgiven.

The immense contrition for her sins revealed by that incident will probably strike many people as rather exaggerated. It might be, though, that they count hardness of heart normal because it is the common condition. Since one cannot believe that Frances at this early age had been guilty of a sin of any seriousness, it must be assumed that the sensitivity of her conscience was part of her preparation for holiness. Father Ignatius Jeiler, her first biographer, gives it as his opinion that these temptations were, if not caused by excessive scrupulosity, at least intensified by it. The poor child must have worked herself into an overwrought condition when she dared not look at the most innocent picture — even one that represented a sacred object — for fear that it might suggest an impure thought. This was something that she outgrew completely, though she tells us that two or three times in later life, when she was debilitated by fever, images of a similar sort recurred, to be dealt with then with greater courage and more solid sense than she was able to muster as a child. Her scrupulosity was replaced by self-understanding and confidence in God. It is not so very strange that a little girl should have been terrified by her phantasms. While it is indeed desirable to avoid scrupulosity, that neurasthenia of the soul, there is no merit in treating small sins — and those of Frances must have been very small, if sins at all and not rather painful temptations — as of no account.

Looking back upon her childhood Frances was to write: "I perceive on my part a great inclination to evil, from which serious unfaithfulness resulted; and on the part of God inconceivable graces and proofs of His love." Father Jeiler, modi-

15

fying this as one experienced in the direction of souls and as a friend of Frances in her later years, says: "God took occasion, from the faults common to ignorance and thoughtlessness in childhood, to form in her a contrite and humble heart, the essential condition to receive future graces." He deals with these matters both with spiritual insight and common sense. In so far as there was scrupulosity, he deplores it, knowing that this can proliferate into an evil as great as the sins one has committed, or that one fancies one has committed. But since the scrupulosity, far from hardening into a settled habit in this case, was overcome, he extenuates it as due merely to inexperience and treats it as a stage in spiritual development that was in the end productive of good, because it prepared Frances for the work she was destined to do.

Considered in that light we may understand better Frances's compunction when one day, caressed and kissed by a seamstress who used to go frequently to the Schervier home, she let the good woman see all too plainly her distaste for this show of affection — though she admitted that the woman intended no harm. The seamstress was naturally hurt, but recovered from what seemed to her an unaccountable repulse, for it was this same woman, in years soon to arrive, who figured often as aide and abettor to Frances in her surreptitious deeds of charity. What the Italians call *casto pudore* was being manifested. Her early extreme sensitiveness about this was overcome; at any rate she transformed it into something strong, simple, and practical. At this point in her life it should be treated, along with her preoccupation with her "sinfulness," as being part of her preparation for the future.

If there was in her at this time any tendency that some people might consider a streak of melancholy, I should be inclined to find it in her sensitiveness rather than in that fantastic "suicide" project she entertained as a means of getting all the more quickly to heaven. Children are often very strange little creatures. Even St. Teresa of Avila, of whom Crashaw was to write, "She's for the Moors and martyrdom," but who became a rock of good sense, once ran away from home, when a little girl, in the hopeful expectation that she would be killed by the infidels. That was essentially suicidal and came a good deal closer to realization than Frances's musings along somewhat the same lines. Fortunately Frances confided her plan — that of drowning herself — to her brother Karl. Since he was three years older and better instructed, he managed to give a convincing explanation of why what was in her mind would be exceedingly wrong. She regretted that she had told him about it, for she believed that if she had actually killed herself, God would have recognized her good motive and taken her at once to Himself! The quaint, impetuous little moral theologian had at least enough good sense to admit that in Karl there spoke the voice of reason and of the moral law.

What Frances probably had more reason to reproach herself with — though here too her offences could not have been very grave — was her propensity to anger. She was a vivacious child, and as such the favorite of her vivacious French mother, and this perhaps meant (among other things) that she was quick tempered. But the only explosions we hear about — except for what she called "violent outbursts, especially towards my younger sister" — are the times when she found her teasing elder brothers too much for her. We all know how annoying boys can be in this way, even when they are not ill-natured, so we may condone the child's flashing into momentary rage against her tormentors and then, no doubt, giving them the satisfaction of seeing her burst into tears. As for her younger sister Pauline, some incidents recorded of her when she was a nun in Frances's Congregation suggest that she may well have often been provoking when a child.

If there ever was such a propensity in Frances it was completely conquered. But I suspect that, as in the case of the exceedingly sweet-tempered St. Francis de Sales, who accused himself of the same failing, there was some exaggeration. Vivacious St. Francis was to the end, and vivacious people, being highly strung, are prone to be somewhat sharp in retort, saying what sound like malicious things without malicious intent. In Frances Schervier, so far as her later life is concerned, it was seldom that she permitted herself much vivacity, perhaps in fear as to where it might inadvertently lead. Her habitual tone is one of mild serenity. Whatever inclination she had to irritation when her brothers passed all bearing or when Pauline was being intractable was certainly soon overcome. Frances herself says that as soon as she was aware of this fault she set herself to conquer it. It is not claimed that she was already perfect or that she ever reached perfection, unless perhaps an approximate perfection. Nevertheless I must say that (on the same principle) her self-accusations go too far. She may be blamed for some things in her childhood, but the heaviest blame attaches to her scrupulosity and that perhaps may be blamed on her too rigid training. Yet in saying this, it seems to me that all the more credit has to be accorded to her self-conquest. If ever she is officially enrolled among the saints — and this now seems not at all unlikely — she will assuredly have to be accounted as among those whose youth was most blameless. In due course she learned that a thousand temptations do not necessarily mean a single sin. If in youth she thought otherwise, it must have been because of a conscience more sensitive than it was, as yet, well instructed.

Her acute sense of guilt must have been removed when the time came for her to make her first confession. Just when this happened she does not tell us, for the simple reason that she does not recall the exact date, except that it was when she was about eight or nine — that is, about the time when she was obsessed with her sinfulness. A pious relative — there were many relatives in Aachen and all of them were more or less pious — during a call at the Schervier home said in Frances's presence that she thought it was about time that the child and her elder sister Julia, nearly two years her senior, should be prepared for their first confession. One wonders why their parents had neglected to attend to this in the case of Julia, or had even to be prompted about it with regard to Frances. The explanation doubtless is that their mother considered them both very good little girls and had perhaps forgotten that even good little girls, upon reaching the age of reason, should be led to the confessional. Catholicism was about to leap into vivid activity in Aachen, but after the exhaustion of the wars it may still have been a bit somnolent, perfunctory, and formal.

The words spoken before the alert Frances (probably there to help her French mother over the difficult German phrases) stirred her more than anyone knew. Confession, that was what she had been longing for! She could hardly wait for the hour to arrive when she would be put to bed and left to her solitary thoughts. Then in the darkness of the night she traced on her pillow the figure of a priest, and to this she confessed the minute enormities she had committed. What could these have been? Her petulance? Filching a taste of jam from the pantry? But why should we enquire? As she confessed to this imaginary priest — again we see the doll-notion — she was so overcome that she sobbed her heart out, making her pillow so wet that she was afraid that it would be noticed in the morning. At last she fell asleep, later to wake in what she described as unutterable happiness and peace. To her great relief her pillow was quite dry. Possibly it had never been so drenched as she fancied.

Going to confession to a real instead of to a make-believe priest relieved her immensely. And we may suppose that the priest, though he may have been slightly surprised at getting anything beyond the ordinary glib accusations that children make of their tiny sins, certainly absolved her, much to her happiness of heart. She would have gone more often to confession had she been permitted. But her father had his own notions about such matters. Children should not bother the priests; once a month was ordinarily enough, and during the seven weeks of Lent once was enough, as the confessionals were thronged at that season. It may be that the brisk businessman had sometimes been kept waiting by an interminable line of children before he could get into the box. But deeper than this was another reason: he did not wish his children to be too pious. Very improperly he tried to control their religious life, confounding a parent's duty to see that his children attend to their duties with the notion that it was for him to mark out the limits of their spirituality. What should, however, in fairness be said for him is that in his ideas on this subject he would probably have been supported by most of the priests of his day. Not until the reign of Pope Pius X in the first decade of the twentieth century was the frequent reception of the sacraments officially encouraged by the Holy See, though this is not to suggest that it did not have its earlier advocates.

The specific tenets of the heresy of Jansenism, in particular the suggestion that it is well-nigh impossible to make a worthy Communion, had been condemned by the Church, but its pernicious spirit lingered on in France, and from France infected, to some extent, the Rhineland. Herr Schervier may not have been affected by its heresies, but he was unconsciously Jansenistic to the extent of holding that even pious people should be moderate in their devotional exercises. He would certainly have disapproved had he known all that was going on in the soul of his little daughter.

The father and mother had little directly to do with Frances's First Communion, which she received when she was ten years and nine months old. The prompting for this came from Canon Deboeur who, although only the proxy for her godfather, the Emperor Francis I, had perhaps a right to feel that he had a special obligation in the matter. Very early one morning in May or June, 1829, he called on the Scherviers, with whom he had become increasingly friendly, and took his hostess out into the garden for some private talk. After a while Frances's mother called to her. Then the Canon, taking her hand, said, "Child, I had a very peculiar dream about you last night. You must be prepared as soon as possible to make your First Communion."

Her mother answered for her: "Well, she is still rather young. Yet she is not a stupid child, so I shall make no objection. How soon do you think, Canon, that this should take place?"

About the date the Canon was set in his mind. He did not give his reason, but in all probability Frances's name had decided him. He said: "It must be on no other day than the Feast of St. Francis, October 4th."

When they returned to the house an almanac was consulted, and all were delighted to see that in 1829 two feasts of the Church happened to fall on the same day — St. Francis of Assisi and Our Lady of Victories. The second of these was always celebrated with special solemnity in their parish church of St. Paul's. Since one of Frau Schervier's names was Victoire, it was a name-day feast for her. She clapped her hands, delighted at this, crying, "Of course there could be no better day for Frances, and Julia too, to make their First Communion!"

One of the parish priests prepared the girls during the following months, and, when October 4th arrived, the Canon himself insisted on administering Holy Communion, which the whole family received that day. When he came to Frances, his favorite, his tears flowed and his voice almost failed him as he murmured, while putting the Host upon her tongue, *"Corpus Domini nostri Jesu Christi custodiat animam tuam in vitam aeternam. Amen."* Her tears flowed also, but, with characteristic honesty, she wrote in her autobiography, which she began over 30 years later on another coincidence of the same two feasts, that she did not know whether she wept for joy at receiving her Lord or because she saw the Canon in tears. It may be that both factors operated.

Even at that time Frances's piety manifested itself as charity; loving Christ she had to love the poor. There was as yet only one thing that she could do for them: with her pocket money she purchased cotton yarn and began secretly, while lying in bed in the early morning, to knit stockings for those in need. She was to write: "Scarcely had I heard during instruction at school that our dear Saviour had a special love for the poor, and had Himself become poor and lowly for our sake, when I felt impelled to a great love of the poor and was grieved that I did not belong to their number." She added that she wished that everything could be taken from her, in particular the pretty dresses she had liked so much. As that could not be, she sought out and made friends with a girl at St. Leonard's who was of an impoverished family.

One day at the entrance to the school, just as she was going in, she was so overwhelmed with her love of poverty that for a moment she felt as though she were being lifted from the ground. "Similar occurrences," she recorded in her calm and somewhat matter-of-fact way, "happened at several other times in my childhood. I have mentioned these only because it seems to me that our dear Saviour intended to prepare me by them for what He required of me, and what was to be observed later in the Congregation." The same may be thought, to a greater or less extent, of everything that befell her during these years of her childhood and those that lay immediately ahead.

3

*

On the Shoulders of a Child

WE ARE NOT TOLD whether Canon Deboeur was a friend of the Scherviers prior to his acting as proxy for the Emperor of Austria at Frances's baptism. It would, however, seem likely that there was at least an acquaintance, and it is certain that as the Canon watched Frances progress he took an immense fancy to her. He was an aristocratic old man, also one of considerable wealth. Already the idea had begun to form in his mind of making her his heiress, taking her as his adopted daughter if circumstances should ever make this possible and spending his declining years with her, even though he had a sister living in Aachen. For some years he had been buying the child valuable pieces of plate on the slightest pretext or on none at all, and he had already deposited with her father 10,000 thalers,* which, he allowed it to be understood, was an earnest of much more to come. By the standards of a small German city inhabited by frugal people, Frances was well-to-do and would one day be rich.

One wonders a little at these transactions, for the gifts were much more lavish than those usually given by a godfather, especially by one who was only a proxy. But perhaps the

* The thaler was worth about three marks or three shillings. When, after 1871, the mark became the standard of currency in the German Empire, the thaler, because of its importance, was allowed to circulate until 1908, fixed at a three-mark valuation.

23

Canon managed to insinuate that he was acting for the Emperor. Perhaps his generosity was not altogether disinterested, he may have regarded what he was doing as a kind of insurance against the years of the locust.

Herr Schervier may have acquiesced all the more willingly because he was not a very rich man. He possessed, it is true, his needle factory, but the profits of that were spent, one has reason to suppose, as soon as they were earned, in operating a rather large domestic establishment. Moreover he maintained a school for the children of his employees, and this must have cost a good deal. And he was the kind of man who tends to neglect his own business for concerns that bring him no personal profit. Being the deputy burgomaster of Aachen may not have involved a great deal of work, but one surmises that the public-spirited citizen served on all kinds of committees and that the sessions in the fourteenth-century *Rathaus* — the astonishing edifice built on the site of Charlemagne's palace — involved spending loquacious and ponderous hours over trifles, hours that he could ill afford to spare.

Frances's father had a number of children — a daughter by his first wife and two sons and four daughters by his second. To provide adequately for them all would not be easy. Fortunately Karl had already begun his preliminary studies for the priesthood and would be supported by the Church. The factory would eventually be taken over by Henry, but Herr Schervier knew that it would not be the gold mine that people supposed — not unless Henry made it one by his own energy and ability. There would be barely enough to provide the girls with adequate dowries. Under the circumstances it seemed fortunate that the Canon had undertaken to leave his wealth to Frances; her father was glad to accept those 10,000 thalers for her.

Her mother also accepted the plate for Frances. She did even more: she helped the Canon select his expensive purchases, which may suggest that he did not want his sister to know what was happening. But in this case the matter is more understandable: presents of plate are one thing, money is another. If Frances's eyes shone with pleasure when these gifts were given, it was for a reason that the Canon did not suspect. She intended to give all these things away as soon as an opportunity occurred.

Then in 1830 Frances's mother came down with tuberculosis. Since she had several servants to whom she could give orders in her room, she was able to rest and so lingered on for three years — a fairly long time under the conditions that then prevailed. However, she did not know what precautions to take with her family, and her children, except Frances and Henry, who were not brought into too close personal contact with their mother, also developed tuberculosis.

After 1830 the Canon's gifts for Frances were selected by himself. He still did not ask for his sister's assistance and advice, but by this time he may have acquired a knowledge of what kind of plate to buy. His presents were as opulent as ever. They may even have been more opulent, for one imagines that Frau Schervier, in mere delicacy, would have tried to restrain him from spending too much on her little daughter. As for Frances, she felt these rich gifts to be so many fetters, putting her under a kind of obligation to her proxy-godfather. Yet though she was embarrassed by what was being done, she was resolved not to be permanently bound. If she accepted the presents, she accepted them as a kind of trustee for God's poor. As soon as she got the chance she would coin them into alms.

There are a few letters written by Frances when she was about twelve — apparently the earliest letters we have — that are worth drawing upon at this point, for several reasons. One is that though she shows herself a pious little girl, the piety expressed is no more than normal. Another is that she has the same enjoyment of "fun" that other girls of her age would have. "Haven't you recalled the first night you were with us? My, how we laughed!" To make this friend of hers, Hannchen Geller, who was at the Ursuline convent school at

Düren, laugh again, she relates how the donkey of the Schervier children had escaped and had run down the street, until
it was driven back to its stall. There are one or two private
(and therefore obscure) jokes: "I hope you have discontinued the use of Aachen German." We hear that Pauline
has just made her First Communion, that Karl is at the Gym-
nasium, that Henry (presumably already in his father's business) is away on a trip, and that Lise's (Elizabeth's) baby has
had the ague but is getting better. Mostly these letters are
signed not "Franziska" but "Françoise," which may have been
a childish affectation but which more probably reveals that
Frances thought of herself as French rather than German. It
was similarly in this mode that her mother would have addressed her.

As for Frances's mother, Frances has to stop in the middle
of a letter to go to her. A postscript written by Julia to one
of these letters tells Hannchen that her mother "is still in
the country because her severe cough allows her no rest."
From another letter we learn that she, together with Louise
and Julia, was at Liège, perhaps in a sanatorium. But a letter
written on January 10, 1833, exclaims, "Oh, who would have
thought last New Year's that Mama had only a few weeks yet
to live!" And on February 20, 1833, Hannchen is told:
"Julia is ill too; she has been bled; but I hope she will soon
be well again." In this she expressed hopes that were all too
soon to be falsified.

It is not perfectly clear whether it was during the period
of the mother's illness, or after her death, that the Canon
went to live with the Schervier family. Frances, while very
precise on some details, rarely ventures explanations, and always she avoids discussion of motives. But we do know that
he came to be installed in the Scherviers' comfortable house,
presumably as a paying guest. But as he was a close friend of
the family by now and as his gifts had put them all under an
obligation to him, he could not be refused harborage. This
constant contact with the little girl made the old man very

happy: it was the first move towards what he had long wanted. He dearly loved Frances, and he felt that he would now attach her all the more firmly to himself. She was almost his daughter now. Under her care he could be sure of a comfortable home for the rest of his life.

To Frances the loss of her mother was a great shock, although her death had been long expected. She was consoled by the reflection that the one lying dead on the bed was a most virtuous woman, so that she could say: "I knelt and offered my dear mother with my whole will and with all my heart to God. The sacrifice did indeed cost countless tears, but nevertheless it was sweet, because it was offered to the Lord." At the age of twelve she had already discovered that what one returns to one's heavenly Father is not lost.

Feeling her need for a mother, with charming naïveté she asked the Blessed Virgin to take the vacant place. She meant this in more than the ordinary sense — that in which all Christians cast themselves upon Mary's maternal heart. What the bereaved child was asking was that Mary direct her in the new responsibilities that fell upon her, all the more now that her two elder sisters were evidently soon to leave this world. She felt that she did indeed receive help from that source, though (again one must note her candor) she records that she later omitted to say the special prayer she had composed at this time. The omission, however, was one that no doubt the Blessed Virgin excused. For this particular prayer was intended to ask for the needs of a particular period. After she had founded her Congregation, her many duties, her many acts of charity, and also the many community prayers drove the earlier prayer from her thoughts.

But that she needed Mary's help in a very special fashion appears at once when we hear of new sorrows and new burdens. On July 12, 1833, her sister Julia died, and five days later Louise. As her elder sister Elizabeth — the only child of her father's first marriage — was married by now, the care of managing the household fell on Frances's shoulders. She

27

was taken away from St. Leonard's and set to this task. She was only thirteen and a half years old.

It would seem that this decision was rather inconsiderate. Servants in those days were easily procurable, and so, it may be supposed, a competent paid housekeeper could have been found. There may, however, be an explanation of which we do not know. Perhaps the widower could not bear the thought of a stranger discharging his dead wife's duties, or perhaps he was at that time pressed for money and felt that he could not afford this additional expense. But also it could have been that he perceived Frances fully capable of rising to the emergency. Possibly all these motives operated.

There is at least no need to deplore that Frances's education at St. Leonard's was terminated. She never finished her course at school, and yet she was already as well educated as were most girls of the upper classes of society. She could not have gone beyond St. Leonard's, unless by private instruction, for universities at that time were not open to women. No girl was educated to earn her own living, though of course now and then it happened that some of them, through some misfortune, had to become teachers or governesses. Frances, though her studies were left uncompleted, never struck anyone as lacking in general culture. She had already acquired all that she needed for her special purposes. Though the management of her father's household fell heavily upon her, it proved to be the best of training for her life's work.

In the beginning Frances was, naturally enough, very diffident about her ability to cope with the domestic duties suddenly thrust upon her. With her bundle of keys strapped to her waist, she had to give orders to the servants, orders she feared they would not be very inclined to carry out. Indeed, many times she preferred to do things herself than to tell others to do them. However, the servants did obey her, not only because they had already been brought to love her but because she showed herself efficient. Without their good will she could never have executed the charitable plans that came into her mind with her new authority. At any moment they might have reported her to her father, and though we do hear of one of them grumbling, "The child will eventually give away everything," this remained a private complaint, probably mixed with some admiration. The servants were, in fact, to a great extent her accomplices. And while we cannot affirm that they guarded her secret generosity with absolute faithfulness — for some hints may have been dropped — upon the whole they went no further than to hide food or clothing lest these necessities be given to the poor.

Herr Schervier was himself a charitable man — within reasonable limits — and he may have had some inkling as to what was going on; he may even have approved, up to a point. While Frances was congratulating herself upon the successful stealth with which she distributed her alms to the poor, he probably had some knowledge of it, but was too awed and too kindhearted to interfere. Besides, men are notoriously unobservant, and how should he know what was in the larder?

What is surprising is that he seems not to have noticed that the Canon's plate was gradually vanishing, being cautiously sold piece by piece by the seamstress of whom we have heard, or that there were depredations upon the Canon's thalers. The money must be presumed to have been in a strongbox in his room, the plate in a special place. Even a man lost in sorrow for his dead wife would, one would think, have noticed that there was some evaporation. And had he not noticed anything, it is hardly conceivable that reports about the sold plate should not have reached him from friends and neighbors. Nevertheless he did not intervene.

Apparently the explanation is that stern, aloof, and austere as he may have seemed to be, he concealed a soft heart under a forbidding carapace. No doubt he thought — and correctly — that Frances requested the recipients of her charity to pray for the repose of her mother's soul. That would have commended itself to him. Frances, writing over 30 years later, remained under the impression — was it not rather the illusion? — that her father never guessed what she had done. One applauds her simplicity; one must applaud less her perspicuity. Of course she was writing of a child's memories.

In the shouldering of her responsibilities the girl developed very early into womanhood. She quickly acquired maturity of judgment and independence of action. This independence was something which, at this time, she guarded not only from her father but her father-confessor. In the confessional she contented herself with listing her failings (such as they were), but she did not seek a spiritual director. Instead she relied upon what may be called instinct but which was rather divine guidance directly imparted. She came to see eventually that this was a mistake, and in later years she was notably submissive to guidance and counsel, though to the end she often relied on God's directive words to her. At this stage, however, her spirit of independence was an advantage. In this way, too, she was being prepared for the work that lay ahead.

So far as is known no photograph exists of her as she was when a child. The earliest is one taken some time before 1855, and in it she is shown with her brothers and sisters. Pauline (by that time Sister Paula) is sitting by her side, the image of her, even with her head tilted to the left in Frances's manner. Her brothers' heads, however, are held erect, and Karl was handsome, though in an unspectacular way. One can see that Frances herself had good features, and her eyes are alive with intelligence. She was French brunette rather than German blonde, small and daintily formed, but yet capable of heavy work, even of a physical sort. Her look is candid, and she suggests a good deal of charm.

The old Canon, now so contentedly installed in the house, was in full accord with the father about the inadvisability of excessive religious devotion. In the face of their opposition, it is a matter for wonder that Frances did not submit to their sage advice. But though she never openly contested it or was disobedient, she kept her own counsel and usually contrived to go her own way. She had long before this dedicated herself

to God in the way of charity. She was already a lavish benefactor of the poor; what she wanted was to be of the poor
— and that of course was something beyond the comprehen-
sion of the Canon and her father.

From the responsibilities of her position Frances derived
the compensation of liberty — not of course the liberty of the
young in these days but certainly more liberty than most girls
of her upbringing were permitted at that time. Restrictions
to be sure remained, but they do not seem to have hampered
her a great deal. Now and then her father had to go away on
business. At once she seized these chances of visiting the sick
poor. At other times, when her father was home, Frances
asked the Blessed Virgin to take her place in the home, to
assume her face and figure so that she herself might have an
hour or two for an errand of mercy! But though she quite
expected this to happen some fine day, it never did. She had
to use such natural opportunities as presented themselves.
These were fewer than they might have been because her
married half-sister Elizabeth had a way of dropping into the
house with her small children when she was least expected.
She gave herself all the airs of her position and seniority.
Frances divined that Elizabeth would be quite out of sympathy with her charitable projects, and so had to proceed with
the utmost caution.

Even so Frances had more freedom than she had known
before, though not enough to satisfy her. She was fairly safe
regarding her charities, for the servants abetted her. To go to
weekday Mass called for finesse and stratagem, for this was
one of those exercises of piety of which her father — and
the Canon too — did not approve. In order to prepare for the
Communion she hoped to receive when she was able to slip
away, she had to toy with her food at the breakfast table and
to seem to be eating something while actually eating nothing.
Usually her father, buried in his newspaper or his sad
thoughts did not notice this little performance. St. Paul's
Church was not much further away than round the corner,

and to go to Mass she received her father's reluctant permission, as she was careful not to say anything about intending to go to Communion as well. He quite supposed that would be impossible after breakfast. When she could not get to church for Mass, she sometimes persuaded one of the priests to give her Communion at some other time. For the sake of what were considered the proprieties she had one of the servants accompany her. There was a kind of pious conspiracy against the head of the household.

That this was so certainly shows that Frances was beloved by the servants over whom she ruled. If her father may sometimes seem a bit rigid, it is only fair to say that his attitude was that of the majority of the conscientious fathers of that age. Possibly he was willing to wink at a good deal, so long as he was not asked to surrender his principles. Gossips must often have told him, "Oh, I saw Frances out this morning." But after all, the worst that could be said of her was that she was exceedingly devout, exceedingly charitable. That she had become so highly competent a housekeeper may have acted as a deterrent: so long as she ran his house well, he was hardly in a position to object. It may be that he was himself a kind of embryo saint (indeed, aren't we all?); at least he was an upright man and a staunch Catholic, according to his lights. He must have been more in sympathy with Frances than he would ever have admitted.

Thus the situation remained for several years, during which the larder and wardrobes were generously looted, the Canon's plate sold, and the fund of thalers was gradually depleted. What is not quite easy to see is how Frances managed to get her hands on the money, or why it was kept in a strongbox in the house instead of at a bank. Further one must admit that all this has some not altogether pleasing aspects. Though the money (like the plate) belonged to her, she was still only a girl and as such not really entitled to manage her own estate. It is clear that legal technicalities did not bother Frances! The poor had to be helped, and as she had means at her disposal for helping them, they were freely, though with due circumspection, used.

The Canon was in the house and had to be circumvented. Perhaps he said now and then, "Yes, *Liebchen Franziska*, if you know of some family in great need, by all means sell a bit of the plate I have given you." There was no need for her to tell him just how much of the plate she was selling, and she could stretch his permission to cover an occasional handful of thalers. But he could not have known that the hoard was being used to the extent that it was; he must have imagined that it was merely being nibbled at along the edges.

Strictly speaking, one cannot quite approve of all this, admirable as the motive was. If it comes to that, one cannot give full approval to the similar treatment St. Francis of Assisi accorded *his* father, objectionable man though Pietro di Bernadone was and glorious as was the goal of the Saint. Probably in neither case do we have enough information to pronounce a definite judgment. That the intentions in each case were excellent must be allowed to cover the matter. There are many situations in life that are insufficiently provided for by the copybook maxims.

At least Herr Schervier was a far better man than was Messer Pietro, and he must be accorded respect. It is a pity that Frances in her autobiography says little about him. We get the impression that she was in some fear of him, though (if so) not of excessive fear. He was assuredly no harsh tyrant. While holding her in check to some extent, it must be admitted that he did as much to further her plans as might be expected of him. The story has to be filled in with many conjectures, as Frances was often reticent, and there may have been much of which she, as a child, was unaware. I can only hope that my conjectures are not too wide of the mark and that my judgments have not been unjust.

The Yearning for Contemplation

IN FRANCES SCHERVIER, as in many, perhaps all, holy souls, may be discerned two apparently conflicting tendencies: the desire to work for God and a longing for nothing except union with Him. Only a few of these souls are ever able to disentangle themselves from all mundane concerns so that they may devote themselves to the contemplative life. Frances was not of their number; the life of active charity proved to be her vocation. At the same time she never ceased to long for retirement. It must be added, however, that the contemplative spirit informed all the works of charity to which she was called. She saw, a little sadly, that she was to be a Martha and not a Mary.

Yet Mary and Martha were sisters and have a strong family resemblance.

> If bustling Martha, saint and scold,
> Served neither love nor supper cold,

doubtless Mary usually did her share of the necessary housework, except on the one occasion when she drew Martha's somewhat tart complaint. Similarly Martha, when she had leisure, was glad to sit at the feet of Christ. Though they stand as opposing types, there is no very real contradiction between their vocations. To be a good Martha one needs a strong infusion of Mary.

The longing for contemplation, as the enormous success of the recent books by Thomas Merton demonstrates, is far more widespread than is commonly supposed, though it is in the vast majority of cases rather vague and intermittent. The famous cry of St. Augustine, *O solitudo beata! O sola beatitudo!* echoes (and very fortunately so) in many besides Catholic hearts. It is the affirmation of a deep human need — the need for the supernatural. Solitariness can be merely morose if it is not Augustinian solitude, the solitude of the mystic, for that is filled with God. The desired withdrawal is not to get away from people, who should be loved more than ever, but to find communion with the Divine.

The striking fact about Frances Schervier is not that she never ceased yearning for contemplation — for that is a common enough state of affairs — but that this yearning preceded her works of charity, except in so far as she could perform these on the very small scale then possible to her. When she was only eleven or twelve she had a strong desire to become a Trappistine nun, and confided this to the pious seamstress about whom we hear so much. She also told her brother Karl about it, and he responded by revealing that he had a similar desire for the Trappist life. One evening, when their parents happened to be visiting some friends, Frances persuaded Karl to go with her to talk about the matter with a priest noted for his piety. She calls this a very daring undertaking, as the Schervier children were never allowed to go out unattended without permission; therefore we must call it a breach (if not a very great one) of obedience. But we must not be pedantic; the emergency existed, the opportunity was seized.

Karl, as Frances admits, was dragged out without being fully aware of the object of their mission: he was fully informed about this by his younger sister only while they were walking to the church. He was probably a bit bewildered and half inclined to turn back. This Frances would not permit. She reminded him that he had told her often enough that he wanted to be a Trappist. Here was their chance to do something about it. He yielded to her stronger will.

Karl did in fact become a priest, though never as a member of any religious order. Nor did Frances become a Trappistine. The priest they consulted said what any wise priest would have said: "Dear children, do not be ridiculous. You are much too young to be thinking of matters of this sort, especially you, Frances. I am not saying that you have no vocation to the religious life; but from what I have seen of you, yours is not a Trappistine vocation. Have you ever thought of the Sisters of Charity?"

Frances tried to explain that none but the strictest of all religious orders would suffice to expiate her monstrous sins, but at this the kindly and sensible priest smiled gravely. "No, no, no," he must have said. "What terrible sins can a child like you have to expiate?" He may have led her into the confessional and checked her with each of the Ten Commandments, concluding: "There, you see, dear child, you have no serious sins upon your soul. If you want my opinion, your life, if you insist upon the religious life, should be with the Vincentians in their works of charity."

At the word "charity" Frances's heart leaped; that she knew was what she really wanted. In fact it must be said that the more her spirituality grew the more she felt impelled to the active works of mercy. But that evening the advice of the priest seemed to dampen her enthusiasm, although she continued to cling for several years to her Trappistine idea. Much of the same sort of advice was undoubtedly given to Karl, when his turn came.

Lord Macaulay has praised the Catholic Church, even while attacking it, for its genius in making use of fantastic and visionary people, those for whom a sedately respectable Protestantism can find no niche. Actually, of course, the Catholic system is very levelheaded and tends to discourage

36

eccentric outbursts. Frances and Karl received that night a salutary dose of cool Catholic common sense. The boy and girl were warned that neither of them was as yet nearly old enough to be accepted by any religious community. They were gently told not to make fools of themselves but to go home and wait a few years. Rather crestfallen, they saw the force of the good priest's arguments. All too well did they know how insuperable an opposition they would encounter from their parents. Yes, they would wait; their minds remained unchanged. And yet the advice showed much insight. Frances, though she was never to wear the Vincentian cornets, had a vocation not dissimilar to that of a Sister of Charity. And Karl found his life's priestly work in Aachen.

It will be noticed that in this interview Frances showed herself once again to be obsessed with her sense of sin. Only the rigors of Trappistine life would suffice as a penance. Whether the Trappistines are actually the most rigorous of women's religious orders is a question, for one would suppose that, except in the matter of perpetual silence the Second Order Dominicans, the Carmelites, and the Poor Clares are equally severe. However, little Frances had got it into her head that only the Trappistines would do for her, and there is no need to argue against the imperfect knowledge of a child. One cannot refrain from a smile. Even had the priest not told Frances and Karl to be sensible, their father would have put an immediate stop to anything so silly. Moreover, Canon Law would have prevented their acceptance. Needless to say, the whole project was fantastic. The important fact it brings out is Frances's deep attraction, both as a child and throughout her life, for the life of pure contemplation. Though it was shown not to be her vocation, she nevertheless provided for such a life within the recesses of her own Congregation, when it was founded, though that Congregation was dedicated to the performance of acts of mercy for the sick poor.

One more point might be made: Frances at this time appears to have thought of a life of external severity as offering her in that severity itself what she primarily sought. In this, of course, she was slightly in error, for while mortification — not necessarily physical asceticism but asceticism of some sort — is a necessary condition of contemplation, it is a means rather than an end. Frances explains: "At that time external mortifications had a great attraction for me, and I devoted myself to them as far as I could." She came to have a truer view of the matter, and yet it must be said that, when she drew up the Rule of her Congregation and theoretically allowed mitigations that are not to be found in the contemplative orders, she herself rarely would avail herself of them. In this respect, too, her life was all of a piece. Her development went forward uninterruptedly from the place from which it started.

The advice the priest gave was, it will be seen, not all of a negative sort. Apparently he recognized that this young girl, already well known to him, did in all probability have a religious vocation. And he came rather near the mark when he suggested that she should become a Sister of Charity. Naturally he did not imagine — and neither did Frances — that she would found a new congregation with a specialized form of charity as its purpose. Frances, for her part, was so impressed with what he had said that, without renouncing her original idea, she returned to him regularly for confession. He repeatedly advised her to give up the idea of the Trappistines and the penitential life, but she said she neither would nor could abandon a resolution so dear to her.

Frances, as we shall have many occasions to see, was in some ways inclined to be very independent. It was only relatively late in life that she put herself under a spiritual director. Ordinarily she did no more than confess her sins, taking any special problem that arose to whatever priest would, in her opinion, be best able to help her. Eventually she was brought to abandon her early wish to join the Trappistines.

Meanwhile Frances had spoken again to her friend the

seamstress, who suggested that she should consult another priest, the pastor of her own parish. As that did not seem possible — for it was not safe to risk another unauthorized expedition — the seamstress undertook to speak to him about the Trappistines and to ask for a book that might enlighten Frances. The Schervier household was not well stocked with books, and of the religious sort there were only a few missals, prayer manuals, and a copy of *The Imitation of Christ*. The priest must have been rather puzzled by the request made to him, through an intermediary, by a child. Without actually talking to her he could hardly venture any definite advice, but he did pick out from his shelves a volume that he thought might be of some help. It was a book telling the story of some of the first Visitation nuns. This might look like an arrow shot into the dark, but showed more insight than might at first appear. Though St. Francis de Sales wished the order to be one for contemplatives — one which, because it was not quite so rigorous as Carmel, might provide for women in delicate health — the very name, the Visitation, indicates that there was an intention to unite adoration with active work among the poor. St. Jane Frances de Chantal had even placed her Congregation under the patronage of St. Martha. It is clear that what was in the mind of the priest now consulted was the idea of leading Frances's thoughts to a midway point between the Trappistines and the Sisters of Charity.

The book thrilled Frances. It cannot be identified now, but, however poorly it may have been written, no work in which St. Jane Frances and her friends SS. Francis de Sales and Vincent de Paul figure could have been barren of interest. At any rate the day that the book arrived Frances was so excited that she could neither eat nor drink, at which she was greatly embarrassed, probably fearing that this would only serve to harden her father's conviction that she was carrying devotion to unhealthy extremes. But nothing seems to have been noticed, and from this book, the first of the kind that Frances had ever read, she learned of the wonderful ways by which God prepares souls for their vocations. Reading it greatly increased Frances's desire to serve God alone; everything else struck her as mean and insignificant.

But by this time the child's mother was slowly dying, and when a couple of years later she was carried to the grave, soon to be followed by her two elder daughters, a final end appeared to have come to all of Frances's chances of becoming a nun of any sort. When at last she found an opportunity of consulting the priest who had loaned her the book, he listened to what she had to say, asked some questions, and then said: "Well, as you ask my opinion, I will give it. Make a sacrifice to God of this desire of yours to become a Trappistine, and obey the directions of your confessor, who believes you are called to the active life. I do not say you have no vocation to the Trappistines; I do not know. But of one thing I am sure: if it is God's holy will, there will be ample time for you to become a Trappistine later."

The interview calmed her. When she got home she sat down and carefully thought over all that the priest had said. What impressed her most were his remarks about the will of God. He had asked her only to make a temporary renunciation, which did not rule out the Trappistines as an eventual possibility. But he had also told her that she should follow her confessor's advice, and her confessor had been from the beginning quite positive that she was called to the active life. Suddenly she saw that she had been obstinate and self-willed. Now she would make reparation; she would make the sacrifice without reserve. To seal it, she knelt before a crucifix and surrendered her Trappistine ambition once and for all. "I offered," she wrote, "and desired to offer it absolutely, even should my heart, in which this idea had taken so deep a root, bleed to death." While she was praying in tears a light suddenly flooded her soul. It seemed to her that from the Cross itself had come an assurance that God had accepted the immolation of her will. Now that she had made her act of renunciation she felt inexpressibly happy. All hesitation had vanished. "A fire of holy charity," she went on, "was enkindled in my soul, and from that moment I felt an ardent desire to serve and love our Lord in the poor, the sick, and the miserable. In that solemn moment, moved by divine grace, I offered myself to God for the service of suffering mankind." With this she had been brought to accept her true vocation.

Even so she had to wait a number of years before the vocation planted in her soul fully blossomed, though it can be seen budding all that while, as indeed a discerning eye had seen it budding before. This did not mean that her yearning for contemplation ceased. From time to time during the rest of her life, after her Congregation had been firmly established, she tried to resign the responsibilities of administering the active work and to join the contemplatives in her order. Each time she came to see that this was not God's will for her. The renunciation she had made as a child had to be repeated over and over again.

Frances, when she became a Franciscan, took St. Elizabeth of Hungary, who had been a tertiary living in the world, as her patroness. But a Dominican tertiary, Catherine of Siena, who also lived in the habit outside the cloister, she regarded as her model. There was not much similarity, one would think, between Frances and this ecstatic and politician who hectored popes and recalled them to their duties. But Catherine's achievement — half nun, half lay-woman, very much in the world's turmoil — provided the inspiration that was needed. In some ways St. Catherine seemed closer to her than even dear St. Elizabeth.

Thomas Merton (Father Louis), the Trappist poet, in a remarkable article in the twenty-fifth anniversary number of the *Commonweal*, points out that there are many "masked contemplatives" both in the world and in the so-called active religious orders. "They are mystics," he says, "but they do not know it. And generally, even if you tell them so, they will not be inclined to believe you. They will always fear that you are joking, and that a term so exalted as that could not possibly apply to them. The truth is that they are the little ones who will perhaps turn out to be much higher, in heaven, than many who seemed great by more manifest graces of prayer."

Father Louis goes on to point out, as have many other writers on the same subject before him, that the mystical life is not something specialized but one to which all Christians are called. It is the life for which we are created, and if we manage to scramble into heaven, our capacity for contemplation will be more intense than that enjoyed by a St. Bernard, a St. Francis, or a St. Philip Neri while they were still entangled in mortal coils. There may be something slightly amusing in thinking of a stockbroker or mortician spending eternity doing nothing but gaze on God. But so, poor men — most blessed men! — they will, if they enter heaven at all. And if they do arrive there it will be only through the redemptive work of Christ and by the operation of grace, whose chief channel is the sacraments. All this is mystical; indeed what could be more mystical than the branching of Christians in the Vine, their membership in the Body of Christ. In short the Christian life is always a supernatural life; and if a few chosen souls are called to a loftier degree of contemplation by the special grace of mystical prayer or infused contemplation, it also remains true that the ordinary pious life — that by which the ordinary Christian is saved — is a mystical life.

It is not being asserted that Frances Schervier was a "masked contemplative." Nobody knows enough about her personal spirituality to offer any opinion. But this can be said without undue presumption: the priests who advised her amply proved — whether they spoke out of special insight, or general experience, or mere common sense — that they were right about her vocation. This is why her renunciation must be looked upon as the crisis of her life.

Though we hear no more after this about the Trappistines,

we shall encounter recurringly a longing for the main features of the Trappist life — contemplation and penance. That longing gave added value to Frances Schervier's life of unceasing activity, for at the core of everything was a rapt attention to purely spiritual concerns, even if we can glimpse this only now and then. As Frances's holiness manifested itself in work it might be well to recall to those of the active as well as the contemplative mode what Benedict XIV, who reigned as Pope from 1740 to 1758, set forth as the means of estimating the worthiness of those put forward for canonization. There were four marks, so he said, and they are these: the first is that their deeds should surpass the ordinary strength of human beings; the second, that they be performed promptly and easily; the third, that they should be accompanied with supernatural joy; and the fourth, that these manifestations should have been evident not occasionally but frequently. There is no intention of putting Frances Schervier forward in these pages as a saint — for they are written in submission to the decrees of Urban VIII and several of his successors; their aim is merely to tell her story. It is one of boundless charity, the performance of works of mercy. But it may be permissible to remark that One greater than Urban VIII or Benedict XIV has told us who are those blessed of His Father: "For I was hungry, and you gave me to eat: I was thirsty, and you gave me to drink: I was a stranger, and you took me in: Naked, and you covered me; Sick, and you visited me: I was in prison, and you came to me." The words are a literal description, and in sufficient detail, of Frances Schervier's program of charity. And all was done as to Christ; the poor were Christ's; in the poor she always saw Christ.

The Goad of Charity

IT IS HARDLY POSSIBLE to write a life of Frances Schervier in strict chronological order, at least not for its early period, as we have nothing to go on except what she herself wrote. These autobiographical fragments were written reluctantly and are therefore most reticent, especially concerning her secret thoughts. And since she wrote long after the events she mentions, she cannot be expected to be always perfectly sure as to dates. But this much drops into our chronology: when Frances was about fifteen her youngest sister, Pauline, who had been away at boarding school, returned home. The fact is important, because Frances at once started to initiate her, by degrees, into the domestic duties she had hitherto been performing herself. As Pauline proved competent and cooperative, Frances found herself more free for the external charities she wished to perform.

We also find the "pious seamstress" — most aggravatingly left unnamed — flitting in and out of her life. We get the impression that the seamstress, because she was so often close at hand, had, at this stage, more influence over Frances than any priest, for while Frances had already attained a greater latitude of freedom than she had dared to hope for, she could not often slip away, even to consult her confessor. The head of the Schervier household was still looked upon (perhaps

44

unnecessarily) as an object to be circumvented. The prying half-sister Elizabeth was actually more dangerous. But as Henry was in his father's needle factory, learning the business from the ground up, and as Karl was in the minor seminary, the two girls were left to their own devices, controlled mainly by what they knew to be prudent. It was very difficult to be prudent and impetuous in charitable impulses at the same moment.

The months and the years had drifted by without much change. Frances was — she had to be — a good housekeeper, punctual, methodical, attentive to duty. But though she had renounced all idea of becoming a Trappistine, she was forming by slow but definite degrees a project of devoting herself to God through works of charity in some religious community. The project had necessarily to be vague, for Frances as she grew older became all the more clearly aware that she would never obtain her father's permission for anything of the kind; it was probably for this reason that she had no particular religious community in mind. Though she did come to consider several of them a few years later as possibilities, it is rather curious that never once, so far as we know, did she ever picture herself as a Sister of Charity, the vocation suggested to her by her confessor.

The situation was, however, changing. About 1837 there came to Aachen — always in a sleepy and rather offhand way a very Catholic city — a revival of Catholic life. The Archbishop of Cologne, Clement August zu Droste-Vischering, was imprisoned by the Prussian government for his refusal to comply with certain oppressive governmental decrees. And though this persecution was not particularly severe — as compared with what was to come later under Bismarck, Hitler, or the ferocious Communists — it had the effect of making the Rhineland, which was Catholic and very un-Prussian in tone, leap as though touched with an electric wire.

Let there be no exaggeration. Most of the Catholic Rhinelanders did not lose a single night's sleep in worry. But there were some thoughtful and conscientious people — and of these Frances's father was one — who were troubled. Just what was in his heart we do not know; he pursued his usual course of rather stiff and formal piety, but at least this much is evident: he came to show himself willing to allow Frances a further latitude in her devotions.

The Feys' house became a kind of center of resistance, even if the people who gathered there could not do much except talk about the difficult times. But such talks are not always so ineffectual as is commonly supposed. From that house there were to go out three young women — Clara Fey, Pauline von Mallinckrodt, and Frances Schervier — to found three new religious congregations. And there too were the Fey brothers — one in process of becoming a Redemptorist and the other a secular priest. The whole group seethed like yeast with Catholic projects.

One of these was for a charitable society to work among the poor, the organization that was to point the way to Frances's lifework. Had her father suspected that this would be its result, he would not — despite his recent but controlled fervor — have permitted her to join it. But as he suspected nothing of the kind, in 1840, much to her surprise, he gave his permission.

Frances had taken for granted that she would be opposed and so had not asked what she supposed would be refused. But one of Frances's friends, Anna von Lommessen, soon to join the Religious of the Sacred Heart, called upon Herr Schervier and persuaded him to give his consent. This consent was not revoked even when some of the numerous Schervier relatives, all of whom had very rigid ideas about the behavior of young ladies, strongly protested against it. "No," he answered, "I have told Frances that she may join and I am not going to take back my word."

The first meeting of the new organization was held in Anna's house, and at this the care of the sick poor was assigned to Frances in her own parish of St. Paul's. When

Frances told her father about this, he was displeased and alarmed. Though he would not withdraw the permission he had given, he now restricted it: Frances was free to attend the meetings of the society; she might even have them sometimes in his house. But he seems to have thought of the organization as a sort of directive committee, similar to the many to which he himself belonged. He had not pictured these well-born young women going out and soiling their dainty hands in personal work among the poor. "If you do that," he exclaimed, "you will be bringing sickness into the house. You must not do that."

The man cannot be altogether blamed. Not so many years before he had lost his wife and two of his daughters from tuberculosis; and though little was known about this disease, or of the nature of the contacts that might spread it, people were at least aware that it was contagious. So also were the typhoid, smallpox and diphtheria that were endemic to the Rhineland. The most that he would consent to was that the seamstress should go on Frances's errands of mercy. While the seamstress came into the house regularly, she did not live there or have, on her days of work, very close associations with the members of the family. In any event, the seamstress would do no actual nursing, of the kind that Frances had proposed to do, but would merely carry alms of money or food.

The compromise was not very logical, as Frances was quick to point out. She feared that everything would be lost, except liberty to attend meetings — which would mean only talk — unless she managed to persuade her father to let her go out herself. To this he was eventually brought to consent, but only on condition that she was accompanied by the seamstress — and that proved the thin edge of the wedge. Before very long she was permitted to go out alone on her charitable missions. Her father grumbled at this from time to time, but he recognized that Frances was doing a good work and decided to treat the matter with dour humor. When one day he said, in Frances's presence, to an acquaintance, "My daughter has succeeded in emancipating herself," Frances made a light jest in reply, after which there were no further grumbles. She had won her point. He had been brought to complete if not very comfortable acquiescence.

When the priest who had tried to turn Frances's thoughts from the Trappistines to the Sisters of Charity heard of her new activities, he was delighted. But he made the somewhat surprising remark, "Now you won't want to join the Sisters of Charity!" though that had been the very thing he had been urging upon her. He probably meant no more than that she had found the equivalent. It pleased him for he saw what difficulties Frances would encounter at home had she attempted to join any religious community, and he did not wish to be at loggerheads with a man so important in the city as was Herr Schervier. But Frances later took his words as prophetic: even at that time she felt convinced that what had been in her mind so long, brooded over day and night, would be brought to full accomplishment, small as this beginning was. She had, as yet, no clear notion as to where she would be led; at the same time she was sure that at last she was on the road.

Frances, as will already have been noticed, was exceptionally skillful in getting her own way. This would be not a very admirable trait in a young woman in her situation — and not very admirable in anybody — were it not for one fact: she was entirely engrossed in God's service; she was asking absolutely nothing for herself; she was trying to contrive means to give, not to get. Even so, she might have made many mistakes out of excessive zeal. That she did not make these mistakes must be attributed to God's guidance. If she "got around" her father, so also she got around her confessor — to him she confessed her sins without seeking his spiritual direction. She concluded later, while admitting that her practice laid her open to dangers, that perhaps God had permitted this in order to leave her free to act. "For," as she says, "a director would have been compelled on reflection, and according to the dictates of prudence, to prohibit many things to which my ardor impelled me." She adds, "Therefore I went my way in great liberty and independence." At this experimental stage much good eventuated in her being free; but it was not a safe state to be in.

That she avoided its dangers must be set down to the fact that she had more clearly than ever an entranced love for God. In the poor she saw Christ as though He were physically present. She was serving Christ in His personal necessities. This was why her hunger to help the needy sometimes grew so intense that, as she relates, the only way she could get control of herself was to run at top speed through her father's garden. One does not quite understand why this should have had a calming effect, but apparently it did.

Several of the young women with whom she was associated in this charity organization became nuns, either joining one of the existing religious orders, like Anna von Lommessen, or, like Magdalen Hermans, joining Clara Fey, whose work in the school for the poor founded by her was already in process of developing into a religious congregation. All of them agreed that their natural leader was Frances, for she had not only the keenest enthusiasm but the practical good judgment which is rarely found with enthusiasm. In spite of what she tells us about her well-nigh delirious moments, she struck her associates as calm, well-poised, resolute, and very discreet. Such certainly was her manner when she was confronted with a problem or with work that had to be done. Her management of her father's household, her direction of the servants, had taught her a great deal. The advantages of this were immediately apparent, though we must suppose that she had a gift for such things, and that it was his recognition of this that had led her father to put her in charge of a fairly large establishment when she was only thirteen and a half.

Her methods in the charity organization were similar to those she used later in her Congregation. She called on people whom she knew to be fairly well off and persuaded them to give meals, or the means of purchasing these, to particular people on stated days in the week. For special cases of destitution she sought subscriptions of money, collecting these herself. She had so moving a way of soliciting alms that few had the heart to refuse.

Precisely because she had an unassailable social position she could afford to disregard it. Before many years are out we hear of some really astonishing instances of this. As a "lady," in the strict sense of those times, she was not always obliged to think of the keeping up of appearances. It was not that she traded upon this circumstance — for it would never have crossed her mind to do so; but her upbringing, plus of course her own character, set her free from worrying as to whether what she was doing was respectable. All that mattered was that it was the thing to do and that it needed to be done. In the belief that the patois of the lower orders (what is called Plattdeutsch) would put them more at their ease, she adopted it herself for the time being, reverting to her ordinary High German when she returned home or when she was asking something from the better educated. She did not want to seem superior — still less condescending — when talking to the poor.

No task was too menial for her. When she came across a poor sick person who required what most people would have considered distasteful service, she was most pleased. Frances never allowed herself to think of anything as disgusting. The practical side of her compassion appeared when she found herself at the bedside of some poor woman who was torn with anxiety as to what would happen to her children when she had gone. Frances promised to take care of them, and her promise was trusted. People soon came to discover that Frances lived up to her word; she often did more than might have been expected of her. As for the bodies of the dead, when Frances had occasion to prepare them for burial, she treated them with the most tender reverence, kneeling and praying first with her companion and behaving just as though this were the Crucified taken down from the Cross.

There was, however, one thing that Frances could hardly ever bring herself to do. As the resources of her organization were limited and many calls were made upon the alms available, some choice had to be exercised. Therefore when one of the poor whom she had been helping got a job — even an inadequate job — or when a patient of hers seemed to be on the road to recovery, the announcement had to be made that the help that had been given would have to be discontinued in favor of somebody more urgently in need of it. On these occasions Frances found it more than she could bear to break the sad news herself; so she would send one of her associates with it.

Clara Fey was not the only person to have established a free school for the poor. The conscientious needle-factory owner had long before this opened one, though his was primarily intended for the children of his employees. Frances found time to reorganize it and to introduce, what had been strangely lacking until then, an hour a day devoted to instruction in religion. Compulsory education at the expense of the state was, it need hardly be said, unheard of anywhere. Now if Frances met any ragged urchin on the street she would say, "Do you go to school? Take me to your father and mother and I'll arrange for you to go to school with me." But the first thing that usually had to be done was to put the grimy little boy or girl into a tub of hot water for a thorough scrubbing. Though in 1840 Frances was only twenty-one and looked younger because of her small build, many people were already addressing her as "Mother."

In 1841 the work of the organization — or of Frances's part in it — received an extension. There was at St. Paul's, the parish in which she worked, a young assistant of more than ordinary ability and devotedness named Father Joseph Istas. He was already doing a good deal to encourage Clara Fey with her poor school; indeed, there were few charitable enterprises in which he was not actively interested. Now on Septuagesima Sunday, just after the exceptionally severe winter of 1841–42, he preached so eloquently that, as on a similar occasion which we hear of in the life of St. Vincent de Paul, a group in the parish was immediately formed to deal with the emergency with Fräulein Schervier, of course, being the life and soul of the undertaking.

There was nearby a former Dominican priory which had long since come into the possession of the city of Aachen and which was popularly known as the "Preachers." This building was used for all kinds of purposes, depending upon the needs that arose, and had served as almhouse, hospital, and orphanage. Since it was not being used at the moment, or at least had some of its many rooms vacant, Father Istas had little trouble in getting the city council (with whom Frances's father, as assistant burgomaster, could put in a good word) to let them have quarters in which to set up a soup kitchen. It cost the city nothing, for collections were made both of money and food, and Frances and a group she gathered set to work, since this seemed to be the most pressing of needs.

A soup kitchen does not sound very glamorous, and it was not made more so because of the gloomy rooms assigned to this charity. But Frances never asked herself whether any work she undertook was humanly attractive — still less whether it would give her an opportunity to strike graceful poses; all her practical mind required was that the work be of use. Though her work before long was to expand far beyond soup kitchens, these never ceased to be a part of it, when they were called for. She never asked herself, then or later, the prim question, "Does this man or woman deserve to be helped?" The only thing that mattered was need. If deserts are weighed, charity becomes, if not entirely destroyed, at least diminished. Frances's was the purest kind of charity, and it burned in her from the time she was nine or ten until she was fifty-seven. If people were undeserving — that is, if they were spiritually as well as physically destitute

— that was all the more reason for her going to their rescue.

This soup kitchen at the "Preachers" was criticised by some people, probably because it could be charged that Frances and Father Istas were helping some rather shiftless people as well as those whose extreme poverty was no fault of their own. Frances was not a Franciscan tertiary as yet, and perhaps knew at this time very little about St. Francis, but she was already Franciscan in spirit. Her unromantic soup kitchen was the real beginning of her life's work, unless we think of her childish and perhaps not very effectual charities. Straight as an arrow this life goes — charity to the poor, compassion for the poor, envy of the poor, since they embodied the poor Christ.

Other people besides Frances contributed to making St. John's Kitchen, as it was called, a success, but they were all inspired by her enthusiasm and held to their tasks by her steady determination. Moreover, it will be obvious that Father Istas ("Curate Istas" they style him in the Chronicles of the Motherhouse) could, being a man, not have achieved much without her. She supervised the cooking, for which she had been trained in the running of her father's house. Nor was it only soup that she ladled out, though often enough she had nothing but soup to provide. Whatever fare was offered, it was gathered by her or those who were under her direction.

Father Istas tried to restrain her bounty, with results that hardly need to be related. Good kind man though he was, he considered Frances as too expansive, too lavish. Again her independence appeared. She writes: "When I deemed it necessary to give a meal to this or that family, and could not make him agree, I would hurriedly beg some money and pay for it." She records that when he discovered this, he used to protest that he was acting on principle — just what principle is not very evident — but always in the end he yielded to her charitable impulses, acknowledging them greater than his own. While he remained the nominal head of the undertaking, she was its driving force.

He sometimes used to accompany her in the collecting tours, and in these his position as a priest was of service to her. She did not restrict herself to soliciting alms of money or food or clothing from her well-to-do friends but started the practice of going the rounds of the market stalls, frankly begging for whatever could be spared, obtaining here a half decayed cabbage, there a bunch of carrots or onions or turnips, somewhere else a pound or two of potatoes; and these she lugged happily back to the kitchen to be made into soup.

It is not much cause for wonder that some people jeered at the "eccentric" young woman, but she did not mind a little good natured banter, and it never seems to have proceeded further than that, perhaps because she was protected by being known as the assistant burgomaster's daughter. Nor did she hesitate to make use of the fact that she was the goddaughter of the lately deceased Emperor when the Archduke John paid a visit to Cologne to assist at the laying of the cornerstone of the tower of the cathedral which had been a-building for several centuries and was not to have the final touches put to it until shortly after Frances's death. To make sure that the letter got safely into the Archduke's hands and was not kept away from him by a secretary or attaché, she took the precaution of having it delivered to him personally by one of the Sisters who had joined Clara Fey's Congregation, Magdalen Hermans, a lady who until recently had been working in her own charitable organization. The result was that the Archduke sent 50 thalers to the Burgomaster of Aachen. When that official proposed to use part of this donation for another purpose, Frances objected with such vigor that the whole amount was turned over to St. John's Kitchen. Mild and meek though she seemed, she could be a lioness when it was a question of the interests of her poor.

All this suggests that the whole of the sum of 10,000 thalers the Canon had given her had been used up; either that or she was keeping what was left of it for some extremity. By now she was operating only upon what she could obtain from others. Food she accepted wherever she could get it, but money mostly came from people she knew, friends and relatives. Some of these tried to have a little fun at her expense. One of them said jestingly to her: "Why yes, Frances, I'll give you something but only on condition that you come for it during daylight wearing men's boots." He probably never seriously expected her to do this: either she would not come at all, in which case he would be absolved from giving his contribution, or (more probably) she would arrive in her own shoes and pass over his condition as being merely facetious. But no, she duly appeared next morning, clumping along in men's heavy boots; she was going to take no chances of a refusal. And one suspects that she rather relished the little joke.

A somewhat similar incident occurred one day when Father Istas accompanied her on an expedition beyond the city walls. Usually she went alone, and putting whatever she received into her basket — sometimes a heavy weight for her frail body to carry — she would trundle off very happily. This time she was offered, instead of vegetables, a young pig; but the man said, "I am sorry that I cannot take it in for you, Fräulein, but if you know of any way that you can get it where you want it . . . " .

This was something new in her experience, but she was daunted by nothing. So she asked simply, "Have you a piece of rope?"

When he gave her the rope, Father Istas tied it round one of the porker's hind legs. As the animal struggled hard, squealing desperately, it had to be dragged along backwards all the way into the city, while a good many jeers and much laughter attended the trio. It took until evening for them to reach St. James's Gate, and here, as at all the city gates, toll-gatherers were posted; they guffawed loudly at the ludicrous spectacle. But they knew Frances and Father Istas, and when they heard the story of how they had obtained the pig, they were, without ceasing to be vastly amused, touched by what

55

they could not help seeing was a heroic exercise of charity, and so let them pass with their prize without demanding the usual tax.

Though the soup kitchen had come to take first place in her activities, Frances by no means gave up her visits to the houses of such of the poor as were sick. And though by now the idea of the Trappistines was long since abandoned, Frances's thoughts were still of the religious life. Whatever the reason may have been, she rejected the advice given by her confessor that she join the Sisters of Charity, but she thought of the Borromean Sisters, who were already established in Cologne in a hospital. Even more she wished she could become one of the Good Shepherd Sisters, whose sole work was that of rescuing fallen women, but to join whom she would have had to go to Angers in France. She had already reclaimed some of these unfortunates, but as she had no means of looking after them herself, she turned them over to Father Nellessen, a priest who had established a refuge for women of this sort.

To Father Istas, Frances confided that, happy as she was in the work she was doing as his assistant at the "Preachers," and (as opportunity served) for the sick and the girls who had gone astray, she knew she could never be satisfied until she was able to consecrate herself entirely to God in a religious community. Then this could be just no more than a project kept in reserve, for she felt she would never obtain her father's consent. However, plans could be made for the future, and Father Istas did not discourage her as, in one way or another, the rest of her priestly advisers had done. In this he was very disinterested, for though she was of great help to him and was doing a vast amount of good in the parish, he was not going to oppose a still higher vocation, should it ever become feasible. "But meanwhile, Frances," he said, "go on with what you are doing. Pray to God for guidance, and I shall not fail to pray for you."

Frances was now about twenty-two and therefore could

have regarded herself as no longer under the legal authority of her father. Even less was she under any moral obligation. But she had to recognize that he had been rather lenient, according to accepted ideas, towards her, and even surprisingly understanding. That made her reluctant to enforce any demands of her own, even had she been quite free to attempt this. One thing, however, must always be remembered: in the society in which Frances had been brought up a father's wishes were respected; they were accorded a weight which might seem excessive and, today, even a bit quaint. Even when she was twenty-six Frances did not feel that she could move in opposition to her father. She had succeeded in establishing a large measure of independence; she would never have exercised it so far that it would have involved the flouting of her father's will. That Pauline was at home, and now managing the household, had given her this liberty; but what had happened was mainly due, after all, to Herr Schervier's acceptance, much against the grain, of his daughter's desire to devote herself to charity. In the face of such complaisance, Frances considered herself bound. She saw, as Father Istas did, that she would have to wait until God Himself opened the way for her.

6

★

The Germ of the Idea

It will have been noticed that the general idea of Frances Schervier's lifework had already taken shape, although she was not free to carry it out for some time to come. She still needed further preparation, which came in an exceedingly strange form: it was a grave illness coupled with a recurrence of those impure imaginings which she records as having assailed her when she was a little girl, twelve or thirteen years earlier.

A few words of comment might be given in advance. There is perhaps nothing very unusual in one who contracted fever — in this case typhoid fever — being in the state of debility that brings on such fantasies. It is a common enough experience of good people that when the body is weakened the mind becomes more or less temporarily unhinged; in such a condition one is peculiarly vulnerable to all kinds of phantasms. The old rhyme, "the Devil was sick, the Devil a saint would be; the Devil was well, the Devil a saint was he," is often wide of the mark, psychologically speaking. When one is ill, especially when one has a sickness that disorders the brain, one is most susceptible to the weaknesses of fallen human nature. No blame can be attached to the matter. These new imaginings are far more understandable than similar torments that overtook Frances, so she records, when she was only nine. Since then she had been as free from them as it is possible to be; now they returned with a force greater than ever.

She says in her autobiography that she could point out the exact spot where she felt herself suddenly attacked with the fever. "I felt," she wrote, "as if a dagger were thrust into my brain and into my heart." She had nursed several people the previous year who were suffering from typhoid and had come off scot free. It was not from that source that she had been affected.

The attack came very early in the morning, about five o'clock, when she had already arisen. And though she at once took to her bed, she rose again at seven so as to be able to attend Mass, first making her confession to Canon Kloth, her pastor, a priest of whom we shall hear a good deal more in connection with her affairs. When she got home she hurried back to bed, and in bed she remained 26 days before the crisis came. The doctors who were brought in subjected her to the treatment then in vogue, cupping and leeching, thus leaving her all the more weakened, so that the only nourishment she could take was in the form of liquids poured down her throat. She lay day after day with closed eyes, insensible to the outward world, with all her senses, except that of touch, completely paralysed.

The worst part of the illness, to her, was that the temptations now seemed too strong to resist. "Every breath," she wrote, "every movement seemed to me a consent of sin." The heavens were blotted out and, she adds, "My spirit was so oppressed with fear of yielding to the enemy that the vagaries of fancy usual in this sickness did not occur." Frances did not yield, but she was overwhelmed with fear that she might yield. Father Istas visited her almost every day, standing at the head of her bed where he would say the Litany of the Most Holy Name of Jesus and some other prayers. Once when he did not begin to pray as soon as he had arrived, she managed, by opening her eyes, to convey her wish that he should pray. Herr Schervier, who was present, noticed this and told the priest, "I think Frances wants you to do something." At this Father Istas bent over and asked, "Do you want me to pray? I thought you were too weak." She managed to make some sign of assent and after his prayers she felt calmed.

Suddenly these temptations departed, having made her suffer intolerable anguish. They were succeeded by temptations even more terrible, temptations against faith in God. They too were ineffectual, for Frances fastened her eyes upon the crucifix in her darkened room and interiorly made the act of faith: "If everything else is taken from me, I believe in God and in everything taught by the Catholic Church." With this the temptations vanished and she was at peace, though after this from time to time her mind wandered a little, only, however, into harmless fantasies.

The experience of this illness was to be of immense value to one whose main work was to be that of serving the sick. She was brought to realize that these imaginings were only due to her weakened condition, so that when she saw other people similarly assailed, she understood that this was caused by weakness rather than by positive wickedness. The knowledge was of great use to her when she had to deal with such cases. She had discovered that it was only when she was sick that she had to suffer these things and that in health she was free of them. This subject is the theme of one of Francis Thompson's most remarkable essays, the one entitled "Health and Holiness."

Yet Frances Schervier judged herself severely. She had barely held her ground, and this was a source of deep self-humiliation. She was able to console herself with the reflection that, had she died then, she would have "just succeeded" in being numbered among the elect, but that she could have gained heaven only after a long purgatory. That she had not died made her very grateful to God: this gave her a new lease of life and a new time of grace. Father Jeiler admits that many would regard this as "morbid self-deception," but he concludes that it aided her to arrive at supernatural illumination, for she had been shown the depths of human misery and the sublime heights of divine purity. Again we can see, as she came to see, an important stage in her preparation.

One other circumstance of this illness should be noted. No sooner had the temptations departed — and with this came the crisis of her long illness — than what she calls "a luminous picture" presented itself to her soul. "It seemed to me," she continued, "as if a beautiful woman surrounded by dazzling light and royal splendor stood at the head of my bed. She bent over me and gave me my health." Though Frances's mind may not have been quite free from the last phantasms of her illness, it was at least clear enough to enable her to avoid all suggestion that what she had seen was an actual apparition of the Blessed Virgin. Her characteristic honesty makes her write: "I believe it was only an effect of my imagination; yet it produced a great impression on me and caused me to shed copious tears." Her conclusions were that in such illnesses as typhoid fever, "the mind is often not so bound up in the body as when in its usual condition; and therefore it is better adapted for the reception of spiritual impressions, both of a good and an evil kind. In such a state we may be visited by apparitions of light, and by dreadful ones of darkness." She saw now why it is at the approach of death that Christians are especially in need of spiritual assistance and prayer.

Her trials were not over, though the following incident, which she assigned to about the year 1843 may have been part of her illness of 1842, for in the nature of things her chronology is often not perfectly definite. In any event it reveals an extremely overwrought condition, though this was soon to pass away, never to return. She says that she had just returned home from church and was changing her dress when she found (or thought she had found) that she had suddenly lost her sight. As she had never had any trouble with her eyes before, this was naturally a great shock. But as she adds that she remained quiet and that the blindness soon passed, we must regard the incident as something very different from what at the moment she thought it to be; it was probably some temporary nervous affliction.

Though at first she was filled with unutterable sadness, soon after she was seized with a fit of uncontrollable laughter, which was so contrary to her ordinary serenity that she fancied that this marked the onset of insanity. She even fancied that she heard a demoniac voice telling her that she was about to become demented and that she would be compelled to curse and blaspheme God in that condition. She was filled with horror and felt herself on the edge of a terrible abyss. Scarcely able to breathe for her terror and imagining that within her there was going on a tremendous conflict between two opposing forces, she quite expected to go out of her mind the next instant.

Our generation has become so psychiatry-conscious — rather too much so — that any of us could have told the poor girl that she had no need to worry. The very fact that she feared insanity at a moment's notice proves that she was only in a nervous condition, due almost certainly to the fact that she brooded so constantly over her vocation. But she showed, as before, her fundamental spiritual balance by the way she dealt with this momentary crisis, which, by the way, she says had occurred once or twice before, though without the same degree of fierceness. Nothing was more dreadful than the thought of losing her reason; she kept her hold on it (if she were really in any danger of losing it) by making then and there a firm resolve to submit even to its loss, should this be God's will. Falling on her knees before a crucifix she prayed: "If it be Thy will that I become demented, let it be accomplished. But this one thing I implore: that Thou wilst not permit me to blaspheme and curse Thee while I am in that state." At once a great tranquility of soul flowed over her. She was able to perform that day's work and that of the days that succeeded with a more profound recollection of spirit than before.

The acute mental sufferings she had to undergo served, like her temptations, to which they were undoubtedly related, to strengthen her spiritual life. They made her all the more holy; they also served to fit her better for the work that lay ahead. In short, what she believed was the frustration of her vocation turned out to be an indispensable part of that vocation.

The biographer of Frances Schervier is obliged, even more than most biographers, to fall back upon conjecture, because of the definiteness of details at some points and the indefiniteness at others. Only in this way is it possible to bridge the gaps and to place matters in orderly sequence. With regard to the dates, it is perhaps enough to say that the years 1841 to 1843 were of peculiar difficulty for Frances. Though one is disposed to group together the things that have been related up to the time of her fever and convalescence, one cannot be at all sure that this is correct.

Another factor must be allowed for. Though it is quite possible that her father was more unobservant than most men, he could hardly have failed to see that Frances was in an extremely tense state. He had probably given her her freedom not altogether out of Christian zeal but because he saw that this was necessary to Frances's well-being. And Canon Deboeur, who looked upon himself as Frances's second father, as a priest should have had a special insight into states of the soul. The two men may be presumed to have discussed the situation together anxiously and to have reached the conclusion that the only safe course was to slacken the rein for Frances. What neither grasped was that she was not given enough freedom. Each man — father and proxy godfather — was resolutely opposed to the radical solution of making Frances completely free.

Frances did not open her mind to either of them, because she dared not do so. Her father had given his reluctant consent to her charitable activities. She could not bring herself to ask for more lest she get the answer, "No, Frances, you are not to become a religious. See where my leniency has led!

First I let you operate through the seamstress. Then I stretch things, or you contrive to make me stretch them, by letting you nurse people in her company. Finally you have managed to go out alone, begging in market places among very low-class people, from whom you come back dragging pigs to be cooked in your precious soup kitchen. I have known more than you suppose of your doings. I know how you have sold all your plate and used your dowry to give money away, often to utterly worthless people. The time has come for me to put my foot down and to forbid absolutely these eccentric activities of yours."

He did not say anything of the kind, but Frances probably feared that she would hear something like this from him if she had disclosed what her full ambition was. Therefore, knowing how useless it would be and torn between gratitude for the freedom that had been accorded and a hunger for a complete consecration that her father would never allow, she did not speak.

It is possibly true enough that a soul more perfectly resigned to the will of God would have waited with more patience than Frances showed. But one would be unfair to expect from a young girl, very independent of mind, yet rather timorous in some ways, sensitive, as yet inexperienced, and without any systematic spiritual direction, the perfectly rounded holiness of a saint. If it comes to that, the saints themselves did not attain holiness at a stroke, but only after struggles and mistakes. If in the face of what appeared to be insurmountable opposition, Frances now and then — not always, but now and then — cried out in agony and her sense of frustration brought her to the very verge of a serious nervous collapse, it is not to be wondered at. What is to be wondered at is the way she always recovered at the last moment by committing herself and all her concerns to God. That He had never ceased to have her safe in His keeping she came to see clearly; she also saw how all her trials and temptations and tribulations were necessary to her spiritual development and fitted her for the work she was to do.

After the crisis of her illness, during her convalescence, the doctor advised her to take a short walk. This she did in company with Magdalen Hermans, her chief helper in her charities. The two women at once went to church and there, though it was not time for Mass, Father Istas administered Holy Communion to them. Then as the doctor advised a complete change of scene and occupation, Frances went to a village in the Belgian province of Limburg. He saw that she would never get completely well at home, where she would be constantly fretting about being unable to resume the labors of her charities. Herr Schervier and Canon Deboeur thoroughly concurred; they may even have hoped that, when she returned home, she would drop all her former activities.

Though it is not easy to fix all dates with precision, we know one thing for certain: this change of scene occurred towards the end of 1842, for on January 3, 1843, shortly after Frances went back to Aachen, Father Istas, her great friend and a tower of support to her in her perplexity, fell ill. His was some disease of the lungs which the doctors attributed to overexertion in preaching. It was, however, so serious that it soon became apparent that, short of a miracle, the good priest was going to die. Frances saw to it that the poor whom he had befriended in St. John's Kitchen made novena after novena in St. Paul's Church for his recovery; she also organized a pilgrimage to the shrine at Salvator Berg, just beyond the east wall of the city. It was all to no avail; on the day after Ascension Thursday he died, with Frances at his deathbed.

What he said to her at that time she does not record, except to say that she would never forget his words. Had she not accepted his loss as according to the will of God, she would have been in danger of another breakdown. Possibly Father Istas foresaw this likelihood and guarded against it with his last words.

What we know positively is this: after his body had been clothed in sacerdotal vestments for burial, Frances was granted the special privilege of praying beside him for an hour. She invoked him as a saint, asking his prayers for the poor and for herself. In memory of Elias giving his mantle to Eliseus she asked that he would give her his spirit. During his life he had never once touched her hand with his; he had an adroit way of giving her money or of taking money from her so that their hands never came into contact. Now she raised his hand and placed it on her head; so lying in his coffin, he was made to give her his blessing.

The work of St. John's Kitchen now more than ever devolved on her. A young priest of the parish was appointed to take the place of Father Istas, but one gathers that he was merely officially the head of the undertaking and never did very much; it is certain that he never showed anything like the zeal and energy of his predecessor. The real responsibility rested upon Frances's shoulders.

This responsibility, valiantly accepted, steadied her. So also did a dream she had after a long exhausting day of ladling out food to the poor. In this dream Father Istas appeared, transfigured as though he were an angel. He looked at her with a grave and benign aspect and said: "Do not weep, my child, but keep your affairs in order. I shall soon come to take you away." After that, though Frances knew it was only a dream, she was greatly consoled and no longer mourned his death. She also settled down to her work in a quieter way, though it was a busier way than ever, not worrying unduly about her vocation, but accepting the immediate tasks as God's will for her, believing that if He willed more for her, He would bring it about, without any fretful striving on her part.

Her father showed himself most kind and considerate, exhibiting a gentle indulgence not so evident in him previously. But Frances knew that on the point of her joining any religious community he would never budge an inch. So she ceased to think about that any more, leaving all to God. And in this way she went her serene way for nearly two years.

Then on February 26, 1845, her father died. Though Dr.

Rey says that the cause of his death was pneumonia and pleurisy, the suddenness of his passing, as described by Frances, points to a heart attack. She says that acute pains came on him during the night and that he fell to the floor. She alone of the family seems to have kept her head. She sent out her brother Henry to find a doctor, and Karl, who had been a priest since 1840, gave conditional absolution to his father, an indication that he was already unconscious. Frances herself ran out into the night to summon Father Fey so that he might bring the holy oils for Extreme Unction. A couple of rough men tried to stop her, probably imagining that, as she was out alone at that hour, she was a very different kind of person from what she really was. Through her tears she exclaimed: "My father is dying, and he has not received the sacraments!" At such a conjuration they fell back abashed. But when Father Fey arrived, simultaneously with the doctor, Herr Schervier had already breathed his last.

Frances mourned her father, all the more because she could not help being grateful to him, especially during the last years of his life when he had softened so much. At the same time she saw instantly that his death had set her completely free, and at that she rejoiced. Thirteen or fourteen years later, when the memory of her grief had mellowed and when she was able to trace distinctly the way she had been led, she was able to write: "I understood, after the death of my father, that all interior, as well as exterior, circumstances in which the Lord had placed me, had been only preparations for me to become an instrument for the fulfillment of His eternal plans."

During her hurried journey through the night in search of a priest, Frances had pressed a crucifix to her breast, imploring God that her father would not die unprepared. This consolation she did not have. And yet she was by no means left without hope. She remembered how upright and charitable a man her father had been, and how regular in the practice of his religious duties. She said that his unexpected death was a bitter chalice for all his children and added that it was the most harrowing experience of her life. "We leaned together upon the cross. The power of the Lord was manifested in our weakness and did not permit us to be confounded. The firm confidence in His mercy was balm to our hearts."

It took Frances several months to find her bearings. From a sorrowing family she could not at once separate herself. So she went on living at home, meanwhile attending to her work at St. John's Kitchen. Moreover, there were family affairs to settle, and these turned out to be rather involved. Frances lets it go with the laconic remark that her father was not a very good businessman. Henry, who was already his father's partner, took over the needle factory. Karl had a good position as teacher of religion in the schools of the city and so needed no other provision. Frances, though she had long since used up the money given her by the Canon and had sold all the plate, was assured of inheriting the Canon's fortune and could all the more readily renounce her share of the little her father had left. There would be enough to provide for Pauline when she came to marry. It seemed best to leave the needle factory under the sole charge of Henry; only by retaining that, the main if not the sole investment, undivided would there be much chance of Henry's being able to straighten out the complexities of the situation. Such at least would seem to be the only possible inference from such facts as Frances has recorded. If she ever did get anything from her father's estate, it must have been no more than, at most, a few hundred thalers.

She had already taken a step which was to indicate more definitely the path she was to follow through life. A sick widow, a very pious woman, whom she had nursed during 1843, had often urged her to join the Franciscan Third Order, to which she herself belonged. The suggestion was attractive, though at that time Frances knew very little about Franciscanism. What held her back was the knowledge that her father would be displeased. He had a prejudice against tertiaries because he had known some who, so he considered, were not all that they should have been, which may actually have been the case. What he should have grasped was that the faithfulness with which tertiaries living in the world, and preoccupied with their secular activities, carry out their obligations varies a good deal. Some are exemplary; others only partially and perfunctorily fulfill the requirements. A few of them may be only nominal tertiaries, as they are only nominal Christians. It does now and then happen that people join the Third Order during a fervent period and afterwards virtually forget that they are tertiaries. And Frances, knowing that if she herself became a tertiary she would feel bound to perform all that was theoretically required — the saying of the Little Office every day, and the keeping of the many fasts that are recommended rather than enjoined, was reluctant to add to her difficulties at home.

She struggled in this frame of mind for over a year, without coming to a decision. Then when the pious widow she had been nursing recovered her health, Frances no longer had occasion to visit her and so was freed from her importunities. Upon this, she dropped the whole idea of becoming a Franciscan tertiary.

Or so she thought. But on the feast of St. Anthony of Padua, June 13th, she attended the Franciscan Church of St. Nicholas, where Father Van der Meulen, the director of the Third Order, preached. His eloquent description of the Saint's life and of the Franciscan idea so deeply stirred Frances that, at the conclusion of the service, she went to the altar of St. Francis and there, to Francis himself and the Blessed Virgin and St. Anthony of Padua, she vowed to become a tertiary as soon as possible. All her doubts and hesitations had vanished at a stroke; so also had all fears as to what her father might say. Tears streamed from her eyes and she felt an ineffable peace.

On leaving the church, her first thought was to go at once

to the widow who had first suggested that she become a tertiary to ask what preparations had to be made for her reception, and what was the mode of application for membership. To her great surprise she found this widow walking beside her; she too, not unnaturally, had attended church that day. Pledging her to secrecy, Frances begged her to see Father Van der Meulen on her behalf. At the same time she gave her the trifling sum of money which would be needed for the Franciscan cord and scapular which, as a tertiary, she would have to wear under her dress.

The next day her friend reappeared. She had just come from seeing Father Van der Meulen. He had consented to enroll Frances among the tertiaries but he had assigned a date for her admission which, to her impetuosity, seemed a long way off. It was that of the Vigil of St. Peter and St. Paul, June 28th. To Frances it seemed an almost unbearable delay — one of two weeks! Father Van der Meulen must have known something about the religious zeal of Frances, otherwise he would hardly have accepted her without at least a preliminary interview. But he probably had heard that she had a reputation for enthusiasm, and he prudently left an interval sufficient for its subsidence, if it were only aroused by his sermon. However, her enthusiasm remained as ardent as ever, and on the appointed day he invested Frances with the scapular and cord in the presence of the pious old woman who had so often proposed that she become a tertiary.

Frances did not rest there. Now that she was a member of the Third Order she sought to get some of her friends to join it too. Among these were Catherine Daverkosen and her sister, and Gertrude Frank. Just how soon after her own reception they were received we do not know, for Frances merely says that it was "shortly afterwards." This may have meant a few weeks or a few months, or it may not have been until the death of her father made it possible for her to carry into execution plans which, until then, had necessarily remained rather vague. She was much in company with these ladies and also with a Joanna Bruchhaus, a seamstress living in such retirement that she never left the city except to take part in the annual pilgrimage to the shrine at Kevelaer, about 40 miles to the north, and once, in 1844, a still longer journey to the south to Trier (Treves) to venerate the Holy Coat exposed in the cathedral there on rare occasions.*

Joanna was of a lowly station in life; the others of the group were well to do. Catherine Daverkosen was even something of a society belle, though anything but empty-headed, for even then, she read a good deal, especially in the poets. As for Gertrude Frank, she was the daughter of a factory manager at near-by Laurenzberg. She had already been in a convent, the novitiate of the Good Shepherd Sisters at Angers, but had not remained, perhaps because she was something of an eccentric, with a very forthright way of speaking, but more likely because she was destined to carry out a mission for which her rugged bluntness qualified her. She was to play a decisive part in the formation of Frances's Congregation, which indeed, had it not been for her, might never have come into being.

Frances and these four friends of hers often talked of forming themselves into a religious community. But at this stage it was only talk and might have gradually evaporated had they not been spurred into action in a most extraordinary fashion.

Not all pious young women enter convents, and most fortunately so; but it is of course true that a good many of the pious, whether women or men, are given religious vocations. Thus Magdalen Hermans, who had been Frances's chief assistant during the early days of her charity work and whom Frances would have certainly tried to enlist had she been available, had several years previously joined the Congregation that Clara Fey had founded for the instruction of poor children. She ended her days as the superior of a convent of the Con-

* The Holy Coat has been exhibited only three times in the past 110 years: 1844, 1891, and 1933.

gregation of the Poor Child Jesus in England. Another for whose company Frances hoped strongly was Anna von Lommessen; Frances even thought of her as the superior of the community she had in mind, and she said, "I will join it as the very last and least!" But Anna had other plans. To Frances's appeal she could only answer, "Oh, how gladly would I join you! But I cannot, I dare not. Something in me restrains me and urges me to go elsewhere. It is a great sacrifice to tear myself away; it seems to me a mystical death." She stood firm and not long afterwards carried out her intention of joining the Religious of the Sacred Heart. The situation is illustrative of the wide variety of religious vocations.

But however much these zealous young women may have talked, there seemed no possibility of putting their plans into effect. Frances's father was not the only one who stood adamantine against them, and since in 1844 he was only sixty years old and apparently in excellent health, there was no evident reason why he should not live for another 10 or 20 years. Much the same was true of Catherine Daverkosen and Gertrude Frank: while their parents might not have been too unyielding, it was well understood that they would give no financial support. And without some money — it did not have to be a great deal, but *some* money was necessary — how could a start be made, even if Frances were free?

There was one other possibility: Frances knew that the Canon meant to leave her his money, and he was reputed to be very wealthy. But old and infirm people such as he often live a long time. And Frances certainly did not want him to die, for she was fond of him. In any event nothing could probably be counted upon from that source for years to come. It was a possibility but no more than that.

Small wonder that Frances was daunted. She now had a tiny group of Franciscan tertiaries around her, and their idea was to operate as a group, if this were feasible, one devoted to charitable enterprises, especially the nursing of the sick poor. Yet Frances was far from anxious to put herself forward as their leader, for when Anna von Lommessen would not accept that position, Frances thought of Catherine Daverkosen in that capacity. All that could really be said at this stage was that a band of friends existed, all of them devoted to the same objective.

The situation seemed, however, to be taking shape quite independently of their volition. Frances had long ago discarded her Trappistine ambitions; she had thought of the Borromean Sisters and also of the Good Shepherd Sisters, but had come to see that her vocation did not lie among them. And though she looked upon St. Vincent de Paul as a personal pattern, she was — for reasons that do not appear, though we may surmise a divine inspiration — not in the least attracted towards the Sisters of Charity. (The natural explanation here may be that her independent spirit resisted the pressure that her confessor had brought to bear at this point.) Clara Fey's Congregation does not seem to have been considered even for a moment, though as Clara was a friend, one might have expected that Frances would have felt drawn to throw in her lot there. But no, this was a Franciscan group, and though each member of it would have been perfectly free to each join a different order, they held, as though by some mysterious instinct, together.

And yet — such is human inconsistency! — even after the way had opened, even after unmistakable word had come from God as to what Frances was called to do, her reluctance to lead was so great that we shall find her trying, at the very last moment, to avoid her commission by joining another congregation. At the last moment, too, she turned again to what she recognized as obedience to God's will. She could therefore say with the fullest possible assurance that the work she came to accept was not of her choosing, that her Congregation was founded not by her but by God.

7

A Message from God

IT CAN BE IMAGINED in what disquiet and anxiety of mind
Frances found herself. The death of her father had indeed
made her her own mistress, but it had not supplied her with
even the slight material resources that seemed indispensable
for the carrying out of what she had in mind. But about her
own feelings she says little, indicating them only in very
restrained and detached language. Her fragmentary autobiography ends with the words: "All external circumstances
and internal conditions wherein the Lord had placed me were,
as it were, a preparation ordained by God to form me to what
He had decreed from all eternity concerning me. Therefore
I can only be sorry that in general I corresponded so negli-
gently with grace. Because God makes the development and
multiplication of this precious gift depend on faithful coop-
eration, I must in truth confess that there is scarcely to be
found on earth a more foolishly perverse and relatively more
culpable person than I was and still am. This is the verdict
of truth, proceeding from my most intimate conviction."
That she honestly believed this is beyond question; as to how
much objective truth there was in it will appear from what
will soon be related.

She had never wished to found a new religious community,
and though her circle of friends had been discussing the pos-

sibility of such a foundation, Frances had always taken it for granted that — should this become feasible in the face of all apparent probabilities — somebody else would be its superior. God simply had to force her hand to carry out His will.

Rarely has a religious founder acted so clearly under compulsion from on high. Usually, as in the case of St. Benedict and St. Ignatius, disciples gathered around, and circumstances gradually led to a formal organization. Francis of Assisi did indeed hear a voice from the Byzantine crucifix in the little dilapidated chapel near the city in the Umbrian hills telling him, "Rebuild My church," but he took the command in the most literal and most limited way as an order to repair that particular edifice. Only much later, after disciples had come to him, did it begin to dawn on him that the command had a much wider application. In the case of Frances Schervier, on the other hand, she had her disciples first, though she did not regard them as such. It was in fact one of these disciples who told her what she must do, not because this was her personal judgment but because she bore God's direct message.

It is all a very strange story, and one might think that a delusion was involved were it not for several sound reasons to the contrary. For one thing the outcome was so manifestly good, so manifestly blessed by heaven. For another, Frances was a woman of great caution in matters of this kind; she would not act except after several proddings and several consultations with her priest-advisers. Finally, the bearer of the message — most emphatic though she was on this occasion — never set herself up afterwards as a prophetess or as one endowed with extraordinary powers. The only subsequent prediction she was to make concerned herself: that she would never live to wear the habit of the Congregation and that she would die at the very age at which she actually did die. This very fact served to demonstrate the authenticity of her momentous message.

But first let us see what might possibly be urged on the other side. Frances had had such vivid dreams in childhood that she might have taken them as genuine apparitions; she did nothing of the kind. Again, when she was suffering from fever it seemed that the Blessed Virgin came to her; but Frances was careful to say that she saw nothing with the sight of her eyes. Finally, though she had undoubtedly come very close to a serious "nervous breakdown," she had avoided it by casting herself upon God. In any event since the death of Father Istas, two years before, all such manifestations had ceased. Since then she had worked quietly, doing the things that needed to be done immediately, and had left everything else to the divine guidance. Her becoming, after long hesitation, a Franciscan tertiary and persuading some of her friends to follow with her had been the only new development. That proved to be a step of utmost importance, and yet was in itself nothing very unusual. This gave her, it is true, the nucleus of a possible religious community, but several months passed after the death of her father before any definite attempt was made to bring it into being. There had been a good deal of rather vague talk about this, but everyone knows what a vast difference exists between talk and action, a hope for something and a determination to bring it about. When Frances was at last brought to act, it was reluctantly and because she dared not do otherwise.

What decided her was a message that was brought on Pentecost Sunday, May 11, 1845, by her friend, Gertrude Frank. Gertrude was of a family, all of whose members were devout and who lived at Laurenzberg, a village within short walking distance of Aachen where her father was the manager of a factory. Gertrude was of a taciturn disposition, with a notable abhorrence of anything savoring of untruth or detraction. She spoke only when she had something that really needed to be said, and she spent much of her time praying at the *prie-dieu* in her bedroom. It was there that occurred what is about to be related.

She had tried her vocation with the Good Shepherd Sisters at Angers in France but left, partly because her German temperament did not happily accord with a French community; partly because she was a bit too bluntly outspoken (or so one must suspect); but also partly — and here we do not have to guess — because the Good Shepherds, austere though their manner of life is, did not provide her with sufficient austerity. When she returned home it was to the displeasure of her parents, for though they had not wanted her to go in the first instance, they were apprehensive of what people might say about an abandoned vocation. They carried their disapproval so far as not to admit her into the house for two weeks; but when they at last relented and allowed her to cross the threshold, all was forgotten.

It was only on Sundays as a rule that Gertrude went to Aachen. There she attended several Masses and received Holy Communion, breakfasting at St. John's Kitchen (where she had become acquainted with Frances), and helping afterwards with the distribution of food to the poor. On the Sunday in question she found Frances busy with the preparations for the funeral of the father of one of the priests of the parish, a favorite charity of hers then and throughout life. She was so busy that she did not have an opportunity to talk to Gertrude. When she invited Gertrude to help, the excuse was made that it was late and that it was high time that she went back to Laurenzberg.

Early in the evening a furious storm, bringing torrents of rain, sprang up. Frances could not delay her return home because a friend of her brother Karl's, a Professor Floss, was to be a guest for the night, and she had proposed that the daughter of the dead man, Sibilla, should also stay with them. It was therefore a bit inconvenient when Gertrude arrived, drenched through and through, at the Schervier home.

"You here, Gertrude?" Frances exclaimed. "I thought you had gone to Laurenzberg."

The reply came, "I did set out, Frances, but I was overtaken by the storm." That would have been a perfectly adequate explanation in the case of anybody else, but Gertrude was the kind of masterful woman who would not have allowed an earthquake to deter her. Frances wondered where she was going to put her friend up for the night. She decided that Gertrude should sleep with Pauline and that she would take Sibilla in with her.

Dry clothing was found and some food. But this food was something of an embarrassment, for Frances knew that it was Gertrude's custom to take only a little bread and water at night, a custom she feared might cause some comment among the other guests. To her relief Gertrude that evening broke her usual rule and ate the same supper that was placed before the others.

The meal was hardly over when Gertrude's brother arrived. He said he had been sent by his parents, who were naturally anxious, to take his sister home. But Gertrude said she wanted to stay where she was; she was so very positive about this that in the end her brother departed alone.

By now it was eleven o'clock, and when Frances said, "It is too late to have an additional bed set up by the servants, so you had better sleep with me, Sibilla, and Gertrude will share Pauline's room," Gertrude quickly interposed: "No, Frances, *I* must sleep with you." As it was evident that Gertrude had made her mind up, Frances did not contest the point. After all, it did not matter a great deal. The great French bed she used had ample room for three, if necessary. She was sleepy and did not want to argue about so trivial a point.

Frances said her prayers quickly and climbed into bed, leaving Gertrude still on her knees and apparently intent on remaining there a long while. "Well," said Frances to herself, slightly irritated at Gertrude's dictatorial way, "Well, pray as long as you like!" Turning on her side, she at once fell fast asleep.

She had no idea how long Gertrude did keep at her prayers, but when Gertrude at last lay down beside her, it was to say, "What! are you already asleep, Frances. I want to tell you something."

Since Frances wanted to sleep, not talk, and was rather annoyed at being awakened, she said a little sharply, "I am asleep or awake, just as you please." To this Gertrude returned, "By the command of the Lord I have something to tell you."

This of course explained Gertrude's behavior, but it filled Frances with fear. Had Gertrude gone out of her mind? In any event she must be suffering from some delusion. Instinctively Frances did the right thing by praying silently, "Preserve me, O Lord, from deception and every vain sentiment accompanying it; and help me that I may not resist Thee by obstinacy." As she prayed, she folded her hands over her bosom as though to guard herself. Then with bated breath she said to Gertrude, "Well, now speak."

Gertrude told how she had had a vision of Christ as He was after the scourging at the pillar. When she bent to anoint His wounds, He had said lovingly to her, "If you would heal Me, you must fulfill My command." When she promised to do so, she was told to tell Frances to leave her home and family "to found a community which is to heal these wounds."

Gertrude went on to say that she had tried to give Frances this message at a previous meeting, but she had not known how to begin and so had gone home without having spoken. A few days later, Christ had appeared to her again with the same command, but as she had not been able to go to the city until the following Sunday, she again had found no opportunity of talking in private with Frances, which had made her very dejected. A third time Christ appeared, and this time she weepingly promised to do what was required of her. But she ventured to ask, "But will she believe me, Lord?" To which the answer came, "That is My affair. Yours is to comply with My will."

Gertrude went on: "When I came today and found you had no moment for me because of the funeral, I did not know what to do. My only consolation was that, as tomorrow is Pentecost Monday, I would be coming to the city again then.

But on my way home that dreadful storm began, and finally when I saw a thunderbolt strike the road I was about to take, I feared that the next flash would strike me down if I did not return. Now tell me, Frances, what shall I reply to the Lord? He expects your answer."

The rest of the story illustrates the simplicity and candor of both young women. Frances might have replied that she would make her own response to Christ. Instead she said mildly: "Gertrude, if you had only known me better you would have made objections to the Lord. You are not sent to *me*. A soul that has offended God so often cannot be of any use for such a purpose. Besides, I am awkward and ill-fitted for everything. Say this to our Lord the next time."

To this Gertrude returned in her plain-spoken way, "I have already told our Lord that, of my own accord."

"And what did He say?"

"The Lord said that by this very fact the work would be known as His and not man's." She added her own comment: "The lower and more insignificant the person is whom He has selected for His purpose, the more will the honor be given to Him, to Whom alone it belongs. It is for Him to choose His instrument at will, and also to sanctify and exalt it."

Gertrude continued to speak, simply but powerfully; she said God had shown her by a series of images what He purposed. She had seen a gnat, and as she gazed at it, it became a lion. A virgin — one very small and insignificant — was also shown; "and you," said Gertrude, "were this virgin. Soon afterwards you stood with a palm in your hand, at the head of a long procession, so long that I could not see its end; and all of them carried palms. Again a tree grew before my eyes and spread into an arbor protecting these virgins, and this changed into a splendid palace of crystal — crystal on the outside and gold within, like the New Jerusalem." Other things also had been revealed, but Gertrude said she was not sure whether it was permitted her to mention them.

From the marvellous outcome of this midnight talk, it

would seem that Gertrude really had spoken as God's mouthpiece: at the time, however, Frances in her humility reserved judgment. However, impressed with the sense of her own nothingness, she felt it safe to ask Gertrude to tell Christ, "I am ready to do everything He wishes. If He has selected the insignificant and the unworthy, He must be responsible for the result. If it actually is His will that I undertake this task, He should make it clear to me Himself. Remember, Gertrude, I would fear delusion, even if an angel from heaven had brought me this message."

The forthright Gertrude accepted so forthright an answer. She commented: "I am content with what you have said. For the rest God will provide." Then the two friends went calmly to sleep, for such of the night as remained to them, and were up in time to assist at the five o'clock Mass at St. Paul's and to receive Holy Communion.

In the morning Frances appeared to be more confused in the presence of her friend than she had been the night before. She was glad that Gertrude went home immediately after breakfast, making no further allusion to what had happened. That in itself was a good sign, but the more Frances thought about the matter, the more she felt the need of consulting some wise priest. This, however, she could not do at once, for she had to make preparations for the dinner that the family of the dead man were to share in the Schervier household. Nevertheless, she felt pervaded by a happiness similar to what she had experienced when she was confirmed. These were no doubt, she considered, at least in part, Pentecostal joys, but in part they were due to her already having answered Gertrude's summons, though she needed corroboration before she would act. Her peace upheld her during what would otherwise have been a difficult and distraught day.

With nightfall, however, a sense of unbearable oppression bore down upon her, the inevitable natural reaction to what she had gone through. She decided that the next morning she would bring the whole affair to the attention of Father Van der Meulen, the director of the tertiaries. As Gertrude's confessor he was probably already informed. Whether or not he had been, he was an experienced director of souls and a man of strong common sense. If there was any delusion here, he could be counted upon to recognize it as such and to correct it. Frances knew that Gertrude was very obedient to him. In every way Father Van der Meulen seemed the best man to consult.

After early Mass, at which Frances received Holy Communion, she visited him. He was surprised that she had called on him so early, and so as not to let him suppose that she was going to take up much of his time Frances remained standing, as did he. When she spoke of the divine message brought to her by Gertrude Frank, he smiled in such a knowing way that Frances surmised that he had heard about it already, though of course he did not say so, for whatever Gertrude had told him had been under the seal of confession.

The interview was brief but much to the point. He said, "To the Cross, to the Cross! Thence you must receive counsel and aid. The outcome will show whether this is an inspiration of God." He added that, for his part, he had nothing to say against it, though he would not commit himself to the other side either. He said further: "Gertrude is a pure, pious soul, and not easily moved to enthusiasm. She always takes a direct course, even if she should be obliged to crush something in her way. That is what I praise in her." He might have added that, forceful in character though she was, she was not the kind of person who puts herself forward as a leader.

Frances already knew that much about Gertrude's rather strange character. Her function seems to have begun and ended with bringing Frances the message that resulted in the formation of her Community. Never was she thought of as one to take command of anything. This may have been due to the fact that she was inclined to be eccentric. On the other hand, it may have been because she did not show much imagination, though this inclined those who knew of her message to believe in its authenticity. Still standing, Father Van der Meulen had a parting word of advice: "Go on, but beware of cloister fever!" He realized that the ardent desire these young women had for a community life might lead them to believe that heaven was confirming by revelation what they were hoping to gain.

When he said this, though the tears stood in Frances's eyes, she had to smile. The whole conversation had lasted only a few minutes. But though the priest had been rather noncommittal and even a trifle brusque, Frances felt relieved. He had not suggested the possibility of delusion but had merely advised her to seek further guidance from God Himself.

Taking him at his word, Frances decided that she would visit, as far as possible, all the churches of the city in which, in turn, the Forty Hours' Devotion was being conducted. There before the exposed Blessed Sacrament she would pray.

One afternoon a few days later Gertrude made one of her very rare midweek visits to Aachen. As Frances knew that this was specially to see her, she was uneasy and disturbed, for she was not yet ready to give any definite answer. She took Gertrude into an arbor in the garden where they could be alone, and Gertrude immediately came to the point, asking: "Have you done anything about this matter, Frances?" When she heard of the visit to Father Van der Meulen and was told by Frances that at the moment she had nothing further to report, Gertrude was not at all satisfied. "That's all very well, Frances," she said, "but it is not enough. You must go forward resolutely and without hesitation. I shall be able to have no rest — I am scarcely able to eat or sleep at present — until I know that you have decided to give yourself to this project without reserve." This was pressing rather hard, but shows Gertrude's deep conviction. She spoke not only of the loving and suffering Redeemer Whom she had seen in her visions, but of His faithful follower St. Francis, and Frances felt her to be indeed a messenger from the Saint, of whom she was vividly reminded by the yearning expression on Gertrude's emaciated face. Frances again insisted on her unworthiness and made some humiliating confessions which she supposed would prove this. At the same time she assured her friend that she was taking the matter seriously and would pray earnestly about it. She had to wait for further light, but after Gertrude had left, she leaned back in the leafy shadows of the arbor, folded her hands in resignation, and looking up to heaven said, weeping, "My heart is ready, O Lord, my heart is ready. Do but grant me the necessary light, and the requisite grace and strength."

There were other similar interviews, Gertrude always trying to push Frances on and Frances always feeling pained and embarrassed in her presence. What was being proposed seemed so heavy a cross that it could be accepted only from the hand of God. In these interviews Gertrude brought other revelations which, writing many years later, Frances had to regard as divine communications. But she also records — and this is very significant: "Sometimes she would mix her own observations with the most sacred and important things; then I would express myself plainly and strongly regarding her folly. If my replies had reference to her own views and observations, she always remained calm and easily yielded; with regard to the real issue, her supernatural communications, she remained inflexible." In other words, Frances had the good sense to distinguish clearly between Gertrude's personal opinionativeness and the essential matter; and so did Gertrude, when challenged. Both young women were keeping their heads and showing perfect sincerity and humility.

It will be remembered that Gertrude had first spoken on the night of May 11th; it was nearing the end of June before Frances obtained what she felt to be necessary, a direct assurance from God. She had been praying all that while, but without getting the answer she sought. Then during the Forty Hours' Devotion, at St. James's Church, at a time when very few people were there, her eyes fell on a banner near the altar. It represented Christ embracing the Cross with one arm, and as Frances gazed at it, it seemed to her that Christ looked straight at her.

The sight of the Saviour and the Cross so affected her that she implored Him with all the more fervor to enlighten her regarding His will. (She did not suggest, by the way, that she beheld more than the pictorial representation of Him; on the contrary she tells us that at first she was left in total darkness and that, when the answer came, it was in her soul, not by visible or audible impressions.) * But as she prayed, hoping against hope, light began to flood her. To quote her now: "It seemed as though a fair aurora had dawned in my mind, becoming brighter and brighter, until finally I discerned, as in the strongest midday light, what the Lord desired. The Lord spoke to me in spiritual communication even more explicitly than if He had addressed me in words, saying: 'Behold Thy Redeemer! Behold how I have submitted to all the hardships and fatigues of life, especially during the three years of my public ministry. See the Cross which was my portion from the first moment of my earthly life until I gave up my spirit into the hands of my Father . . . Wilt thou cowardly shrink from what I have embraced, for love of thee and all mankind, with so fervent a desire?' "

Now at last she was convinced. She was ready to begin her work and felt sure that she would find the way, if only she confided herself entirely to the guidance of Providence. Though she had taken six weeks to reach her decision and another three months had to elapse before she was able to

* It is with some hesitation that I quote the words that Frances records as spoken to her — not by an apparition but by something perceived interiorly. As in the case of St. Margaret Mary Alacoque, the language of Christ as quoted here does not correspond very closely to the magnificent style of the words of Jesus as recorded in the Gospels. I suggest that these latter (and private) revelations are filtered, as it were, through the human medium, so that while the substance may be accurately conveyed, it is also clouded. Or we may use the simile of a perfectly straight stick which, if put in the clearest water, still appears to be bent, the result of the refracting element.

put her plans into execution, she looked upon Pentecost, 1845, as the date of the founding of her Congregation.

It is worthy of note that she made a last-minute attempt to escape from what seemed to her a crushing obligation. Father Fey suggested that it would be well for her to stay three weeks during August in a convent so as to get a clearer idea as to just what community life involved. Accordingly she went to the Sisters of the Holy Cross * at Liége. These Sisters had only recently been founded by Canon Habets and Joanna Haase (who became their superior as Mother Teresa), and as theirs was a vocation Frances proposed to follow, Father Fey believed she could with profit study their mode of life. It appealed to Frances so much that, for a short while, she felt strongly moved to join that community. She asked God to release her and to let somebody else make the foundation He had commanded.

She laid her views before Mother Teresa and also Canon Habets, asking them to receive her as a novice, which they were quite willing to do. But when she went on to request that a house of the Congregation be established at Aachen, she was told that this would not be possible during the immediate future. Yet hope of this was not altogether taken away, so that Frances tried to convince herself that by a roundabout means she might carry out God's will. That she herself should be a foundress was most repugnant to her.

That afternoon she went again to the chapel to pray before the Blessed Sacrament, making the most solemn promise to serve Christ until death, if He would but permit her to remain as the least of the Sisters of the Holy Cross. In the silence of the chapel she broke into sobs until suddenly there came a Voice from the altar — this for the first and, so far as we know, for the last time a Voice that was heard by her ears. She lifted her face, which had been buried in her hands, and

---

* They are not to be confused with the women's branch of the Congregation of the Holy Cross founded about the same time by Father Moreau at Le Mans.

looked towards the tabernacle. Nothing was to be seen, but the voice came again: "Simon Peter, lovest thou me?" Frances made Peter's response: "Lord, Thou knowest all things; Thou knowest that I love Thee."

It was the end at last of all struggling against the will of God. She felt transported for the rest of that day, insensible to all external things. At Benediction that evening she wept so freely that Mother Teresa spoke to her afterwards, only to get the reply, "I am a poor captive of the Lord." She did not bring up again the request that she be admitted to the Holy Cross Community, nor did she mention the words she had heard. Years later she told a priest about it and she thought, but was not sure, that she told Gertrude at that time. Everything was now settled in her mind. She employed the remaining time in Liége in making a rough sketch of some of the rules in vogue there and of the rules she thought her own Community should adopt.

But ways and means had still to be discovered. When Frances consulted Father Sartorius, the closest friend of the Father Istas who was no longer there to advise her, she says that "he expressed himself very soberly and coldly concerning our plan." In short, he was dubious about the whole affair, seeing more clearly than she did what difficulties lay ahead. It does not appear that he was given her confidence with regard to the message that Gertrude had brought but was merely asked to advise as to how they should proceed.

Nor were Frances and Gertrude in very close agreement as to what should be their mode of life. Gertrude maintained that they should follow the Rule of St. Francis to the letter, which, had they done so, would have resulted in their being strictly cloistered like Poor Clares. Though Frances did not as yet have any very clear concept of the spirit of St. Francis, she maintained that a cloistered life would make all works of active charity virtually impossible. She insisted that St. Catherine of Siena should be their model, though that was also rather wide of the mark, except in the sense that St.

Catherine was a Dominican tertiary living in the world.* The friends argued one day so heatedly in the presence of Father Van der Meulen that he laughed and said, "If you ladies wish to settle this, you had better step outside." In the end Gertrude conceded that works of charity were not to be omitted. They were in fact the main object the group proposed to seek.

Frances admitted later that she had submitted to the divine will only out of fear of Hell; it was the first and last time that she was actuated by this motive. Even so, as the time drew near for her to leave her family, she felt so strong an attachment to her two brothers and her sister — and also the Canon — that she felt she could never bring herself to the separation. Indeed, she could argue, why should she? She was now perfectly free to carry out her works of charity without the slightest restriction. Why make any change in her mode of life?

Just before she had gone to Liége she had experienced a strong revulsion of feeling. Gertrude was visiting her and, as usual, calling upon Frances to do what was required. Under this pressure she feared that she would angrily explode. The only way she avoided this was by going to her room, throwing herself upon her bed, pressing her face into her pillow, and giving free vent to her tears. The emotional outlet relieved her. She returned to Gertrude an hour or so later, greatly calmed. It was in great peace of soul that the two friends went that afternoon to confession in preparation for the Communion they intended to receive on the morrow, St. Dominic's day. But up to the very last moment Frances felt it hard to leave home.

When the time came for her to do this, she broke the news to her family and Canon Deboeur, who had now lived for several years in the Schervier home, by letter. She had the

* She wore, as did St. Rose of Lima, and of course some other forgotten tertiaries, the Dominican habit, something now worn by secular tertiaries only in the grave. Frances probably was only vaguely informed at this time about such matters.

excuse in the case of the Canon that a letter would be better than shouting through cupped hands into the ears of a deaf man, though the real reason — as appears in the family also being informed in this way — was that she would have to face none of them. Her brothers and her sisters were, however, very sympathetic and had probably been expecting something like this to happen. They said they were sorry to see her go but would put no obstacles in her way, since she felt she was carrying out the will of God. They also promised to help her so far as they were able to do so; and this promise was redeemed by the two brothers with donations (a little later Karl also served her as an unpaid chaplain). As for Pauline, she threw in her lot with her sister before long.

The poor Canon, however, was stricken to the heart, which was what Frances had feared. Yet he could not have been really surprised, though he had clung to the hope that his dear Frances would take care of him for the rest of his life. He was already old and in poor health and dependent upon the services the Scherviers gave him. When Frances's letter arrived he was so upset that he locked himself into his room and would see nobody that day. It was not until the following day, when his friend Father Classen (who had been Frau Schervier's confessor and who was to become auxiliary Bishop of Cologne) called to see him, that he calmed down and resigned himself to the inevitable.

Frances and her friends had decided to go forward, even in the face of what appeared to be insuperable difficulties. They were a very small group, and Frances's mainstay was not (as might have been expected) Gertrude Frank but Catherine Daverkosen, later Sister Mary, a tall stately young woman. But Catherine's parents were unyielding, so she had to extract their consent by the exercise of a guile which one wishes it were not necessary to record. As she could think of no other way, she asked her father and mother for permission to visit her married sister in Mannheim for the summer. They agreed to this, and then at the moment of parting they were told by

Catherine that when she returned to Aachen she would not go home but be joining Frances in her new work. Just why this "stratagem," as Jeiler calls it, should have been successful is not easy to see. Herr and Frau Daverkosen could, presumably, have stood firm, and might have been pardoned had they been annoyed at the trick played upon them. But as the visit to Mannheim had already been arranged they let her go, no doubt counting upon being able to deter her by letter while she was there, while Catherine counted upon being better able to withstand pleas made to her by letter than those made in tearful conversation. She seems to have been the only one of Frances's followers who had any money, but it was only the pitifully small sum of 200 thalers. Gertrude did not have even that much, for her father and mother, pious people though they were, tried to prevent her from making what they considered a harebrained move by cutting off supplies. If Frances had anything we do not hear of it. The Canon's plate had long since been sold and all of his 10,000 thalers given away. Her brother Henry may have given her a small sum, but that could, at best, have been all that she had available.

Their poverty, far from being a hindrance to the young women, was actually preferred. They would be obliged to trust completely in Providence. Frances would not have been averse to using the inheritance which, so she had often been assured, was to have come from the Canon, as that would be useful in the buying of a house for a convent or for building one; but she felt that she would show distrust in God if she waited for this.

Even so, they could hardly have acted had not an elderly widow named Beissel, devout and wealthy, come to their rescue with an offer to pay the rent of a house in any part of the city for three years, adding that she hoped to be able to pay the rent for them even after that. "Would that be of any help?" she asked. Frances at once answered, "It is more than enough; it is too much. Well, now we are ready."

The house taken for them was number 12, beyond St. James's Gate, that is, just outside the ancient fortifications. It was near St. James's Church and not far from Frances's old parish church of St. Paul's; as such its situation was well suited to them. Since it was rather roomy it was also well suited to needs which were soon to become apparent. One must suppose that it must have been at least partly furnished, for 200 thalers — if that was all they actually had — would not have gone far towards buying even the cheapest sort of secondhand beds and tables and chairs. But furnished or not, Frances and her friends were not going to lose this opportunity and so eagerly accepted Frau Beissel's offer.

The house was rented for them from September 1st, but they did not get into it, as it happened, by that date, as the family in occupancy could not find another house and so their tenancy was extended by a month. Meanwhile, Frances and Catherine and Gertrude had the promise of the seamstress Joanna Bruchhaus that she would join them, and a girl named Catherine Lassen, who had hitherto lived at home helping her mother with the housework, also came forward. This meant that instead of starting with a community of three (including herself) Frances would have a group of five. It would, Frances saw, make a good deal of difference in their effectiveness. Already God had shown that His blessing was on their undertaking.

Frances, Gertrude, and Catherine agreed that they would go to Cologne for a private retreat, and while in that city they arranged to occupy some rooms used by students who were at that time on vacation. One imagines the furnishings of these rooms and the pictures on the walls did not seem very appropriate to young women about to begin a religious life, though duelling swords crossed on the wall and steins on the mantelpiece could be tolerated.

Why Cologne was chosen is not at all clear, unless it was that the three friends — Frances was twenty-six, Gertrude thirty-one, and Catherine not quite thirty — wished to get away from a town where they were well known and in which they might have had the intrusion of visitors who would not have been welcome just then. Though Frances had already sketched out while at Liége some rules for their guidance, she realized that these would not be quite adequate. She therefore got together any books that she could lay her hands on that might give some inkling as to the nature of the religious life. Meanwhile Joanna Bruchhaus and Catherine Lassen were assigned the task of getting the house at Aachen ready for their arrival. When its occupants departed at the end of September, they left it in an untidy condition; there was much work to be done.

Frances and Gertrude and Catherine had gone to Cologne on September 24th, intending to stay a week. It turned out to be longer than that, for on the 28th Frances came down with an attack of erysipelas. Her face swelled out frightfully, so that she was hardly able to open her eyes. The date of October 1st was now out of the question. A doctor was summoned, and he did what was necessary, with such effectiveness that he was astonished at the rapidity of Frances's recovery. On October 2nd Frances was well enough to leave her lodgings for a walk; the next day, early in the morning, they started for Aachen.

Catherine Daverkosen had brought such a pile of baggage with her from Mannheim that they were obliged to take a wagon. The journey took the entire day, so that it was half-past six when they lumbered into Aachen to take possession of their new home. As they drew near the city they heard bells ringing from every steeple; it was to announce the Feast of St. Francis of Assisi on the morrow. Had it not been for Frances's erysipelas, they would have been there on October 1st; as it was these Franciscan tertiaries began their community life on St. Francis's day. No day could have been more fitting.

Establishment

It MUST BE understood from the outset that this group of five young women did not constitute, as yet, a religious community in the canonical sense but only a voluntary pious society. Many religious congregations have, however, begun in much the same way. Thus in our country the Maryknoll Sisters, who are Dominican tertiaries, but who wear a uniform of practical gray instead of the beautiful black and white wool of St. Dominic, were at the outset no more than a band of secretaries helping the editors of a missionary magazine. Then in private each took a "religious" name, Mary Joseph, Anna Maria, and so forth, but did not use the appelation of Sister until their canonical recognition. Frances and her first group did not even adopt religious names, except that Catherine Daverkosen, in order to escape confusion with Catherine Lassen, decided to be known as Mary. But all addressed one another as "Sister" except for Frances, who from the start was "Mother." For that matter she had been "Mother Frances" to the poor of Aachen she befriended for some years past. The titles had at that time no official signification.

As soon as the three who had arrived from Cologne were greeted by the two who had been getting the house ready, they all knelt for a short time in prayer, commending themselves and their undertaking to God; then Gertrude, never one to lose a moment's time, asked Frances to assume the superiorship. Frances quite properly refused, saying that a superior must be duly elected. So after invoking the Holy Ghost, votes were cast, and Frances was inevitably chosen.

She tried to evade office, pointing out that she was small and that since her typhoid fever her hair had not fully grown again, making her look more like a child than an adult. She used other arguments — that she was ignorant and uncultured and deficient in all the necessary qualifications; but it was all useless. She herself cast her vote for Catherine Daverkosen, whom she knew to be thoroughly capable and of stately bearing and captivating address. But as the others had elected her, Frances submitted, though with feelings of anguish. Upon this Gertrude Frank — who, though she was never considered for office, took it upon herself to be a kind of tutelary genius — informed the others that they must now always address Frances as "Mother Frances."

None of this, of course, canonically speaking, meant that the group was now a religious community — a point to be borne in mind in view of other happenings soon to be related. There is, however, a practical point of view to be considered here. Every human group — and the same is usually true even of animals — needs some leader, some person in authority, if order is to be preserved. And it must be remembered that this little band of women was already looking forward to the time when they would be recognized by the ecclesiastical author- ities, something that would be all the more speedily obtained the sooner they presented the formation of a religious com- munity. This, in their manner of life, they were from the Vigil of St. Francis, 1845, though Frances preferred to push back the date to Pentecost of that year, when at about one in the morning Gertrude Frank brought her an astounding message from Heaven.

There exists a paper in Frances's hand, which has every appearance of having been written during the days of her seclusion in Cologne during September, in which she sets out the purpose the group held before themselves:

Having resolved of our free will to observe the three evangelical counsels, living in conventual community, and to devote ourselves to the service of the sick and poor, and to the reformation of fallen women, we bind ourselves to order our life and work according to the following rules:

Christ, our divine Spouse, is to be our model, our life, our strength, the inspiration of our souls; Mary is to be our Mother; St. Francis our Father; St. Vincent de Paul, St. Catherine of Siena, and St. Mary Magdalen are to be our special patrons. Convinced that we must have a Superior to obey, who is to direct and manage everything, being above us in position, but equal to us in everything else, and who is to walk before us in the practice of poverty and humility, in the faithful observance of the rule and in love for the Crucified and His members: we intend, with the assistance of the Holy Ghost, to elect one. And in the presence of God we promise Him, our God, most punctual obedience in the person of this our Superior. *Veni, Sancte Spiritus!*

As that is hardly detailed enough to constitute a "rule," properly speaking, we must suppose that the actual drawing up of their eventual rule was deliberately left to a later period, when experience would have shown what was most advisable. What we have here is a statement of the purpose of the group in general terms. For the rest, the Rule of the Third Order, which went back to 1221, sufficed. That indeed said nothing about begging, but as its heart was the spirit of poverty and as they could support themselves only by begging, begging became an integral part of their mode of life. The regulations as to how often meat might be eaten had little application to women who rarely got enough to eat and hardly ever any meat. The saying of the Little Office of Our Lady was also provided for. This they said in German, not Latin. About all that they needed to do was to go on as before. Almost the only thing added at this stage was the community life.

They lived together in an obedience freely tendered, but

not an obedience promised under vow, for they were not bound in any way, except by the obligations they had accepted when they became Franciscan tertiaries. As they had no chapel in the house and no permission to have the Blessed Sacrament reserved, they went together every morning, very early, to St. James's before beginning their rounds of begging and nursing. Frances still had charge of the St. John's Kitchen at the "Preachers," which was an activity of St. Paul's parish, and soon afterwards they set up another soup kitchen for the poor in St. James's parish.

There was possibly a shade less of the informality that had characterized their work only a year or so before. Thus Frances, when at one time she was nursing at night a consumptive, who was so weak that she did not want him to use his voice and perhaps bring on a fit of coughing, said, "Now listen, Jacöbchen (Jimmy), you are not to call when you want anything tonight. Just beckon to me and I'll come at once. Remember, Jacöbchen." But at midnight she heard a call, "Franzchen! Franzchen!" She hurried to him and said, "Now, Jacöbchen, did you forget? You ought not to call." And Jacöbchen answered, "But Franzchen, I have been beckoning you for more than two hours!" Overcome with weariness she had dropped off to sleep in her chair. After October, 1845, however, Frances and her friends, though their relations with their patients were not less intimate than before, were looked upon as a species of nuns so that Fraenzchen became Mother Frances, which was what many of the poor had called her even when she was a quite young girl.

Even from this time she paid special attention, as she did throughout her life, to the daily instructions regarding vocation and the religious state which she gave the "Sisters." And in their formation she was also helping in her own formation. They were, after all, all of them novices together. They had much to learn and nobody to guide them except the confessor that each individual member of the community chose.

It will be noticed that in the statement of principles drawn up by Frances in Cologne, the result of consultations between her and Catherine and Gertrude, the reformation of fallen women was specifically mentioned as a part of their work. Frances had long been interested in this, but until now she never had a shelter available and so had been obliged to turn over such girls of this class who wished rehabilitation to a priest who maintained a small rescue home, which was obviously not a very satisfactory arrangement. It was different now; she meant to care for them herself.

Yet it was a month before they received their first penitent, and she came to them by a seeming accident. A wealthy young man, who had been living with a mistress, suddenly died. Before he passed away a priest was summoned to hear his confession and to administer the Last Sacraments. He took this occasion to exhort the young woman, who was now in a chastened frame of mind, to turn from her former life. At his recommendation she sought out Frances and was warmly welcomed into the house beyond St. James's Gate. Soon — nobody knew why, except that word must have gotten around — 20 and even 30 young women flocked to the house, until Frances and her associates hardly knew where to accommodate them. Probably few of these were of the most abandoned type, but were for the most part girls who had been betrayed by their lovers and cast off, with nowhere to go. They had recoiled at the first false step and were only too glad to accept the kind hand stretched out to help them, without which most of them might have relapsed in despair into a life of sin.

Frances and those who had worked with her had already received criticism in certain quarters for their disregard of the conventions in working for the sick poor. People of their own social circle looked askance at the way they laid what is called respectability aside in going after the destitute. To drag a squealing pig through the streets by its hind leg could be looked upon as eccentricity and merely laughed at. It was another matter when she and her friends went out begging for food and money to support the disreputable girls to whom they were giving shelter. People were, or pretended to be, horrified. Frances notes the talk about "the adventurous young women who, instead of attending to their duties at home, associated with persons of ill fame, and even asked their benefactors to feed them." In at least one instance, when applying to a wealthy woman who had given liberally to St. John's Kitchen, Frances was met with abusive language. That lady was won over when she observed how her tirade was received in silence, but in other quarters the criticism continued. Mischievous boys, sometimes egged on by their elders, tried all kinds of pranks. The house where these women lived became something so mysterious that curious people tried to peer in through the basement windows, in the hope of seeing something "spicy." Needless to say, they saw nothing at all.

The criticism of the respectable, and even of the genuinely pious, including some priests, mounted to such a height that Frances thought it best not to ask for donations herself for this work, but to find persons, not connected with her activities, who would be willing to serve as her agents. Frau Beissel was one of these, and we may be sure that one so generous herself gave freely of her services. Frances and her associates, while continuing to look after their penitents, restricted their begging to help for the kitchens and the sick poor.

Fortunately Dr. Gregory Kloth, the pastor of St. James's Church, went publicly to their defence, commending their work from the pulpit and giving further support by privately asking some of the ladies of his parish to contribute. Father Fey, of St. Paul's Church, did the same. And as Dr. Kloth himself went out with Frances on her begging tours, the objections of the "unco guid" appear after this to have died.

One wonders, however, whether even Dr. Kloth would have approved of an incident somewhat guardedly related by Father Jeiler; it also appears in some of the other biographies of Frances Schervier. I do not know that I am prepared to call it very judicious, nor would I hold it up for imitation (though there is small chance of many people doing the same thing), but I certainly would call it one of the noblest and most courageous actions of Frances's life. Some of her penitents did relapse, possibly because they found it dull in a house full of women, possibly because their vicious instincts revived. Far from despairing when one of her girls returned to a bawdy house, Frances acted at once: she put on a man's clothes and went into the house in question. Just what happened there we do not know — and it might be best not to try to imagine — but it is certain that Frances took the girl away.

The intrepidity of this act takes the breath away. The "madam" of the place must have been indignant, and she could have summoned one of her bullies to throw the intruder out into the street. But perhaps Frances was recognized as she was departing with the rescued girl; and even depraved women often have a kind of good nature which, in this case, may have made the proprietress indulgent towards one so well known for her charities. Perhaps there was a look in the face of Frances that overawed everybody, so that they dared not interfere with her. But she could have had no assurance when she made her daring entrance that she would not emerge with her face beaten into a pulp.

Father Jeiler gives us this much further information about the matter. The girl was of great beauty and had been converted some years before by Frances. Then in 1850, shortly before the Community received the religious habit (even Frances would hardly have laid aside her habit to perform this exploit), she met the girl by chance, by chance found in what kind of a house she was, and persuaded her to go to her shelter, only to have her slip away again. One hears (though Jeiler may have a somewhat similar case in mind) that the rescued girl this time persevered in virtue and died a pious death a few years later.

Another case reveals the bold methods of another kind that

Frances was ready to adopt when necessary. Father Schneider of St. Paul's Church, who subsequently became a Jesuit, sent Frances a girl who, so he thought, showed a sincere desire of reformation. Frances received her kindly, but after a while, the girl grew bored with what she may have considered a humdrum existence and so left Frances to return to her evil courses. But of these, too, she soon tired, for she could not but remember the calm and holy atmosphere of the house she had left. Back again to Frances she went of her own accord, promising that this time she would remain virtuous. Her nature, however, was fickle: she was drawn to good, but evil also had its attractions, so again she fled. Or rather she was preparing to leave and had announced, somewhat defiantly, that she was going back to a house of prostitution. Upon this Frances told her: "Rather than that, you shall become lame." Even those words made slight impression on her, but she was packing up her belongings when she did suddenly become lame, so lame that she was confined to her bed, helplessly crippled. Nor did the lameness depart: God was taking no chances with her. She resigned herself to her condition and turned to a life of almost continuous prayer. As for the bitter cross laid upon her, she was sometimes able to say with a smile: "Mother Frances lamed me!" She joined the Third Order of St. Francis but not the community, and the Sisters looked after her until in 1857 she was transferred to another institution.

Frances in her autobiography writes of her work for her penitents as being "without all human aid." She even says that she did not wish such aid, but on the contrary feared that it might involve interference. She presumably meant that the civic and ecclesiastical authorities made no donation, for of course without support of some kind she could not have supplied her household of 30 people with food and fuel and clothing. It is easy to believe that, as she says, "Our penitents were more devoted to me than children to their own mother." She gave most of her time to this charity, instructing the girls as a group and holding long interviews with each one individually, when she spared no pains to get at the root of her personal troubles and trials. "To speak candidly," she wrote, "I neglected, on account of this cherished occupation, the duties of my office as Superior of the Sisters; but I am under the impression that God so willed it."

As a Superior Frances suffered somewhat in the beginning from the fact that she had had no conventual training, nor any model to set before herself except what she had seen among the Holy Cross Sisters at Liége, and there she could not have penetrated much below the surface of things in a brief three weeks. But that she really neglected her duties, as her self-accusation says, is hardly to be believed; actually such faults as she had were rather on the other side. In later years she was notable for the mildness of her rule — though this mildness was always accompanied by firmness — but at the start she did not take human frailty fully into account and expected from those associated with her a degree of austerity equal to her own. In fact, the more potential perfection she saw in anybody, the greater were the demands she made upon that person. This fell specially hard on Sister Joanna who, simply because she was so zealous in the performance of her duties, received severe reproofs for the slightest fault and had many mortifications imposed on her. Thus during the very cold winter of 1846–7 Joanna went with some of the other Sisters to attend Vespers at the Aachenerdom, which was situated in the center of the walled city, a long walk from the house outside St. James's Gate. They were not very warmly dressed, and they felt so cold that Joanna suggested that they step into St. Mary's Hospital on their way back, so that they might thaw out a bit. The nuns in charge offered them some cake and coffee — all of which one would think was harmless enough and which even Frances probably would have passed over in the case of one less perfect than Joanna. As it was, she sternly reprimanded that good soul for taking such a liberty. Frances as Superior still had a good deal to learn.

This fault of excessive strictness is one often seen in religious founders in whom experience has not yet tempered an inclination to be exacting.

The presence of so many penitents in the house brought an unusual privilege, one obtained from the Archbishop of Cologne by Canon Kloth. He had championed Frances and had silenced most of the criticism; even so, he could see that it was not very desirable that a procession of 30 fallen women should go to Mass on Sundays and holy days, for people stared at them, and there was danger of adverse comments. The Archbishop accordingly permitted Mass to be said in a room that was fitted up as a little chapel and the Blessed Sacrament to be reserved there. There Father Müengersdorf, one of the curates at St. James's, who afterwards became the Provincial of the Vincentians, used to go at five with his server, who was his young brother; the early hour was necessary because he had to be back to say the six o'clock Mass at his own church. It was also arranged that Father Fey should go to the house to hear the penitents' confessions, so that they would not be obliged to walk through the streets. This was not only a great convenience to Frances but a great consolation. They could now say their Office in the presence of the Blessed Sacrament and make visits during the day when opportunity occurred.

The establishment of this chapel brought them a benefactor in Frau Henry Nellessen, the mother of two young women who later joined Frances. They were known as Sisters Gabriela and Paula, each of whom in turn served as head of the work in the United States, when Frances extended her operations there. She came with her daughters and presented Frances with an alb and a communion cloth, the first articles of the sort she had received. So affected was she by the poverty she saw — a poverty accompanied by the most scrupulous cleanliness and order — that from that day forth she became one of the Community's greatest benefactors.

Housing so many people was a difficulty. The attic was

given over to the penitents as a dormitory. At first, when there were only a few of these delinquents, beds could be provided, the Sisters surrendering their own and sleeping on straw pallets on the floor. But later the pallets had to be given to the penitents; then the Sisters slept on the bolts of cloth they bought to keep these women employed, thus helping to maintain them. For pillows they used bolts of linen.

The comfort of the penitents always came first, though they too lived in anything but the lap of luxury. Since whatever food that came into the house was food that was begged, the rations were irregular and never very abundant, and most of it had to go to the soup kitchens Frances was still maintaining. Their dinner, eaten at midday, was usually only soup with some beans or peas or barley, though doubtless the penitents had to be fed a bit better to induce them to stay. According to the Rule of the Franciscan Third Order, meat was supposed to be eaten no more than three times a week ordinarily, though not all tertiaries observed the additional fasts. The Sisters, however, kept the Rule to the letter. Indeed, they might almost as well have maintained perpetual abstinence, for when they did get meat it was chopped up in very small pieces and mixed with the vegetables, so that whoever got even a particle of meat counted herself lucky. All through those early years no Sister ever got a whole egg. For supper there was only bread, and by the time the penitents had finished, often there was not enough left for every one of the Sisters to get so much as a slice. Then there was a contest in generosity — this Sister protesting that she was not hungry, no, really, she was not; that Sister protesting that she was better able to go without food than another whose constitution was less robust.

Frances all through her life ate like a bird, and the ascetic Gertrude Frank had made it her custom to take only plain bread for supper. They set the example for the others. Yet one wonders how they managed to do so much work on such meager food. In later years, when the work was better established and the Sisters fared better, we sometimes hear them confessing to having hearty appetites. Such appetites must have been among the first group; yet they went uncomplainingly hungry most of the time.

An absolute poverty was their ideal, for they were trying to mould their lives in complete accordance with that of St. Francis. They owned nothing, not even the house they lived in, and the rental of that was guaranteed by Frau Beissel for only three years, after which they had no idea what they would do. It was their principle that they should live on alms, and these alms were gathered for their poor and their penitents, only the barest margin being reserved for themselves. Begging was looked upon as a devotional exercise of immense spiritual value to the mendicant; it was also a means of putting the mendicant on the track of others who might be in need. As Frances wrote later: "The questing of alms is part of that silent sermon by which St. Francis, wherever he trod, led souls to their Lord and God, the creature to the Creator."

Hardships such as these, far from being a deterrent, were a positive attraction. Any one of the group was perfectly free to leave at a moment's notice, for none were bound in any way. But none did leave. Instead of that, during 1846 and 1847 six other young women were inspired to join a community not only young, but one that flourished in some mysterious way on its destitution.

Because of these recruits new work could be undertaken. On November 19, 1846, Frances undertook the nursing of syphilitic women in the "Preachers," owned by the city, the same building in which she and Father Istas had started St. John's Kitchen. It was a rambling structure used for a variety of purposes. Only the arrival of recruits made it possible for Frances to take charge of a soup kitchen in St. James's parish, during a winter of great severity, following a partial failure of the crops. The penitents and the sick poor were still the main object of Frances's work.

But this was not all. An extension occurred, with two new enterprises, each of prime importance. Each sprang from an apparent accident. One evening a girl completely unknown to Frances called upon her — an indication that her reputation was spreading. She confided that she had escaped from a Belgian prison and begged for shelter. This Frances gave without hesitation, surrendering her own room (for at that time she still had a bed) to this fugitive, and with such joy that she had difficulty in concealing her feelings. A divine Voice seemed to be speaking in her soul: "It is I whom you have received. I desire to be served by you in the person of poor convicts in the future." We shall hear some astounding stories of her services to them a little later. The inspiration for this was the turning of that girl to Frances, imploring her not to let the police know of her whereabouts.

The other new work came as an unforeseen result of a begging tour Frances made in nearby Holland during the Lent of 1848, accompanied by one of Catherine Daverkosen's relatives. They started on the north bank of the Rhine at Nijmegen, having little luck, and going on to Amsterdam and Scheidam. Rebuffs were so plentiful that Frances's companion gave up and returned to Aachen, leaving her to beg alone, which she did for three weeks. But at last in the Hague she fell in with Father Opdenkamp, the Superior of the Franciscans, who helped her himself and passed her on to the friars of his order at Rotterdam. She also received the support of Frau Hafkenscheid, the mother of a well-known Redemptorist. Though Frances had to describe her tour as being, on the whole, a terrible experience, she was also able to say that it was in Holland that she first learned the value of hospitality. What is amazing is that she should have dropped all her work and gone out to collect money for one of her penitents who wished to become a Trappistine.

The proceeds of this tour were rather disappointing. It was not very obvious, even to the pious, why they should contribute to such a cause, when they had so many charitable calls made upon them in their own country. But when it turned out that the young woman in question, Catherine Lindauer of Heidelberg, was of too delicate a constitution to perform the heavy work in the fields which is a distinctive Trappist feature, Frances decided that she should be allowed to join the contemplative group already in process of formation in her own community, and which she herself over and over again wanted to join. This group, originally known as the Clarisses but now called the Recluses, not only still exists, but is regarded as the heart of an otherwise intensely active community. The first actual members were Sisters Bernardin, Maria Antonia and Josepha, and not until a little later was Catherine Lindauer assigned to this spiritually select company, though Father Jeiler gives her the honor of having been the very first member. The matter is mentioned here to show how resolute Frances was that Catherine's contemplative vocation should not be thwarted despite her material circumstances and her past history. Frances herself, still at heart a Trappistine, wished to be a Mary, but knew her calling to be that of a Martha. In this new group she hoped that her longings would be vicariously fulfilled.

9

*

The Way Opens

THE WAY OPENED with what seemed to be the complete stop-
page of what was now Frances's main work. She was indeed
occupied in many other ways, for there were still poor sick
people to be nursed in their homes, the hungry to be fed in
the two kitchens she had in operation, and the patients in the
city hospital of the "Preachers." But the penitents had taken
up most of her time. They not only had to be drawn to a
love of virtue and confirmed in their new life, but they had
to be provided for, and providing for 30 women by begging
was an onerous task. While it is true that they helped to support themselves by sewing — Joanna Bruchhaus and Catherine Lassen, getting up before day dawned, cut out and prepared what the penitents were to sew — sewing alone hardly
sufficed to keep them. It was chiefly useful in giving these
girls something to do, so that time should not hang on their
hands and they might regain self-respect.

Then in 1848 a house of the Good Shepherd nuns was
established at Aachen. This had not been possible before because the Prussian government excluded all foreign orders on
the ground that they might be a danger to the state. The
Good Shepherds were French in origin, with their headquarters at Angers, where they were refounded by Mother
Euphrasia Pelletier (since canonized) as an offshoot of a

similar enterprise established during the seventeenth century by St. John Eudes. But though the year 1848 was one of considerable upheaval throughout Germany, King Frederick William IV was persuaded to relax the regulations in favor of nuns doing so admirable a work. A lay commission had made ineffectual attempts to reform fallen women; now, brought to a realization of its own inadequacy, it bought a disused factory in the Bergenstrasse, the funds for this being put up by Helen and Louisa Fey, Clara Fey's cousins. Louisa had entered the community at Angers and now came to Aachen as Mother Euphrasia to head the new foundation. To a congregation whose sole activity was of this character Frances could not but resign her own undertaking.

She rejoiced of course that this work was to be set up on a firmer basis than she could provide, and it was a great satisfaction to her that it should be in charge of a friend of her girlhood. At the same time she was heavy at heart at losing the penitents, to whom she had grown so attached and who had grown so attached to her. When Mother Euphrasia visited the house beyond St. James's Gate, though Frances herself wore a smiling face, many of the girls, when they heard that they were to be transferred, wept openly, and some of them protested that they would not go. It needed all of Frances's persuasive powers to convince them that they would be much better off in the charge of the Good Shepherds. However, she did retain a few of her penitents, among them the girl she had "lamed."

Such exceptions were very few; the penitents as a body finally consented to go to their new home on the Bergenstrasse. Their departure meant that the privilege that Frances and her associates had enjoyed of having Mass in their own house was now taken from them, for it had been given only for the sake of the penitents. And though Frances could hope that before long this privilege would be restored, for she was now confidently expecting that her community would be recognized by the ecclesiastical authorities, she nevertheless gave

Mother Euphrasia the vestments and vessels used in the celebration of Mass, since the Good Shepherd nuns had pressing need of them. It was an instance of her kind of charity, the kind that never would look to ultimate possibilities or her own interests but only considered the immediate good.

The transfer was a most difficult and delicate matter to undertake. Some of the girls went to Frances crying, "If you send me away, I shall go back to my old life!" But she knew that such threats, which often came right on the heels of sweeping promises of reform, were only meant to break down her resolution and were not seriously intended. However, apart from the two or three girls whom, for special reasons, she kept, and a few others whom she placed as servants with families who could be counted upon to look after them properly, the whole group had to go. Frances understood perfectly well that for her to maintain an institution similar to that being established by the Good Shepherd Sisters would not only increase their difficulties but might even make the civil authorities eject Mother Euphrasia on the ground that Aachen did not need her.

On the evening of November 20th and again early the following morning Frances addressed her penitents, exhorting them to perseverance and asking them to go as willingly and cheerfully as they could. "This," she said, "will be the best proof you can give of the affection I know you have for me. Remember the great grace the Lord has given you and believe that the Good Shepherd Himself will reward the sacrifice you are making."

She was listened to, though with sobs and tears, and between five and six in the morning — an hour when few people would be out — she led her girls from St. James's Gate to the Bergenstrasse, taking a roundabout route in the hope of not being observed. She herself led the way and Sister Joanna brought up the rear of the procession of between 20 and 30 penitents. As they walked they recited the rosary.

Frances had feared that there might be some unpleasant

incidents, for she could not forget the criticism she had met when she first took fallen women into her house. Her fears, however, turned out to be groundless. Many who saw these women were, as they told Frances afterwards, deeply moved at the strange sight. The procession passed a group of workmen going into a factory; these all took off their hats respectfully. The old antagonism had long since evaporated.

Father Müengersdorf, who had acted as their chaplain, was waiting to say Mass at the Bergenstrasse. After breakfast Frances took farewell of her penitents, most of whom were once more in tears. So was Frances herself on her way home; when she got to the house, which now seemed desolate, she locked herself in her room and sobbed her heart out. She felt sweetly resigned, although, in her conflict of emotion, she complained to the Lord "for taking my poor children away from me, who had been dear to me for the very reason that they were *His* children, and for whom I would gladly have continued to provide." Amidst her tears and lamentations she felt a great impulse of love for Christ, and in her soul she heard a Voice saying: "Be of good cheer! I shall give you other penitents." She adds, "At that moment the plan of our Recluses was, as it were, visibly revealed to my mind." Yet she had had the plan in some vague fashion before this, for Catherine Lindauer, with whom she intended to begin her contemplative project, was one of the penitents she had retained. She was admitted as a Recluse, under the name of Sister Magdalen, the following February.

The project of the Recluses was at this time in a rudimentary state. It was to be not only a penitential but also a contemplative group, constituted of select members of the Congregation. It may have been for this reason that Frances some years later formed another branch that more closely corresponded to her original idea, though this group, known as the Penitents of St. Margaret of Cortona did not flourish or endure. The fact is that though with the arrival of the Good Shepherds at Aachen, Frances "officially" abandoned her work for fallen women, unofficially she never abandoned it. To this day her Congregation, though it maintains no houses for this specific purpose, is always ready to do all in its power for unfortunate girls that seek its help.

A severe blow now fell on Frances. Frau Beissel had repeatedly asked to be received into the community and had always been refused because she was elderly and, as one used to her comforts, would probably not be able to endure their life, unless with special concessions that might be detrimental to discipline. Frances well understood that the wealth of this lady would establish them firmly, and also understood that Frau Beissel, should she be refused, would probably go to some other convent. If that happened, Frances realized that they would lose their rent-payer. But she had no fear of poverty; she felt sure that the Lord would in some way provide for their necessities. When the guaranteed three years came to an end, Frances managed to scrape together enough money to pay the rent for another three months; after that she and those with her would have no one to look to but God. That was always how Frances preferred it.

A shelter for them was almost immediately offered. The country around Aachen was suffering from a cholera epidemic, nor was the city exempt. The municipal authorities asked Frances to take charge of the infirmary they had set up in the old Dominican building, and Frances agreed to do so on the condition that housing be given there to her community. As this cost the city nothing, it was readily agreed to. It could not be a permanent arrangement, but it helped them over what had threatened to be a rough spot.

Even more of a blow was suffered when Canon Deboeur died at about the same time. Frances was fond of the old man and grieved at his passing. At the same time she had been often assured by him that he was going to leave his fortune to her. Little as she regarded money, she had thought that this would be very useful for providing a convent for her community. On his deathbed he had assured her once more, in the presence of his well-to-do sister and the Alexian Brother who was nursing him, that Frances was to be his heiress. And the Canon's sister congratulated her, professing herself to be very pleased. But after the Canon's death no will was found, so his fortune reverted to his next of kin, that (one fears) rather hypocritical sister of his, who, though she knew her brother's intentions, did not give Frances a single thaler. But though Frances may have been a little hurt, she was not in the least cast down. Why should she complain, she who had sought a life of absolute poverty? She passed the matter off with a jest, saying that she had been deprived of her inheritance by a man in a brown robe, meaning St. Francis.

In the summer of 1849 there was an election for a new Superior. It was all very irregular. Nine new members had been added to the community, among them Frances's sister Pauline, who took the religious name of Paula. And these took part in the election, adding further irregularity to it, though, for that matter, none of the original group of nine were qualified, canonically speaking, as voters. But what was supposed to be the "spirit" of the Franciscan order was invoked to override all technicalities.

Frances insisted, quite incorrectly, that she was not eligible for re-election, and even in the face of the masterful Gertrude Frank her view of the matter was accepted, at least to the extent of having a new election. Gertrude kept on arguing that the rule did not apply in this case, so that Frances had to command her to keep silence and to forbid the others to pay any attention to what she might say. The Sisters all protested, saying, "If we are not permitted to vote for you, we shall be compelled to cast our votes for Sister Mary." Gertrude who, admirable person though she was, was inclined to be a bit domineering, took a somewhat different line: she announced that if she was not permitted to vote for Frances, she would not vote at all. Sister Mary (the former Catherine Daverkosen) implored Frances to spare her, but

Frances remained fixed in her determination, so Mary was elected, as Frances thought she should have been in 1845.

It was with the greatest sorrow that Sister Mary accepted the cross of office, and having done so, she deputed some of her duties to Frances, especially the instruction of the community and the presiding at the weekly chapter at which the Sisters publicly confessed their faults. The whole thing was not only irregular but slightly comical. Had Frances consulted Father Van der Meulen, he would of course have at once informed her that she had misunderstood the situation, but at this stage in her career, and for some time to come, Frances had a way of acting very independently, relying too much upon her own intuitions and personal preferences.

In spite of this her humility must be praised. She was filled with joy that she was now living under obedience. So also we must praise her longing for the contemplative life, which was what was really behind her refusal to be re-elected, though events were to prove that she did not have a contemplative vocation. In any event she could not become a Recluse, because Sister Mary put her under obedience to carry out several of the duties reserved to a Superior.

Another event about this time prevented Frances from dropping the role of Martha for that of Mary. An appeal came from the archdiocesan authorities in Cologne that the community take charge of the Catholic patients in the Protestant hospital at Lennep. It was an opportunity that Frances could not afford to miss; otherwise she might have failed to obtain the ecclesiastical approbation she was hoping for. She had to show herself prompt in responding to her Ordinary, though he had only made a request, not given a command.

At Lennep they found the women patients under the charge of Lutheran deaconesses who lived in a very comfortable house, whereas Frances and her assistant were housed in a tumble-down shack on the hospital grounds. The male patients were under a Lutheran deacon, and with him Frances got on so well that he permitted her to visit even his

113

department of the hospital, which was not part of the original bargain. The Protestant patients, seeing a Catholic nurse in their ward, were at first disposed to be rather insulting, and in fact sometimes used very bad language. Frances soon brought them to heel. The small, slender figure, who looked so childlike and helpless, drew herself erect and said with flashing eyes: "I do not mind any personal affront. But I shall never permit God to be blasphemed in my presence. I have come of my own free will to help you, ready to make any sacrifice. In return I expect you to comport yourselves in a respectful and Christian manner. If you do not do this, I shall report you to the authorities."

Frances's work was very hard, all the harder because of her lack of robustness. Her ward was in the upper story of the building, and, as plumbing arrangements were, in those days, rudimentary, she had to carry upstairs all the water for the baths the doctors prescribed, taken, of course, in hip-tubs or for those very sick, in bed. Her cheerfulness and her instant readiness to answer all appeals won the hearts of her patients, so that the very people who had been most antagonistic were won over. Some of them used to tell her, "Mother Frances, what *is* it about you? We notice something that we cannot explain." At this she used to smile brightly and say: "What you see is the Catholic faith in me; it is the Catholic faith you are admiring, not me."

Frances wrote in her notebook about this period: "It was a blessed, a happy time, that at Lennep. There were difficulties and troubles enough, in truth; but I was strong and easily able to endure the fatigue. In order to give a supernatural direction to my actions, I had to suppress the great natural delight I felt in ministering to the sick. In every patient I saw my dear Saviour. This mental vision overpowered me and caused me to nurse them with tender charity. Hence the patients became aware of the difference between Catholic and Protestant nursing, and they were disabused of the strong prejudices with which they had at first regarded their Catholic nurses." Though she had gone to Lennep to look after the sick Catholics, she did not restrict herself to them. One of the primary facts to bear in mind about Frances is that she would admit no discrimination; all that mattered was need. Those who required her help, however great their unworthiness, received it.

She stayed at Lennep for one month, for the call had only been an emergency summons. But the promptitude with which she answered it and the devotion she showed must have impressed those who had requested her services. Moreover this hospital work, and that which she had done at the "Preachers" in response to the city authorities of Aachen, laid the foundation of what was to become the main — though not the exclusive — activity of her Congregation, the care of the sick poor in hospitals. Until then she had nursed them only in their homes; after this a more systematized mode of nursing was initiated, yet without any cessation of home nursing.

It was after her return from Lennep that Frances, as she put it, "experienced a great desire of earnestly working at my own perfection." She felt that she had not really begun on this, and she admits that she had "sought to avoid as much as possible everything that erroneously seemed to me a circumscription of my efforts. Well do I now see that this was a great imperfection and a serious error." Error or not — and in most cases it would have to be regarded as a mistake — it turned out to be providential at this stage. For had she followed what is called prudent advice, she would never have reached her present point. Even she, looking back upon it all, could write: "On the whole and after all, it may have been well so, because in common affairs I was ruled by a certain sentiment and impulse of grace rather than by so clear a discernment as to enable me to give definite reasons for my proceedings." She concludes, very humbly, that good had proceeded from evil; but we who consider her life as a whole may see the good more plainly than any of the evil of which she accuses herself.

Superior Again

FRANCES had been freed from her superiorship in the summer of 1849, and Sister Mary had, with the greatest reluctance, taken her place. She considered herself, however, only nominally the head of the little community and threw all the duties she could upon Frances, who carried them out under obedience. Her office weighed so heavily upon Sister Mary, now the one responsible for everything, that she fell ill. Tall and stately though she was, she did not have anything like Frances's stamina. Or, perhaps, her decline in health was an indication that God did not wish her to occupy her office.

At this point there appears a man of whom we have not heard before. He was Bishop John Theodore Laurent, at this time in his middle forties, who in 1841 had been appointed Vicar Apostolic of Luxembourg but had been ejected in those troublous times by the civil government. Since May, 1848, he had been living in exile in Aachen. He was handsome and distinguished in appearance and, what was more to the purpose, talented and of considerable spiritual discernment. Frances sought him out, and though he had no authority over her or over anybody else in the archdiocese of Cologne, she voluntarily took him for a guide. He had much to do with the events that followed, for the Archbishop of Cologne, Cardinal von Geissel, sought his counsel on many matters affecting the city in which he now resided.

Frances, though she had refused to allow herself to be elected Superior, was looked upon by everybody as the real if not the titular head of the community. Therefore it was upon her that devolved the duty of drawing up, in a sufficiently formal way for presentation to the Ordinary, the Constitutions of the community she had founded, because it was evident by now that ecclesiastical approbation might be sought. As she was totally ignorant of Canon Law, it was necessary to have an adviser.

She asked Bishop Laurent to act in this capacity. He was all the more willing to do this, for he it was who had pressed upon her the necessity of this step, though he by no means approved all that Frances sought to obtain and sometimes tried to steer her in a direction in which she did not want to go. By way of trying to convince him that she was only carrying out God's will she showed him a memorandum written by her in July, 1845, in which, with Gertrude looking over her shoulder as she wrote, she had given a brief account of what had happened on Pentecost Sunday that year. She also showed him the further statement of the aims of their group which she had written the following September, just before they took possession of the house beyond St. James's Gate. In conversation she amplified all this; the Bishop then asked that Gertrude write out her own account of the message from heaven for him to examine. This Gertrude did, and though what she wrote has been lost, we have from Bishop Laurent a letter written from Loretto, in Italy, to Sister Paula Nellessen on July 9, 1883, in which he confesses himself convinced that "this prayerful and devout soul had really received a divine inspiration concerning the foundation of this community." He adds: "The wide propagation and blessed ministrations of your dear community place its divine origin beyond doubt and ensure its continuation. It is a splendid illustration of the inexhaustible fertility of our Holy Mother the Church and a great consolation amid the sufferings and trials of our godless age." This does not mean, however, that — at any rate when Frances first consulted him — he thought she was right in all that she proposed to do.

We first hear of Bishop Laurent in connection with Frances as intervening with his full personal force — though not, it must be remembered, as having any authority except the authority willingly yielded him — regarding Frances's resignation from office. One infers that he must have visited the Sisters in their quarters at the "Preachers" and had noted that Sister Mary was pining away under the cares of office.

Had that office been conferred on Sister Mary according to the established rules, the Bishop undoubtedly would have dealt with the situation in a way very different from the one he adopted. He might then have suggested that she resign; on the other hand, he might have encouraged her to accept a cross that God had laid on her shoulders. As it was, he did not believe that God *had* laid it there; the resignation of Frances and the election of Mary (under Frances's coercion) was something that he saw to be irregular and invalid, and he said so plainly.

Furthermore he discovered, after visiting and talking to the Sisters, that dissension had arisen on the question of the absolute poverty upon which the community was based. And though the Bishop did not think that this degree of poverty was really practicable, however admirable it might be in theory, it was evident to him that Sister Mary could not cope with the situation but was showing signs of yielding under the pressure that was being brought to bear from outside. The principle, so the Bishop decided, might wait until the Constitutions were actually drawn up, and in these he meant to have a hand. What was immediately more important was that there should be a Superior capable of holding all the Sisters together as a united body. Here only Frances would suffice. Bishop Laurent knew that the only chance the community had of obtaining ecclesiastical approbation — and this now seemed almost within its grasp — was by demonstrating its unity. The Archbishop of Cologne, or any Ordinary, would never approve a religious congregation which already seemed to be in some danger of falling apart.

Bishop Laurent recognized that the trouble lay in Sister Mary. She, good soul, was causing no dissensions, but she was not holding the door firmly enough against dissensions, and her health was rapidly giving way. But still more the Bishop blamed Frances, whom he urged to resume office, telling her that she had acted contrary to the will of God and that she would be responsible for all the mistakes that might result. But Frances at first resolutely declined to follow his advice, very understandably to his annoyance.

As has been remarked, Bishop Laurent had no episcopal jurisdiction in Aachen, so he was not in a position to issue positive commands. He could have washed his hands of Frances but he did not, for while he disagreed with her on some points and considered that she was being rather obstinate, he also believed, in general, in her divine inspiration and could not fail to see that her community was accomplishing much good. Being a clever man, he set to work in a more subtle way. He therefore represented to Frances that Sister Mary was all too likely to sacrifice the principle of absolute poverty. And though he believed that Frances was too extreme on this point, he gained his own point about her resuming office. His mild words struck her, as she was to record, "like a thunderbolt. At a glance I saw that I had acted wrongly in wilfully throwing off my shoulders the cross imposed on them by the Lord." At once she hurried to her cell and fell on her knees begging God's pardon. She implored Him to come to her aid and promised to make any reparation within her power. With this she was flooded with an ineffable sense of peace.

But how was the change to be made? Bishop Laurent, when she saw him next morning, had a plan worked out. He expressed his satisfaction with Frances's "conversion," as he called it, but he gave her a penance that appalled her. As the ecclesiastical authorities would not remove Sister Mary —

they hardly could do so in the case of the head of a small voluntary pious society which, as it was not yet officially recognized, did not fall within their jurisdiction — Frances herself must act: she must depose Mary and resume office. What Bishop Laurent demanded was a revolution, an usurpation.

In this the Bishop had some justification, the justification of dealing with a bad situation in the only way that seems possible when normal procedures have failed. Frances was going to cause Mary's death unless she did as he said. Also Frances was imperiling the central concept of her project. So he said, "At an opportune time — but soon — you must tell her that you did wrong in forcing office upon her, because it was done in opposition to the holy will of God; and that you intend to repair your fault and relieve her of her office." Highhanded though this might appear to be, in Bishop Laurent's view Frances's resignation and Mary's superiorship were not only irregular but totally invalid. Rightfully Frances was still Superior.

This was a heavy injunction to lay upon Frances, who had never wanted to be Superior in the first instance and who spent the rest of her life periodically trying to resign. Despite her courage, she was of a retiring and diffident disposition. As it was she who had coerced the Sisters to elect Mary and had forced Mary to accept the superiorship, it might seem to come with a very bad grace if she should now depose Mary. Might not Mary be very hurt? Might not Frances's own authority be damaged if resumed in this style?

Frances felt her position to be as delicate as it was painful. So instead of doing what Bishop Laurent had advised — indeed, he had taken it upon himself to command — she tried to effect what he had asked by steering a middle course. As might be expected, this only increased Mary's difficulties and her own. What she did was to go to Mary and say, "As you are so ill, I will no longer bother you with questions about what I should do but assume the care of everything." Sister Mary was naturally not very pleased with the suggestion. She had, though much against her will, accepted the superiority, but while delegating most of the work of administration to Frances, her conscientiousness made her feel that she was bound, even though it was from her bed, to exercise a general supervision. This "middle course" of Frances's had totally miscarried.

Mary's illness meanwhile grew worse, and when the doctor called a day or two later, he gave it as his opinion that she would, at best, live only another week. What her illness was we are not told; probably she had nothing that could be diagnosed but was being crushed to death by a burden too great for her to support.

Frances went back to Bishop Laurent, and he at once asked whether she had done what he had instructed her to do. She said she had, which was in a way true, for she had undertaken to look after all the affairs of the community. The Bishop nevertheless was not satisfied, for he had had a good deal of experience of evasive half-truths; he therefore asked bluntly, "Well, have you told Sister Mary that she is no longer Superior and that you are to take her place?"

Crestfallen, Frances stammered out a "No."

At this he was very angry. "Then go back and do it," he said. "Half measures are never going to accomplish anything. Listen, Frances: you have put yourself under my direction, so you must do what I say. Do you understand?"

Frances understood perfectly well, but it deeply grieved her to carry out his injunctions. But this time she braced herself for the ordeal and, going to Sister Mary and kneeling beside her bed, took her hand in hers and told her the whole story. She concluded with: "Dear Mother, you will die if I do not obey, and then, besides my serious fault of forcing the superiority upon you, I shall be guilty of your death." At this Mary drew away the hand that Frances had been holding and embraced her saying, with what seemed an angel's face: "Oh, how you have relieved me! How I thank our good God! Now all is well. I can live again. Yes, now I can live again." Locked in one another's arms they pardoned one another.

It was fortunate indeed for everybody concerned that in the exiled Bishop Laurent they had found a man of strong common sense and decisiveness. He had cut through their difficulties at a stroke, seeing clearly to the heart of what was immediately necessary. After her interview with Mary, no longer "Mother Mary," Frances simply went down to the other Sisters and announced that she was their Superior again. It was to the relief of everybody, even of those who, like Mary herself, had wavered under pressure. Instantly they felt the thrill of knowing that a firm hand was at the helm once more.

What may appear to be a little strange is that Gertrude Frank, who had often been free with her advice, gave none at this crisis. But the reason may have been that she was herself ill. She could not have been in the Sisters' "convent" at this time. For in an attempt to regain her health, after working hard during the autumn and winter, she had gone to her parents' house at Laurenzberg, promising to return as soon as she could. But she never returned: on April 7, 1850, she died, and with her passing the community suffered its first loss. She had predicted that she would not live to receive the habit, which was conferred four months later, and her death occurred, again as she had predicted, when she was thirty-three.

She had long since given up her mission of seeress, exercised only in the message she had brought Frances at Pentecost, 1845, and regarding her own death. And though she every now and then showed opinionativeness, she never claimed that she was divinely inspired. Her function in life seems to have been to start Frances on her destined road; for the rest she had worked obscurely and had spoken her mind freely, so that a good deal was owed to her forthrightness as well as to her early revelations. The future nuns consulted her towards the end of her life as to what habit should be adopted when the impending ecclesiastical approval came, and from the patterns that she was invited to inspect, she picked out the one that was eventually adopted. It departed from the usual Franciscan mode in that it added to the brown serge habit a scapular with a cross emblazoned upon it in red. In her decisive way she said, "This will be our habit," though without any pretensions about special illumination. For the rest she was silent and rather brooding. Before she went home to die she said, "My task is accomplished; I can do nothing more." Everyone who observed her simple spirit of obedience (she was no longer thrusting her views on others), was all the more sure that her previous revelations were proved genuine.

The main preoccupation at this time was with the drawing up of the Constitutions for the approval of the Archbishop, Cardinal von Geissel, with which would automatically go the diocesan approval of their Institute. Yet even so, they did not stand still in their work. In the city of Aachen two new projects were undertaken. They established at the "Preachers" a hospital for incurables, particularly those suffering from cancer, because such patients at that time were not admitted to the other local hospitals. In the other project Frances resumed her work for fallen women. She could do so now without interfering with the activities of the Good Shepherd Sisters, whose hands were already full. A few of her girls had been retained by Frances when the main body of them were transferred to the Bergenstrasse. Afterwards a few delinquents came to her who were disinclined to go to the Good Shepherds, or for one reason or another would not be received by them. These Frances gladly took in. They were God's children who had gone astray; she was quick to perceive the vestiges of virtue left in them. Upon these she built, knowing that in most instances it was not love of vice that had led them into their unfortunate courses, but momentary weakness, accident, or harsh economic necessity. For them she provided a home. At the same time she sought for any opportunity that presented itself for aiding the needy, in particular those who were spiritually destitute.

The Constitutions

IN MODERN TIMES the first step towards getting a religious congregation approved is to obtain the sanction of the Ordinary of the diocese in which it is established. This was not always the case: St. Francis of Assisi and St. Dominic almost simultaneously approached the Holy See direct. St. Francis was just in time to escape the regulation that no new religious rule be drawn up, which left him free to exercise his originality. St. Dominic, just too late, had to accept the Rule of St. Augustine, to which his Order during the succeeding centuries has tacked on its voluminous interpretative Constitutions. St. Benedict, strictly speaking, founded no order at all; all he did was to provide a Rule for such monks as decided to follow it, as almost all monks of the West soon did. Each Benedictine house, being autonomous, may be regarded as a separate religious order. But since the Reformation religious congregations have greatly multiplied, all of them designed for special purposes, so that new Constitutions governing those purposes have also multiplied.

Frances Schervier and her associates, being Franciscan tertiaries, found a Rule ready to hand, the one drawn up in 1221 by the Saint, and ratified by Pope Leo X.* But since this Rule was designed for tertiaries living in the world and

* In 1927 it was revised by Pius XI.

since Frances's group was to be in a more definite sense a religious community, it was necessary for her to indicate the spirit of that community and its distinctive work.

The Constitutions — at first they were described as "Statutes" — proved something of a stumbling block, as Frances feared they might. The main trouble was her insistence upon absolute poverty, an exact imitation of the Saint's own practice in so far as this was feasible to women. Naturally they could not do what St. Francis and his first disciples did, wander at large, sleeping in barns or in caves or under hedges. They had to have a roof over their heads, a settled habitation; but in all other respects they wished to be poor in the sense that St. Francis was poor.

It should be said that even in thirteenth century Italy most people regarded Franciscan poverty as rather fantastic. Even during the Saint's own lifetime there was in the Order itself much controversy on this point, forcing a compromise and the revision of the primitive Rule. But St. Francis's own ideas were illustrated when, arriving at Assisi and finding that a stone building had been erected where there had hitherto been only a collection of stone huts, he began to pull the building down with his own hands and desisted only when told that it was the property of the municipality and had been given merely for the use of the friars. So also upon his return from the Holy Land, when he found some of the Brethren installed in a fine house at Bologna, where they were attending courses at the University, he summarily ejected them all. It was to his mind a gross violation of the poverty to which they were vowed.

Nevertheless under his successors (and he saw the beginnings of this under the new Superior General who took his place after his resignation), the rigors of poverty became somewhat relaxed, until under Brother Elias, who built the magnificent basilica at Assisi, changes were made that so horrified a body of the friars that, a little later, bitter contention occurred, with the party of poverty going to such extremes as to fall into heresy. Eventually a reasonable adjustment was made, with the friars stabilized into three main groups. Poverty — that is, poverty of spirit — remains the guiding principle of Franciscanism. But physical poverty in the primitive sense is no longer looked upon as attainable, not if the friars are to do their work effectively in the great centers of population and as the directors of schools, colleges, and other institutions.

Frances Schervier, however, really did aim at something very like primitive Franciscanism. She did not go, it is true, to the same lengths as St. Francis, who would not touch money, regarding it literally filthy lucre; yet there was no real compromise with principle. In the thirteenth century most ordinary transactions were by barter, so that gold and silver coins seemed to stand for usury or dishonest business methods. In the modern world money has become the only medium of exchange. And while gold is no longer in circulation, paper money and bank deposits are based on gold reserves.

We have seen how Frances began her community life without owning so much as a convent; she merely had the house that Frau Beissel had rented for her for three years. There she and her associates were obliged to sleep on the floor on straw-filled pallets so that the penitents might have beds. And their food was so sparse that most of the time they were hungry. In all conscience they were poor, and so they wished to remain. Early in 1849 the only home they had was the lodgings at the "Preachers," and these were to be theirs only at the pleasure of the city authorities.

First it might be noted that the Statutes of the Sisters of the Poor of St. Francis started with the statement: "Miss Catherine Daverkosen and Frances Schervier in Aachen are founding, in conjunction with other young women of like sentiment, a religious congregation of women according to the Rule of the Third Order of St. Francis for Sisters living in community, but with certain modifications required by its object." The order of the names suggests that this document was begun during the brief superiorship of "Sister Mary," but it should be noted that they did not use the title of Sisters (for canonically they would not be Sisters until they had received Cardinal von Geissel's approbation) but their secular names. Another point to note is that when these Statutes, 25 in number, were at last presented to the Ordinary on May 9, 1851, Frances signed first and Catherine second, indicating that Frances was Superior again. These Statutes were of her compiling, though of course she had consulted the other members of the group.

The decisive article was Number 4, which reads: "The Congregation is determined to possess no property beyond what is indispensable for the convent and chapel and the maintenance of the Congregation; as they work and care only for the poor, so they will also live with the poor and like the poor from the donations of charity." This was later clarified by the statement that the holding of property should be forbidden, not only to individual members of the community but to the community as such. The only exceptions made were that a Motherhouse might be owned and that the dowries of such Sisters who had any were to be held intact in their names until they took perpetual vows, but this money was not to be invested so as to draw interest.

These ideas were laid before Bishop Laurent, who had shown himself such a good friend, and he at once threw up his hands in dismay over the insistence upon poverty of such a kind. "That," he told her, "is no longer practicable but has been long out of date." He was also dubious about the proposal to live on begging or on such donations as benefactors chose to bring. It was one thing for women in secular dress to go from stall to stall in the markets, or from house to house, and another for women in the religious habit to do so. Begging might be all right if looked upon as subsidiary, but for it to be thought of as the sole means of support raised many questions in his mind.

The first draft of the Statutes was sent to Bishop Laurent at Pentecost, 1850. Frances says that it was an exact copy of what Gertrude Frank had bidden her to write. Frances, however, entirely concurred, and in her letter to the Bishop she told him: "There is something so mysterious about the present state of our affairs that I consider it necessary to inform you of it, when God gives me time and opportunity." She was referring of course to the revelation that Gertrude had brought her just five years earlier.

The Bishop remained unconvinced about the absolute poverty. When Frances pointed out a passage in the life of St. Francis of Assisi in which God Himself promised that He would provide for his sustenance and that of his followers to the end of time if they would but adhere to the spirit and letter of his Rule, the Bishop expressed his veneration for such an ideal but also made it clear that in his opinion this was no longer feasible.

Regarding his opposition Frances was calmly to write: "This was part of the plan of Providence and served to fix us more firmly in our purpose . . . for which I cannot sufficiently thank [our spiritual superiors] and the good God, Who thus ordained. For, as in a storm the young trees send their roots deeper into the earth and thereby become more firmly fixed, thus also it happened to us." Whether or not her analogy was sound, she certainly adhered all the more firmly to her ideas about poverty as a consequence of the criticism she received.

Bishop Laurent, while he had no actual jurisdiction in the archdiocese of Cologne, was an influential person; his backing or objections would carry considerable weight with the Archbishop. But Dr. Trost, the Capitular of the Cathedral, was an archdiocesan official, and though he had hitherto shown himself well disposed towards the Sisters, he was decidedly against the taking of perpetual vows (which Bishop Laurent had accepted) and even more opposed to the total prohibition of holding capital. Even the title proposed for the new Congregation he found disagreeable and repulsive.

As he could not budge Frances, he tried to get Father Sartorius, Father Istas's great friend, to see what he could do. Father Sartorius used the argument that perpetual vows and absolute poverty were of minor importance, since they did not form part of the requirements of Clara Fey's Congregation, for which he had sought and obtained the approval of the Archbishop's Vicar-general. As Frances's purpose was very different from that of her friend Clara, she was not much impressed.

Dr. Trost for his part stood as stubbornly to his guns as did Frances, and one day he was rather rude. When Frances told him, "Rather than renounce my principles concerning poverty I will retire," he retorted, "All right; we will let you go!" To which Frances replied, "I am not speaking only in my own name but in that of all the Sisters."

Her threat was not idle: Canon Kloth had spoken to the Bishop of Roermond in Holland about the difficulties the Sisters were encountering in the approval of the Statutes, and the Bishop told him that he would approve them, if Frances and her community decided to transfer themselves to his diocese. They did not want to do that, of course, for they would have been somewhat hampered by their lack of knowledge of Dutch; but they were prepared to go to Holland as a last resource. And as the determination of Frances was by now well known, Roermond could be used as a lever. Cologne and Aachen did not want to lose a group that was doing so much good.

Nevertheless, pressure was brought to bear on Frances from several quarters. One day a priest brought her word that there was no chance whatever of her Statutes being accepted in their present form. To this Frances answered: "I shall never depart from these principles; and if I should do so, I should have to tear every hair out of my head if God did not punish me with sudden death." She spoke with such heat that the priest was not only startled but moved by her evident sincerity. He had already tried to get her to modify what she had written; after this interview he became one of her supporters and promised to use his influence in her favor with the ecclesiastical authorities.

The matter took much longer to settle than was expected, as is commonly true when the heads of a diocese feel it necessary to listen to arguments pro and con. Yet actually the time was rather short, less than two months, and seemed long only because of Frances's impetuosity. Dr. Kloth wrote to Cardinal von Geissel telling him that the Sisters had about given up all hope of obtaining his approval and were seriously considering going to Roermond. It need not be supposed that it was this that made the Cardinal yield, for he had all along been more favorable to Frances's espousal of poverty than were some of his advisers. However, it is possible that his advisers might have prevailed had Frances not been able to exercise pressure. Be that as it may, the Cardinal replied to the Canon that the ladies should have patience, as the affair was nearing its settlement. A little later, after Frances had received the habit, the Cardinal said, on meeting her, pointing to the red cross on her scapular, "Well, you had to fight valiantly for that. I did not personally conduct your affairs, but I was acquainted with all that was going on, and I was convinced that you would come off victorious."

There were others besides Canon Kloth who had been using their influence. For instance, Baron von Boeselager interviewed Cardinal von Geissel on Frances's behalf, saying that he was ready to put at her disposal a house at Bonn, but she would not send Sisters there until she was sure that her Statutes were going to be approved. She had already opened at Jülich a poorhouse known as the Inn of the Holy Ghost, of which her sister Pauline (under her new name of Paula) was the Superior. But she did not want to undertake anything else, if the whole Congregation was to move to Roermond.

Finally, during the octave of Corpus Christi, the Commissary of the archdiocese, Dean Dilschneider, told Frances that her Constitutions had been approved. The date that this word came to her apparently was June 27th, though not for another week did she get official confirmation of this fact — and the Cardinal's signature is certainly dated July 2nd. The delay, short as it was, made her feel suspicious. She considered it strange that the Statutes with the signature of the Ordinary had not been returned to her immediately after the approval that the Commissary told her had been given. She feared that changes had been made, changes that would undermine her central idea. She was on tenterhooks as the days passed.

The reason for the delay was simple enough. What Frances had sent in had passed through a number of hands, and nearly all the priests who had been invited to inspect the document had made so many marginal annotations that the Statutes had become unpresentable and had to be copied out afresh. Another reason for delay was that the ecclesiastical authorities wished for what they described as an "external statute" * to be drawn up, under which the work and organization of the Congregation were to be defined as consisting of ministration to the poor and sick. This, since it presented no problem, had been approved as early as May 9th, even before the Statutes which constitute the Constitutions in bare outline were laid before the Cardinal. They would hardly have been approved at all had not the archdiocesan authorities taken it for granted that the rest would also prove to be acceptable, though no doubt there was some likelihood of demanding modifications at certain points. Finally on September 9, 1853, two years after the Cardinal had acted, the King of Prussia, Frederick William IV, gave the approval of the state, for Prussia asserted some right of control in the guise of providing for the civil rights of cor-

* This was by way of preparing the ground for the presentation of the Constitutions to the Holy See. Its approval was given, according to practice, tentatively on July 22, 1870, with the final approval coming on October 6, 1908. The papal approval of the Congregation itself had come on September 27, 1901.

porations. This had been provided for in Article 23 of the document.

At this point some comments might be offered on the amplification and clarification made by Cardinal von Geissel in 1865 on what was originally decided. Paragraph 28 of what were then called the Constitutions reads: "The Sisters shall neither have nor possess anything in common and as a corporation, except what is indispensably necessary for the subsistence of the Congregation and the necessities of life. They only make use of the acquired civil rights of incorporation for the acquisition and exclusive possession of a convent for a Motherhouse, a garden, and a church. Whenever they take possession of filial [branch] houses they do not consider them their property but only occupy them as a temporary residence, and if these houses are hospitals, also for the benefit of their patients." Looking to the future, Provincial houses were provided for in the same way: they and their novitiates were to be considered as extensions of the Motherhouse. The principle of poverty was thus retained.

Later in the same paragraph we find: "Whatever the Sisters who enter voluntarily donate to the convent will not be put out on interest, but disbursed as the present wants of the house and the necessities of the poor shall require." This is now modified to some extent according to regulations of Canon Law.

Here we might consider a specific instance of Frances's later practice. During the 1870's, while the Kulturkampf was raging in Germany, a young Countess of wealth, Maria von Nesselrode, went to Cincinnati as a postulant. Frances wrote to Sister Vincentia, her American Vicar at the time: "I expressed real joy over what she intended doing for the Bishop of Mainz; what she wishes to do for the Congregation there and here I have disregarded, telling her only that she should decide what is best before God." The Countess, in short, was left perfectly free as to the disposal of her wealth, and Frances was without any wish to try to have her give it to the

Congregation she had joined, a remarkable case of her disinterestedness. As for the young Countess, she was given the habit in Cincinnati in 1876, receiving the name of Sister Paula, but later returned to Germany where she died in 1905. It is pleasant to record that this rich young woman, when she went out begging, rejoiced like a child when the collections were plentiful. The American Annals of the Congregation record how her face positively beamed when she led Sister Antonia (who made the records from which I transcribe) into the convent store rooms in the cellar, showing her how good God had been to His poor.

In America today it is impossible, in most places, to solicit alms from house to house, though in the social service houses it is carried out to some extent and proves, incidentally, of immense value by putting the Sisters in touch with those Catholics who have neglected their duties. Many children are baptized as a result, many marriages validated, many irregular unions broken off, many children recovered for parochial schools.

None of these houses belong to the Congregation. But it has not proved feasible for the Sisters to conduct their hospitals in the United States without owning them. And those working in them are much too preoccupied in other ways to have time for begging. The Sisters are therefore obliged to accept payment from those who can afford to pay, while remembering that their first obligation is to the poor.

In 1918 the new Code of Canon Law was promulgated, in accordance with which the Constitutions of the Sisters of the Poor of St. Francis were revised, in 1930 and again in 1940 with some minor changes, but essentials were left intact. The Sisters observe the Rule of the Third Order Regular of St. Francis revised in 1927 by Pope Pius XI.

In conclusion a word may be said about the Recluses. Though they had been established, in embryo, even before the Congregation received approbation, there is no mention of them in the Statutes of 1851, presumably because the project was as yet only experimental. But the Constitutions of 1865 legislate in their regard. Only a limited number of Sisters who can be spared from the charities of the Congregation are allowed to join, and these may return to the active life with the consent of the Mother. Only perpetually professed Sisters who, in the opinion of the Mother and her council, have manifested a pronounced vocation to the contemplative life, are to be admitted, and these "observe, as far as possible, the second Rule of St. Francis for St. Clare in its mitigated form."

The Recluses were completely apart from the rest of the community, yet they were to take no special vows and were to remain under the direction of the Mother. They did, however, have one of their number, appointed by the Mother, to act as Superior of the group. Though in the early years they were sometimes called "Clarisses" they had no connection whatever with the Poor Clares; they were then, as they still are, members of the Sisters of the Poor of St. Francis.

What Frances expected of this group is beautifully expressed in one of her letters to the Recluses: "You must endeavor in a special manner to assist us in attaining the glorious end for which we are all created and were called to the religious life. You are, as it were, the Moses of the Congregation whose duty it is to elevate and stretch out your arms, yea, to keep them outstretched, that we, battling victoriously, may save our souls, and may, by the grace of God, help to save the souls of many."

Frances Schervier could not but remember that St. Francis of Assisi felt an almost overpowering attraction to the contemplative state and was deterred from a complete retirement only because God's message was brought to him that his vocation was that of working for the salvation of souls. But the spirit of contemplation is an essential part of the Franciscan life, as indeed it is, to a greater or less extent, of the life of all Christians. So now Frances Schervier promoted in her own Congregation that most difficult thing to effectuate, the union of the active and contemplative modes. The Sister most busily occupied in external duties was to perform all her work in the spirit of prayer and to do her deeds of charity as towards Christ Himself; the Recluses were to pray for the success of this work.

12

*

The Habit Conferred

FOR FIVE YEARS Frances and her first associates had been living as a religious community, wearing secular dress indeed, but addressing one another as "Sister" and Frances (as their Superior) as "Mother" and strictly observing the Rule of the Franciscan Third Order. But from the start they had been looking forward to the time when they would be recognized by the Cardinal-Archbishop of Cologne as a distinct religious congregation and permitted to wear the religious habit. Though Frances's thoughts never, at this time, went further afield than the Rhineland, it might be noted that 12 years before her Constitutions were approved by the Holy See she sent a group of her Sisters to the United States, going there herself a few years later. This would indicate that she never had thought of her work as necessarily restricted to being a diocesan undertaking. If she had seemed to demand approbation on her own terms — and had won her point — this was not out of self-will but because of her whole-hearted conviction that she had been directly commissioned by the Divine Will. Less than conformity to that Will would never have been acceptable to her. Father Trost might be blunt and Bishop Laurent bland in the way they tried to induce her to be what they considered prudent regarding her principle of absolute poverty. She could not consider it prudent to disregard the message from heaven, brought to her in so remarkable a fashion.

It has been noted that the Constitutions were signed by Cardinal von Geissel on July 2nd; it was arranged that the habit should be conferred on such Sisters as had been in the community for a full year on the feast of St. Clare, August 12, 1851, a most appropriate date. After that had been accomplished Frances would be able to undertake the charge of the branch house at Bonn that had been offered them and also of the women prisoners in the jail of Aachen, another service which had been proposed by the civic authorities. These activities — and others that Frances already saw looming ahead — could not be accepted until she was perfectly sure as to where she stood with the ecclesiastical authorities.

No formal novitiate had been possible for any of the Sisters, nothing except the novitiate of hard work and devoted charity. But there were 23 young women, besides Frances herself, who had been in the community for the full 12 months that her Statutes prescribed as the indispensable period of probation; these could be immediately clothed as novices and a year later professed. Those who had joined them later were regarded as novices, so their investiture had to be deferred. They were, however, already at work with the others, so that Frances had at her command at least 30 women, not a very large number, to be sure, but a great advance on the four who had joined her on St. Francis Eve in the house beyond St. James's Gate.

We hear of Catherine Daverkosen, who now was going to be entitled to use the name of Sister Mary, having to be half carried into St. Paul's Church, so ill was she still, by the latest arrival, the postulant Louisa Nellesen, who even had to hold the candle for her during the ceremony. But her mind was alert and her face transfigured with joy. She had been drawn back from the very brink of the grave and had several years of usefulness before her as Frances's second-in-command.

They entered the church in a body in their black secular

dresses — a black that had long had greenish hues, acquired through much wear — and walked in procession up the aisle to take their places in the sanctuary. There the Commissary, Dean Dilschneider, sang High Mass, for he had worked hard for their recognition, with Canon Kloth, another staunch friend, as subdeacon and Father Blum, the pastor of St. Paul's, as deacon. We do not hear of his having had much to do with Frances's affairs, but as pastor, he had to take precedence over Canon Kloth.

Father Fey, Clara's brother and the director of her Congregation, preached the sermon, and Clara herself took part in the proceedings, putting on Frances's head a wreath of flowers and assisting in the vesting of the 24 new Sisters. Clara was to live to place another wreath of flowers on Frances's head when she was lying in state awaiting burial.

The ceremony was almost like a family affair so far as Frances was concerned; and of course many relations and friends of all the Sisters, as well as numerous devoted recipients of their charity, were present to witness their serene joy and to offer heartfelt congratulations. The newly established Congregation had a great feast that day by way of celebration: each of them, for the first time in five years — according to the Annals at Aachen — had a whole egg to eat at dinner! In the afternoon the Sisters attended solemn Benediction at the church of the Sisters of the Poor Child Jesus and were then their guests at a simple supper and enjoyed with them a few hours of pleasant recreation.

They went home happy to the old Dominican priory which for the past two years had been their rather uncomfortable and insecurely held lodgings. They much more than paid for the accommodations the city authorities provided for them there, for not only did they conduct a kitchen under that roof but also a refuge for destitute old people and a kind of hospital for syphilitic women. As though this were not enough, three days after they had received the habit the Burgomaster and Aldermen of Aachen renewed their request

— this time formally — that Frances supply Sisters to look after the women detained in the city jail.

Frances was delighted to do so, for this was a work she had looked forward to since that day, a year or two ago, when a girl who had escaped from a Belgian prison came to her begging for shelter. She was before very long to extend this work in a startling style. But Frances always stood ready to expand her activities, so far as this was possible; she added emergency nursing during epidemics and the training of servant girls to what her busy hands were already doing. She had long since discovered that simple country girls coming into the city in search of employment — and perhaps not finding it at once, meanwhile not always having very respectable lodgings — were all too liable to fall into immoral ways, not because of innate viciousness but because they did not recognize their dangers or because they were destitute. While they were being trained for domestic service, Frances either took them in herself or established hostels for them, or (if this was not possible) found them inexpensive rooms with people whom she was able to trust. What was then, and always has been absolutely ruled out, as not being part of her vocation, was educational work. This was not merely because she did not wish to trespass on Clara Fey's field of operations, for when, a few years later, she sent Sisters to the United States, where nun-teachers were eagerly sought, she still would have nothing to do with schools. So also with orphans — she knew that if she accepted them, she would have to educate them. Though after the American Civil War she did, in an emergency, accept a few young children, it was only as a temporary measure. Frances was from the outset very positive as to what was her vocation and equally positive as to what was not.

She still had many problems to solve, and not all of them were disposed of when, a couple of years later, she acquired a Motherhouse. She had begun with makeshifts, and makeshifts had to suffice for some time to come. Thus a canonically established novitiate was as yet out of the question. The "Preachers" was not a convent but only a shelter they were given on sufferance. Since the work was so pressing and there were as yet so few to do it, novices and even postulants were usually sent out to help in one of the branch houses. They returned to Aachen a month or two before they made their profession, and there, in so far as they can be said to have had a novice-mistress, she was Frances. Such an arrangement, of course, was not at all in accordance with present-day Canon Law, which decrees that the Superior of a house has no more than a general jurisdiction over novices, who should live apart from the rest of the community and be under the direction of one delegated to form them in their religious vocation. But such irregularities have often occurred in the early days of a new religious congregation. In short, a good deal of improvisation was unavoidable. Frances did the best she could and then hoped for the best.

It must be remembered that the life of these Sisters was one of unceasing activity, except for the tiny group of Recluses who had been formed in 1848, three years before the habit had been conferred. This meant, in those days, that much of the work had to be done outside of the convent, if the "Preachers" could be called that. All the Sisters took their turn at the begging, which was necessary for their charities and also for their own subsistence. Yet begging served still another purpose: Frances was not one to wait until help was applied for; she wished to find out where there were people who needed her help, and by going out begging they learned about cases, especially of the sick poor, who required their ministrations.

This outside work exposed them to some dangers and, especially as Frances was troubled by the fact that she was unable to give the regular training of a novitiate to those who came to her, she constantly warned them against anything like loitering or idle curiosity. As the present Constitutions put it, "They were to go through the world like holy Father

Francis, as innocent and guileless children, uncontaminated by the world's corruption." So sensitive was Frances on this point that, after she had sent Sisters to America, it was several years before she would permit them to take charge of a small hospital in that "Babylon," as she called it, New York!

Aachen was a sleepy little city, inhabited by a population overwhelmingly Catholic. The tone was one of great respectability, and though this may have been in many instances a trifle smug and stuffy, there was unquestionably a vivid fervor in many quarters. At the same time, it was by no means a city of saints, for we have already seen that it contained its quota of sinners, even if their sins were mostly those of human frailty rather than of downright wickedness. Frances, it need scarcely be said, had no doubt that her Sisters on their errands of mercy would be treated with nothing less than great respect, but she seems to have feared that some of them might waste their time — the time that should be given to the service of the poor — in trivial gossip.

She had also another fear, that some of the more pious among them might, when passing a church, go in and spend an hour or two there when they should be working. They were, indeed, to do everything in the spirit of prayer, but, except for the Recluses, she considered that daily Mass and the community prayers should normally suffice. Therefore in an undated circular letter, which because of its position in the Annals of the Motherhouse, may be taken to have been written about this time, she gives very specific instructions on this point: they must not attend Mass in any church they happened to be passing, unless they had received permission to do so. Meritorious as this act would be in itself, it would not be meritorious for them. She goes on: "For the greater security of the Sisters in order that peace of soul may be confirmed rather than disturbed, I wish to establish a rule of conduct in regard to the practice of adoring and greeting our Divine Lord in the churches which the Sisters pass on their way. If their errand or duty permits, Sisters when out may once during the course of the morning and once in the afternoon enter a church for a short act of adoration and of spiritual communion. If Mass is being celebrated, they should not remain longer than from the *Sanctus* until after the consecration." (That is, for not more than about five minutes.) "If Mass is just beginning when they enter the church they should not wait for the Consecration, but merely make an act of adoration and spiritual communion, and then adore our Lord in the Holy Sacrifice as they do their work or proceed on their way, in the practice of obedience. The same is to be observed in the afternoon: without special permission the Sisters should never attend a service or a sermon, even though only in part. The service of Mary at the feet of our Divine Lord should be sought in the spiritual services of the community; in these let us be very fervent so as not to lose the least fraction thereof, in so far as in ourselves lies." Could anything be more explicit? Could anything be more sensible, when we remember the purpose of the community?

As for Frances's own spiritual life, we know very little, apart from the two autobiographical fragments she left, and they come down no further than to the time her community was approved. But much can be inferred from her conduct, as something may also be gleaned from her circular and other letters, reserved though these usually are. This much also may be added: although from about 1841 to 1843 she was in such a disturbed frame of mind as to come very close to a nervous breakdown, due to her sense of frustration regarding her vocation, all such disturbances completely disappeared after she had formed her community in 1845. She had difficulties galore to encounter as Mother General and also had increasingly poor physical health. But the salient fact is that from 1845 — in fact, from 1843 — on, she showed herself extraordinarily well balanced. She drove ahead on a steady keel in complete confidence in a vocation that had been directly revealed to her by God and with a perfect trust that His Providence would accomplish all that it had begun.

143

Expansion

It is not my intention to write a history of the Sisters of the Poor of St. Francis; nevertheless some details must be given, because what the Sisters did, whether in Aachen or in their branch houses elsewhere in Germany — and in the United States that Frances twice visited — depended upon her and constituted an extension of her own work.

Sister Mary, the former Catherine Daverkosen, with her health recovered, remained Frances's right hand, and, it will be remembered, had been for a short while Superior. Yet even as such her position had been largely nominal, for most of the active direction of affairs had been delegated to Frances herself. The masterful Gertrude Frank had been removed by death in the spring of 1850, otherwise she might have tried to interfere. But her mission had been accomplished; Frances now had a community under her charge that had been recognized by the authorities, and though she had never wished to be its head and from time to time tried to resign, she was, at least while she was the canonically elected and responsible Superior, not going to allow herself to be bothered with self-appointed advisers, though it must be added that Gertrude would never have thought of putting herself forward in this way. With all her eccentricities, she was both holy and humble; if she had been as insistent as she was in 1845, it was because she was entirely convinced that she was commissioned by God. After that she had subsided, except for an occasional mild eruption of her Gertrudian forthrightness.

The first new work accepted by Frances after the approbation of her Statutes and the Congregation itself was in the city jails, and about this we shall soon hear some astounding things. But Bonn was also waiting for her, and there she was being backed by the Baron von Boeselager. It was a much more important place than the tentatively accepted Jülich, a small town on the flat lands between the Rhine and Holland, and promised much greater fruit.

Bonn, though not very large, was an interesting town, situated 15 miles or so below Cologne, with undulating farm lands in between but with the vineyards and the romantic hills and castles somewhat further down the river. It had been one of the main Roman strongholds, and its minster had been founded by St. Helena while her son Constantine was Emperor. There too Frankish kings had been crowned and the Archbishop of Cologne had had his electoral palace. Like Aachen it had suffered a good deal during the Napoleonic Wars, but, again like Aachen, it was making a rapid recovery, helped in this by its university, which contained faculties of law, medicine, and philosophy and both Catholic and Protestant theological schools. It furthermore contained the former residence of the Elector, an observatory, and several excellent museums. From an old bastion on the east side of the Coblenz Gate a good view could be had of the sweep of the Rhine and of the famous "Seven Mountains." Less than a mile from the castle rose a small hill known as the Kreuzberg, which is surmounted by a white church, a conspicuous landmark, and leading to the church were 28 steps of Italian marble which the faithful ascend only on their knees, as they do the *Scala Santa* at the Lateran.

These stairs were of course duly climbed by the three Sisters and the postulant that Frances sent to start their work at Bonn, just as the Franciscan and other churches in so

145

Catholic a town were often visited. But this was only in free hours, for though Bonn was a fairly prosperous place, there was much that needed to be done in the way of nursing the sick poor in their homes, in the establishment of a charity kitchen, and in the support of everything in the familiar way, by begging. The group was placed under the charge of Sister Bonaventure, who might have been considered rather young for her office were it not that few of the Sisters at this time were much older. Baron von Boeselager would probably have deeded them the house he provided for their use had it not been that it was contrary to Frances's principles to possess anything. She wished to be poor; she wished also to be free.

From Aachen Frances guided the inexperienced Sister Bonaventure with advice. What she mainly feared was excessive zeal and the overtaxing of strength, and even more that too much work would destroy the spirit of recollection. Thus on October 6, 1851, she wrote, saying that if this happened, "Your labors would be unprofitable to yourselves and to your fellow men." When a few weeks later she herself was confined to her room by sickness, she wrote again on November 22nd: "Well it is for me to be compelled to escape from the noise and confusion of our daily occupations; it nevertheless appears strange to me not to be with the Sisters. But our dear Lord knows for what this is good, and so I leave the care of everything to Him." Once more she wrote on January 3rd in the new year: "Oh how sincerely I wish to send you assistance! I can scarcely bide the time when I can send you a fifth Sister." Evidently the work was pressing heavily on those whom Frances had assigned to Bonn, and other appeals were being made for branch houses, all of which had to be considered carefully, though to not all of them was she able to respond as she would like to have done.

For the work at the city jail she had sent Sisters Dominica and Jacoba at the insistence of the civic authorities and of Father Mettman, who served as chaplain of the institution. At first the Sisters remained with their charges only during the day, returning to the "Preachers" at night; but afterwards, when they saw that they might be needed at any hour and that in the quiet of the evening they were often able to accomplish more than during a day crowded with many tasks, they took up their residence in the prison itself. The chaplain for the most part gave his attention to the male prisoners, but as he was also the pastor of a church, he could give to this only part of his time. As for the women, it was found that Sisters could often do more for their special needs than a priest was able to effect. In many instances a sincere reformation was brought about, and as the women in the jail were usually there for petty offences and serving only short terms of detention, the Sisters made a special point of obtaining work for them after they were released. This was of the utmost importance, for one of the main obstacles preventing such people from continuing to "go straight" is that it is hard for anybody who has been a "jailbird" to find employment. Later a Sister in the Motherhouse, when it was established, was given this as her sole duty; she conducted a kind of employment agency, a task of considerable delicacy, for she had virtually to guarantee the future good behavior of those employed by families as domestic servants, at that time almost the only kind of occupation open to women of this type, though some of them might find work in a factory or as seamstresses. To act as an unofficial probation officer would hardly have served; she had to make these poor unfortunates feel that she was their counselor and friend.

As Frances could not always feel certain that these former prisoners would persevere, she came to set up in various parts of the Rhineland hostels in which they could support themselves by sewing. The training of young women — either those who had got into some sort of scrape, or might be in danger of getting into one, or who were not as yet properly equipped to earn their own living — became a rather prominent feature of her manifold activities. So thoroughly were they taught to be reliable, neat, and orderly, and their conversions were in many instances so complete, that many families were only too glad to secure the services of one of Frances's girls. She also continued to do some work for fallen women, though these she usually passed on to the Good Shepherd Sisters.

Nor was she content to wait for such women to come to her for help; she went after them. She no longer, it is true, now that she was wearing a religious habit, felt able to make the daring forays of only a year or two before. But more than once when she saw a bedraggled creature wandering through the streets with a baby in her arms, she divined the situation and had no hesitation in engaging the unfortunate girl in conversation and extracting her story, all as a preliminary to reform. Moreover, sometimes in the course of their begging tours the Sisters would hear of a man and woman living together without having troubled to go through the formality of matrimony. To intrude herself into such a case was an operation both dangerous and delicate; yet Frances would not rest until the couple had had their union ratified by the Church; when this was not possible she did her best to get them to separate. All this called for a good deal of courage, but as nearly everybody in Aachen knew of her self-less charity, she was almost always treated at least with respect, and often succeeded in what she was attempting.

If this demanded courage, what shall we say of something else that happened at least seven or eight times? The closest parallel is provided in the life of St. Catherine of Siena, who on one occasion spent a night praying with a young noble named Niccolò di Toldo who had been condemned to death for so-called sedition. Catherine accompanied him to the scaffold, where she knelt beside the block and received his severed head in her lap. The fact that Frances's Sisters were now in charge of the women prisoners at the jail emboldened her to ask the authorities whether she might not pray during the night with a criminal who was to be beheaded the following morning.

At all times her guiding principle was: the more abandoned a soul, the more it needed her help. Never did she think that her ministrations were complete if they were only concerned with alleviating physical distress. Everything she did was without stint, and as her Congregation became better known and greater resources were available, she was able to extend her charities. But her main charity was that of helping the spiritually destitute. It was for this reason that she was, if possible, more zealous in what she did for Protestants and professed unbelievers than for Catholics. All were children of God and potentially heirs of the Kingdom. To them she gave herself freely, and for such work she commonly needed less in the way of material resources than for her other activities.

One marvels that she was permitted to undertake this compassionate work for condemned prisoners. But it was hard to refuse Frances anything. Even unimaginative officials and bureaucrats were so impressed by the warmth of her devotion that they gave her their astounded permission once and then found that it was requested — after the precedent had been established — and had to be granted over and over again.

The chaplain, Father Mettman, had hitherto arrived in the morning to hear the criminal's confession, if he could be induced to make it, and sometimes would give him Holy Communion. But Father Mettman knew only too well from experience that men of this sort often went to their death parading hardened indifference, or were in such a state of confusion and fear as hardly to know what they were doing. What Frances undertook to do was to prepare these men for Father Mettman's coming. To make sure that there would be no last-minute relapse into despair or a railing against God for what had to be suffered, she made it her practice to stay the entire night in the cell of the man who was to be executed, bringing him to a state of penitence, resignation, and even consolation. Not one of these men but was softened by the tender charity he could see in Frances's shining, deep-set eyes and in her gentle voice. She was able to say of those whom she attended over a space of years that the contrition and resignation of them all except one was such that she had absolutely no doubt of their salvation. And even of the solitary exception of whom she was not prepared to say this, she could say that he had at least received the sacraments.

In the courtyard of the jail, where the men took their exercise, a block would be set up. Often a dismal rain would be falling in the dim bleak dawn. It was not so early that the barred windows would not be crowded with faces, looking at the block and the masked executioner who waited for the warder to bring out the man who was to die. There was a sense that the world — or that little lost world — was holding its breath as the prisoner came out, the chaplain walking ahead and Frances coming behind. Father Mettman would have heard the man's confession in his cell, but he continued to read from his prayer book. Then as the man, his eyes bandaged, bowed down for the stroke, Frances would be seen kneeling beside him, murmuring the last words of faith, hope, and charity. She would go back to the "Preachers" in a state of near collapse from the ordeal, but held up with thanks to God that He had allowed her to save a soul. Regarding one such execution — a double execution — she was to write in 1855: "I have just returned from the prison where the two criminals were executed today. I am half dead with fatigue and commiseration. What a grace for those two sinners to have been so sincerely converted! What comfort, what help our holy religion offers! How peacefully one goes to even the most terrible death when one is reconciled to God and makes His will one's own! Pray for those victims of justice today. I think, yes, I confidently hope, that the Lord has been merciful to them."

It is an astonishing story and becomes all the more so from the matter of fact tone used by Frances. Through her rather bare account of the matter we catch sight of her complete disregard of herself and also can surmise the high esteem she now enjoyed in a city that had begun by laughing at her as an eccentric. While she does, in passing, mention her own shattered condition after what she had gone through, it is clear that she all but forgets this in her joy. Without her these men might have passed to death sullen or bewildered or terrified. After her night of prayer with them, they went serenely to death and, so Frances was convinced, to heaven with their sins forgiven.

The Imposter

IF THE ACCOUNT that has just been given of Frances's frequent attendance at the executions of criminals and of the way she prepared these men for their death is sensational, hardly less so, though in a very different way, is what must now be related. On the one side we find a group in the community — and with them some priests — who believed that it was being revealed that Frances should withdraw from the headship of the Sisters; on the other side stood another group — and again some priests — who believed that nothing less than diabolical possession was involved, an attempt of the powers of Hell to wreck the work that had begun so magnificently. However, most of the Sisters probably were not even aware of what was going on, or heard only vague reports of which they could make very little. Most of those who did know of these events seem to have kept their heads and to have treated the matter with cool reserve. What may be confidently said is that whether or not this was an instance of diabolical possession, the effect would have been the same had hysteria been allowed to prevail: the Sisters of the Poor of St. Francis might have gone down in ruin.

Before going further with the story itself, it must be said that while diabolical possession does now and then occur, nevertheless most of the instances of it that have been commonly adduced may be explained in a very different way. Human frailty and human foolishness are such that there is rarely any need for the Devil to resort to extreme and crude measures. The Devil does exist, and one of his favorite devices is to persuade people that there is no Devil; but another of his devices is to destroy the usefulness of otherwise pious souls by making them see a devil in every cupboard and under every bed.

It should be pointed out that, though individual priests are not immune from aberrations, the Church is extremely cautious about any sort of supernatural manifestations. For example: though, beginning with St. Francis of Assisi, there have been many genuine stigmatics, there have probably been an even greater number of stigmatics whose five wounds have been discovered, after careful investigation by the ecclesiastical authorities, to have been either self-inflicted or to have been induced by a deranged mental condition, which is also a kind of self-infliction, though not of a fraudulent character. So also with apparitions and private revelations. While some of these are undoubtedly genuine, for every one upon which the Church pronounces favorably, there are many more upon which no pronouncement is passed, or upon which the judgment is unfavorable. It cannot be emphasized too strongly how cautious the Church is about all such matters.

Father Jeiler, from whom this story was derived (and who derived it from the Chronicles of the Motherhouse at Aachen) while, as always, obviously honest, is, one suspects, rather guarded in what he tells. But by reading between the lines of his account, it is possible to catch sight of some rather lurid lights. The chaplain of the branch house where these things occurred (who was completely taken in), he excuses on the ground that he was "a good priest, but withal rather young and inexperienced in this respect." What is more surprising is that Frances's own brother Karl was among those who came to side with the imposter against his sister.

That he should have done so reveals the extent and depth of the delusion. He was anything but a fool; his position in Aachen, where he taught religion in the schools, a position that gave him the title of professor, shows that he was regarded as a man of some competence. Frances had accepted him as the chaplain of the Motherhouse. It was by virtue of this office that he felt free to speak as he did, though others of no standing at all also were at hand with their advice.

Perhaps even more surprising is the fact that Sister Mary, the Superior of the branch house where these happenings took place, was also befooled. She was, it is true, sceptical at first and therefore treated the imposter's supposititious divinations with severity, but later she was won over, though the divinations proposed the very thing that had nearly caused her death not long before — that she should take over the general direction of the Congregation, which Frances was to resign, or withdraw and found a new congregation. That she was induced to lend herself to this was the measure of her temporary delusion.

Now for the story, which belongs to 1852, just a year after the Congregation had received ecclesiastical approval. Some time before this Frances had rescued in Aachen a girl who belonged to the class for which she had so great a commiseration. As this girl's repentance seemed to be thoroughgoing, she eventually accepted her as a postulant and sent her to work under Sister Mary.

After a while the girl began to walk in her sleep. Her somnambulism should, of course, have been taken (but was not) as a clear indication that all was not right with her. At least it revealed a nervous malady which (in extreme cases) can be a form of self-induced hypnotism, as it probably was in this case. In any event it has nothing to do either with special sanctity or diabolical possession.

Sister Mary, who later was to show herself very sound of judgment as second-in-command to Frances, especially in the direction of practical affairs, at this point failed lamentably.

She did, it is true, bring in doctors to treat the postulant for somnambulism, but they accomplished nothing. A little while afterwards somnambulism developed into what were taken to be ecstatic states. Sister Mary, like the confessor of the house and some of the Sisters, saw the girl fixed immovable for hours at a time and thought that there must be among them a great mystic. In their enthusiasm they even fancied that they sometimes saw her suspended in the air during her ecstasies or trances.*

Frances was informed about these goings on, and her first inclination was to ascribe them to diabolical possession. She witnessed, without any excitement, one of the trances that was staged for her special benefit. The girl was led into the chapel and placed before the altar. It was true; she did "go off"; not only that, her hair stood on end and surrounded her head like a wreath or halo, with her veil ridiculously suspended above her like a kind of roof. Some even thought her whole body was enshrined in light. But Frances was disgusted with the performance. However, as her view of the matter was not shared by the other Sisters in the house, she decided that it would be best to take no immediate action. She counted upon other developments opening the eyes of the postulant's adherents.

Worse was to come before the end was reached. One day, just at the hour when Sister Mary was to give an instruction to the Sisters, the girl, who that day happened to be ill in bed (her general health was far from good), asked her to come to her and then announced: "Send the Sisters here; *I* will

* The phenomenon of levitation has frequently been attested to by much more reliable witnesses. Just what it proves is open to question. St. Philip Neri, who often experienced it, much to his embarrassment, as he also had frequent ecstasies, attached so little importance to such manifestations that he frequently warned people against them. Recently Mr. Roger Babson — backed by a number of hard-headed businessmen — has endowed a scientific institute whose purpose is to find a means of overcoming the forces of gravity. Levitation undoubtedly does occur; much more often people have merely imagined that it has occurred. Quite possibly our postulant was lifted from the ground during her trances. If so, it did not necessarily prove her a saint.

instruct them." Sister Mary consenting, the postulant spoke most edifyingly for over an hour on the Blessed Virgin and her love for the Congregation, but also insisted that Our Lady was speaking through her.

These remarks, however, were now and then punctuated — according to subsequent accounts, which may have been colored by knowledge of later events — with outrageous blasphemy. These were uttered in a different tone of voice, and the girl herself was conscious enough of them to explain that the devil was interrupting her. If this were really the case, the most feeble intelligence should have been able to detect diabolical possession, either that or insanity.

Father Jeiler inclines to the view that the girl was an imposter and was herself imposed upon. She had probably really brought herself to believe that her psychic states were a sign of sanctity, as has happened a good many times in the history of the Church. In a later conference with the Sisters the postulant went so far as to say that the Blessed Virgin herself would be the Superior of the Congregation but (and here was the crux of the matter) would use the speaker, unworthy as she was and a poor sinner, as her earthly instrument. She demanded the habit at once and said that Mother Frances must resign.

Preposterous though all this was, the divinations were accepted as genuine by Sister Mary (who no doubt had heard of the divine message brought in 1845 by Gertrude Frank and so could see no reason why another message from heaven should not be sent). Nuns are usually very level-headed people; even more so are priests. But not all of them are exempt from aberrations of foolishness. At any rate the girl's adherents wrote to Frances demanding her resignation, and when Frances refused, her brother Karl remonstrated with her saying, "So you intend to oppose the will of God!"

Frances did not bother to remind him that Cardinal von Geissel would not recognize a resignation and a new superiorship made in defiance of the Statutes approved by him. What she said was: "If I could discern the will of God in this proposal, I would immediately resign my office. I have shown my willingness to do so on a former occasion." She added: "I cannot recognize the ravings of a demoniac as the expression of God's will. I shall not yield to the Devil."

That last sentence hardly seems to fit in with Frances's treatment of the affair. I conjecture that it was recorded long after the event, when memories, having grown a little indistinct as to details, used imagination to supply what was lacking.

What we know for sure is that Frances thought the best solution was to recall the girl to Aachen. This made the postulant frantic. One day she announced that on a day definitely named by her she would receive the stigmata, and though this did not happen, her prestige still was not shaken among her followers. She continued to give her instructions to the Sisters, and the fact that pious considerations were mixed, as before, with blasphemies and obscenities was explained away by the chaplain: it showed that the Devil was seeking to counteract the operation of the Holy Ghost, and should therefore be taken as a signal proof of grace. Then she threatened to commit suicide if she was separated from Sister Mary. Yet Mary was half persuaded that she should leave the Congregation and found a new one, under the direction of course of the postulant. Really it would seem that delusion could not have gone much further.

Frances remained firm. The girl did not carry out her threat of suicide but obeyed the summons to return to Aachen. There she was kept apart from the rest of the community and so had no opportunities for self-display. As that was not much to her liking, she soon asked to be dismissed. Last heard of, she had turned up in Mainz, barefoot, on a pilgrimage to Rome. Bishop von Ketteler, perhaps the most notable member of the German hierarchy of his time, heard of her, saw that she was manifestly deranged, and (since she was not a subject of his diocese) had her put under restraint and sent to Cologne. There she was placed in an asylum. Probably her imposture was not altogether deliberate; the most likely explanation is that hers was a case of religious mania in an extreme form.

At first Sister Mary was by no means convinced that she had been imposed upon. However, Bishop Laurent got her to promise that she would have no more to do with the affair. But Frances, presumably thinking that a change of scene would do her good, sent her to Bonn not long afterwards to replace Sister Bonaventure. There the Sisters' confessor, Father Lemmertz, heard her story, and while admitting that some of the manifestations she had witnessed were not to be explained "naturally," managed to persuade her that they were more likely to have come from Hell than Heaven. Whether he believed in the literal accuracy of all that she related may be open to doubt. But perhaps he thought this the best line to take under the circumstances. At all events Sister Mary recovered her common sense and until her death in 1858 showed herself an excellent executive. That is, she proved good at managing things; Frances, after what had happened, could hardly have had much confidence in her judgment of character.

However, there was no trace of resentment on either side. Frances might have shown her displeasure by never trusting Mary with any responsibility again; Mary might have borne a grudge for having been proved to have behaved in a very silly fashion. Neither of them showed the slightest ill feeling. For when Frances in 1853 secured a permanent Motherhouse, Sister Mary was put in charge of the extensive renovations that were necessary and held until her last illness the rank of first assistant to Frances. As such she was not only very efficient but edified everybody by her devotion and submissiveness. If the Devil had really tried to disrupt the Congregation, he had been signally foiled.

Frances had never for an instant been taken in by the unbalanced young postulant. But she had learned something from this case of pretended holiness, and her discretion was strengthened and made more acute than ever. A little later she had a somewhat similar case to deal with when another postulant began, so she claimed, to have visions. Frances, far from being impressed, came to the conclusion that this was another instance of imposture or self-deception and made it a reason for dismissing the girl, although she knew that in doing this she would offend the priest who had recommended her. But note the sequel: a year or two later the girl came back with another letter from the same priest, supplemented by an anonymous letter to the priest extolling her virtues. It did not take Frances long to discover that this letter had been written — of course in a disguised script — by the young woman herself!

No great discernment may have been exercised in that discovery, for all anonymous letters must be regarded with suspicion, and few people are capable of disguising their handwriting so well as not to leave some marks of their own identity. Frances's recognition of bogus supernatural manifestations shows how cool-headed she was. This is all the more remarkable because she herself owed much to supernatural manifestations of another kind. The difference is one to be noted. Even Gertrude Frank's message she took with reserve and did not commit herself to belief in it until after consulting other people and praying constantly for several months. And though she heard divine voices speaking in her soul, it would seem that only once did she hear such a Voice with her physical ears — and even her account of that leaves it an open question whether that too was not an inspiration. She had before that gone through a period when overwrought nerves had made her fancy that various calamities ranging from blindness to insanity were on the point of overtaking her. She was therefore armed against all such delusions. It was well for her that this was so, for in distant America, not many years later, occurrences rather like those just cited were met with, as we shall hear in due course. The Sisters there, having learned from Frances's experience, were on guard against pious imposters.

Settled Center

IT WAS NOW a pressing necessity that the new Congregation should have a settled center. One wonders a little that ecclesiastical approval was given without this having been obtained; but of course the Statutes of 1851 in their fourth paragraph had indicated, though in not very precise terms, that a Motherhouse — the only house to be owned by the Sisters — was to be set up, and Paragraph 20 provided that the novitiate was to be in the Motherhouse. The temporary lodgings at the "Preachers" had never been regarded as other than a makeshift arrangement; what was needed was some place that the Sisters could consider home.

Frances had built up no reserve fund against the day when she might be able to erect or buy a house suitable for a convent, and when the opportunity to secure one occurred during the summer of 1852, she had nothing in hand. The building in question was well suited for her purpose, as it had been a convent of Poor Clares until the nuns had been ejected in 1803, since when it had served as a factory. Moreover she had a chance to obtain in this building on Marschierstrasse and Elizabethstrasse * a real bargain, despite some disadvan-

---

* The Motherhouse at Aachen was moved in June, 1893, to the Lindenplatz. Later the old Motherhouse became the Generalate, until in 1946 this was transferred to Rome. In 1937 and 1938 the Sisters were grouped under the jurisdiction of provinces, three of them German, two of them American; in 1947 the Belgian province was established. Cardinal Fumasoni-Biondi, former Apostolic Delegate to the United States, is the Cardinal Protector of the Congregation.

tages that went with it. For only 23,000 thalers was the price asked. But the best of bargains was useless when Frances seemed utterly unable to close with it. She appealed to Baron von Boeselager, the friend who donated the use of the house at Bonn, and he loaned her 10,000 thalers, charging no interest; but that was all she had at her disposal, except for some relatively small sums that she obtained from her family.

She had counted upon Canon Deboeur to leave her his fortune as he had promised, and had he done so when he died in 1848 — about the time when the rent of the house guaranteed by Frau Beissel came to an end — she would then have been able to buy a house. But as no will was found, Frances got nothing, and though this in one way pleased her, as it made her directly dependent upon Providence, she would have had no house at all had not the city authorities given them shelter in the old Dominican building. This, though a godsend at the time, could not be regarded as anything very secure. Moreover the building was not in good repair and their contact with the syphilitic women whom the Sisters undertook to nurse was not without its dangers. The question was how was she going to find the money to buy the former Poor Clare convent?

In her perplexity Frances turned to Bishop Laurent. He, good man, had of course nothing to give in the form of money, as Frances was well aware, but she had counted upon useful advice and spiritual support. Instead the Bishop seized this opportunity to remind her, in his best "I-told-you-so" manner, that he had always been against her ideas as to absolute poverty: now she was finding out how unpractical she had always been. His words, though not unkindly spoken, hurt her almost more than the failure of her plans.

Weeping, she left him. When she got to the "Preachers" shortly before the time of the midday dinner, she told the portress that she would not take anything to eat. Instead she went to her room and gave way to her grief. When at last she got control of herself, she went to the Franciscan Church of St. Nicholas — the same church in which seven years earlier she had knelt before the altar of St. Francis and promised to become a member of his Third Order — and there she prayed for several hours, often in tears, before going disconsolately home. The whole project seemed on the point of breaking down, for she had the option on the old convent for only a few more days.

While she was on her way from St. Nicholas's Church, she encountered Sister Veronica Wildt, a rather new arrival in the community, who, seeing that Frances was in tears and discovering why, made what seemed to be a desperate suggestion. She requested to be allowed to ask a relative of hers, a priest living near the city, whether he would feel disposed to do anything. Frances could see no reason why he would prove a likely "prospect," but at the worst he could only refuse, so there was no harm in trying. Surprisingly, the result was a gift of 8,000 thalers, and now only a relatively small balance needed to be raised. New appeals to friends and relatives obtained the rest that was necessary. A week previously it had seemed impossible that she could raise the money, yet now the whole sum was in her hands. Bishop Laurent was dumbfounded; he had to confess that Frances had been right in placing her entire reliance in her poverty and God's Providence.

This convent, though in general highly desirable, had its inconveniences. It was badly in need of repairs and alterations, and according to the contract that Frances signed she would not be able to take possession until the following year; even after that date part of it would for a while remain closed against the Sisters. The chapel, long used as a storage place for timber, also called for much to be done before it could be restored to its purpose. But Frances felt overjoyed with her good fortune, for she had obtained a habitation which, after some additional wings had, by degrees, been put up, served for the Motherhouse for the rest of her life, and for 17 years afterwards.

The feast of St. Clare, August 12, 1853, which was the second anniversary of the vesting of the first group of Sisters — and the six hundredth anniversary of the Saint's death — was selected as the appropriate date for taking possession of their new home. Though several Sisters were to remain on duty at the "Preachers," at least for the time being, for them too, as for all those stationed at the branch houses, this was their settled center.

Two days prior to August 12th the public were allowed to inspect the convent, and great was the astonishment expressed when people saw how small were the cells, how narrow the passages, and how poor was the furniture that the Sisters were going to use. Some of the visitors were moved to make presents of beds, chairs, and even cooking utensils so as to make the life of the occupants a little less uncomfortable.

Such an occasion is always a great one in the history of any religious community. Dean Dilschneider of the Aachen-erdom celebrated High Mass, at which the choir of St. Paul's Church sang. A charming touch was added by the presence there of one of the Poor Clares who had been expelled in 1803. For 50 years this old woman, who had been a novice when the secular authorities closed the house, had lived in Aachen in close retirement. The joy of this venerable personage increased the joy of the young nuns who made up the new community. That evening every house in the Marschierstrasse was illuminated to mark how the neighborhood felt about having Sisters of such overflowing charity living among them.

Daily Mass in their own chapel was something that they had been obliged to surrender in 1848, when they handed over their penitents to the Good Shepherd Sisters. Since then they had been living in a building belonging to the city government, and full religious life had not been restored, because there were several churches near at hand which they could attend. But now they had a chaplain again, Karl Schervier serving in this capacity, and the Blessed Sacrament under their roof.

Almost a year before this, however, Frances and the 23 Sisters who had received the brown habit with her took their vows on the Feast of St. Louis, the King of France — a notable Franciscan tertiary — and these were received by Dean Dilschneider, the Commissary of the archdiocese, in St. Paul's Church. The date was August 25th. It was on this occasion that all the Sisters were permitted to have the red cross embroidered on their scapulars, something until then reserved to Frances herself and her two chief assistants, Sisters Mary and Joanna. All of them took perpetual vows, though this was after a year's novitiate. Later only temporary vows were taken after a year, and for their perpetual vows the Sisters had to wait for another three years,* not until then being given the red cross. Frances never tired of expatiating on the significance of this cross, saying "[It] should remind us day and night that we should crucify ourselves interiorly and exteriorly," and again, "The red cross is to remind us of the bitter passion of our Blessed Lord and of the rich heavenly reward gained by sufferings borne with love." It became an emblem of the highest honor in the Congregation, the prerequisite to the holding of office or admission to the Recluses. It was not so in the early days of the community.

Though anything like a canonically erected novitiate was not yet possible, the obtaining of a Motherhouse provided a place to which future novices could retire for a month or two before taking their vows. Until then they — and often even the postulants — had to be sent out to work in one of the branch houses. Even this was irregular, but it was the best that could be done under the circumstances.

Though it is an anticipation of events, a word might be said at this point about the distinction that came to be drawn between temporary and perpetual vows. Until 1857 all the Sisters took perpetual vows after a year's probation, but in

---

* Now it is five.

164

March of that year Frances heard that Pope Pius IX had ordained that such vows were not to be taken so soon. Though the regulation was one that was issued by the Holy See with only Italy and Spain in mind, Frances, who wished in all things to conform to the spirit of the Church, even when this was not explicitly declared, made the ruling applicable to her own community.

One or two other matters might be briefly touched on in this place as further illustrative of Frances's desire to have all things done in the most seemly manner. After the ecclesiastical approbation of the Congregation the Little Office of Our Lady was said in Latin, instead of German as formerly. Then in 1857, for further solemnity, Frances prescribed that it should be said standing and with alternating choirs facing one another during the psalms. Previously the Office had been recited with the greatest dispatch so as to gain a few extra minutes for the active works of charity waiting to be done. As for her loyalty to the Pope, when following the seizure of a large part of the papal states the Holy See was impoverished, so that in Vienna the Archconfraternity of St. Michael was founded to provide the Pope with funds, Frances saw to it that every one of the Sisters was enrolled. In order that no one should feel that this was a blanket membership, with the dues coming out of the general treasury, and in order also that the money should not be subtracted from what was ordinarily spent upon the sick poor, she ordered that on the first Tuesday of every month, instead of the customary dish of meat at dinner, something that cost less was to be served, the difference going to the Archconfraternity.

One final thing should be recorded before proceeding to the expansion of her work. In 1858, Frances, prompted in this by the Jesuit Father Henry Behrens, introduced the devotion of the Sacred Heart into her Congregation and encouraged it elsewhere by the distribution of pamphlets. She was told by priests who knew of this that she was well entitled to use the money that accrued from the sale of these for her own enterprises, but she would never do so. Instead she earmarked what was brought in to defray the cost of steamer passage for priests who were on their way to work as missionaries in the United States. She attributed the opening of a missionary field for herself in the same country to a specific blessing sent her from God as a reward for what she was doing.

This American project, which provides some of the most interesting and important chapters in her life, must wait for the moment. What should first be noticed is how innumerable were the calls that came to her from the Rhineland immediately following the recognition of her Congregation. Some of these were only pleas for assistance in emergencies, like the time she sent a few Sisters to Urdlingen during an outbreak of typhoid. Then in a little dilapidated house on the banks of the Rhine, they gave what assistance they could to the panic-stricken inhabitants of the village. Similarly during the hard winter of 1855–56, following an autumn in which the crops had failed, new soup kitchens had to be established at several points in a hurry. One of these, that in St. Michael's parish in Aachen, used to be visited by Frances, and by way of making sure that the soup was really nourishing and tasty, she and the Sisters who worked there as cooks used to take a spoonful or two from a special pot. It was observed that the postulants fell upon what was left, not so much out of a desire to perfect their cookery as to supplement their own somewhat meager rations.

The preparing of these meals came to form a large feature in the community recreations. While Frances delivered a little homily on the virtues of the religious state, the Sisters and novices pared potatoes. Nothing was to be heard except the quiet voice speaking and the dull thud of the potatoes as they fell into the baskets. There were some who humorously compared the performance to the musical accompaniment which sometimes serves to create the atmosphere necessary for the recital of a poem.

As for the branch houses, following the one in Bonn, which was set up immediately after the approbation of the Congregation in 1851, two were established in Cologne in 1852, in the parishes of St. John the Baptist and the Holy Family. The Sisters began operations at Burtschied, now a suburb of Aachen, in 1853, and the houses at Crefeld, Euskirchen, Coblenz,* Mainz, Siegburg, and Ratingen were all founded in 1854. Kaiserswerth was opened in 1855, with Sister Clement (Countess zu Droste-Vischering in the world, a relative of Cardinal von Geissel's predecessor) as the Superior.

Others of these early branch houses that should be mentioned are those at Deutz (1857), a second at Mainz in 1858, Bielefeld in 1859, a third at Cologne in 1863, and Erfurt in 1864. This last was specially dear to Frances because the near-by castle of the Wartburg had been the home of St. Elizabeth of Hungary during her married life. Later it derived a very different kind of interest as the "hide-out" of Luther. It was there that he translated the Bible and there too (according to the legend) that he threw an inkwell at the devil. The plaster where the ink had splashed had long since been pulled off as relics by pious Protestants; the surely no less pious Frances Schervier obtained another sort of relic — a silver cup that "dear St. Elizabeth" had used.

All of these houses addressed themselves to the relief of the poor in whatever way was needed, but some began to specialize in their activities, becoming small hospitals — which later developed into large hospitals — nursing homes, or hostels for country girls who needed to be trained as domestic servants before being placed with respectable families. Most of the houses also had, for a shorter or longer period, a soup kitchen attached to them. And sewing schools were also set up.

* There, a young lady, who had not herself been able to enter a convent on account of her poor health, willed what she possessed to the Sisters. Two priests, Father Krementz, who became Cardinal-Archbishop of Cologne, and Father de Lorenzi, collected funds to furnish it and held the property in their names.

Flexibility was given to her work by Frances's refusal to accept the ownership of the houses she consented to staff. This meant that when it became apparent that there were no very pressing needs for the Sisters' services, or that those services were more urgently needed elsewhere, all that the Sisters had to do was to pack up their few personal belongings and depart. This was all the easier because Frances was, as yet, operating within a restricted field, the Rhineland. The river boats were the ordinary and most commodious means of transportation; for towns further from the river a cart or two sufficed.

The warmth of her heart now and then worked against the cool judgment of her mind. The expansion came upon her before she was ready for it, so that in a few instances she was brought to see that she had made a mistake. These mistakes, however, did not matter a great deal, as no expensive plant or equipment was involved. She could withdraw almost at a moment's notice, if she thought this advisable. But by having to spread her Sisters thin, she may, in some cases, have obliged them to work too hard. When a Sister died an early death she reproached herself for this, though it was usually due to the Sister's own zeal, for Frances was continually warning them against trying to do too much. At the same time it is true that Frances herself was often impelled to accept work which her Congregation was as yet not well enough staffed to undertake. She would exclaim, "Here help is indispensable, at whatever cost!" But if the cost occasionally meant that somebody was worn out before her time, what did the Congregation, after all, exist for, except to work for the poor? "At whatever cost" might have been taken as its motto.

Another cause of self-reproach was that she was not able to give her postulants and novices an adequate training, but had to send them out to work at one or other of her houses. But this does not seem to have been a matter of very weighty consequence, so thoroughly did she — herself one who had gone through no regular novitiate — manage to impress the spirit of St. Francis and the distinctive principles of the Congregation upon the young women who by now were coming to her in steadily increasing numbers. None of them could fail to see what kind of a life it was that they were expected to lead; if they had been actuated only by fancy, that became apparent in very short order. In a house with regular religious exercises and not much else, a lazy novice might escape notice for some time; this could not happen in one of Frances's houses, in which, unless one was prepared to work very hard in the most devoted spirit of charity, misfits speedily grew discouraged or were ejected.

Frances refused during the course of her life no less than 28 places for possible foundations, a larger number than she was ever able to establish in Germany. And several places that she did accept were closed before long. Thus the small infirmary she established at Setterich, which she had opened on the plea of the local priest, Father Wildt — the same priest who had given her the 8,000 thalers without which she would not have been able to purchase the Motherhouse — did not last long. She had opened it against her better judgment because she felt indebted to him. She kept it open for a long enough time to discharge her debt by her Sisters' services; then, as more useful work could be done elsewhere, she withdrew them. It was the same with the house founded at Sayn, established at the urgent request of Princess Sayn-Wittgenstein. A withdrawal of this sort always pained Frances, as did the frequency with which she was compelled to refuse a requested branch house. But her principle was always that of going where the need was greatest, and it was never recorded of her that she failed to respond to an emergency appeal. Somehow or other Sisters were always spared for that, though always on the understanding that they would be recalled as soon as the emergency had passed.

The work of its very nature was very informal and personal. As it was supported everywhere on begging, it was hardly possible to keep very strict accounts. What could have been conveyed by the register of a day's "loot" — six bunches of carrots, two cabbages, a pound of bacon, a bushel of potatoes, a sack of flour, a couple of blankets, an old frying pan and the like? The royal house of Prussia, which exercised some degree of control over religious communities, had fully endorsed Frances's declaration of absolute poverty. This, however, did not prevent some local officials from trying to assert their bureaucratic authority. Thus Herr Kuehlwetter, the Prussian representative at Aachen, suddenly took it into his head that he must be fully informed as to the collections that were made and their disbursement. Frances simply refused, but Herr Kuehlwetter remained stubborn and threatened to have the police arrest the begging Sisters unless his demands were complied with inside of three weeks. Cardinal von Geissel was appealed to, and he effected a compromise: under it the Sisters would, for once only, make a full account of what they had received and as to how they had spent it; this being done, the civil authorities were to leave them in peace. The official "face" was saved; after that the Sisters went their ordinary way with demure little smiles on their faces.

Frances had her own personal troubles and sorrows. Her sister Pauline (one of the community under the name of Sister Paula) died in 1855 and Father Karl Schervier departed this life six years later. He had served without pay as chaplain of the Motherhouse and confessor of the patients at the "Preachers." Of all her brothers and sisters Frances had been most attached to him, for as children they had had the same ambitions, and each had carried these out, although in a somewhat different way than they had expected. After his death she wrote in her notebook: "Adieu, dear Karl! By your death our souls are drawn nearer to each other. You will pray for me, as I pray for you with all my heart. Give greetings to Paula for me. God grant that you find father and mother, and all the rest of our dear ones. R.I.P."

Sister Paula, while serving as Superior at Jülich, showed

great courage and cheerfulness and energy in spite of the disease that was to carry her off. But she was not always judicious, giving away so much — even the Sisters' clothing — as to bring the house into such financial straits that Frances was obliged to send Sister Mary to put things to rights. However, sometimes her rather strange actions brought results. Once a delinquent girl whom she had taken in said she was going to return to her former way of life. Upon hearing this Sister Paula snatched up a pair of scissors and cut off the girl's beautiful hair, crying, "Now you will not be able to go!" When that rather drastic treatment proved of no use and the girl ran out into the street, Paula called two policemen. And though they would have been unable to stop her, they frightened or calmed her enough to make her give up her design. Yet even this was less drastic than the way Frances, as we have heard, once "lamed" a girl under similar circumstances.

Other losses occurred. In 1858 it became apparent that Sister Mary (the former Catherine Daverkosen) was not going to be of much more use to the community because of her increasing infirmities, so she had to be replaced as First Assistant by Sister Gabriela Nellessen. In spite of her foolishness over the ecstatic postulant, she and Frances had the tenderest affection for one another, and her death was a severe blow.

During Sister Mary's illness Frances had a severe attack of sciatica and it was treated — according to the queer medical ideas of the time — by the application of red-hot irons. St. Francis of Assisi had been treated in the same way for his eye disease, which ended in his blindness. In the hope of being cured he submitted to the drawing of fire across his brows from ear to ear, first begging Brother Fire to be kind to him. St. Francis miraculously felt no pain, which was not the case with his daughter Frances Schervier. Yet she continued to direct the community from her bed. She had recently made another attempt to resign, but the Sisters demanded that she remain, and she submitted to their wishes.

Though she could do no active work outside the convent, she refused no spiritual duty; especially did she never fail to preside at the chapter of faults or in giving the Sisters those regular instructions which would fit them in spirit for their arduous undertakings.

At last Frances agreed to accept the remedy that her doctors prescribed, taking the baths at Oeynhausen, a resort near Minden, about three quarters of the way between Cologne and Bremen, a place which is at present the headquarters of the British Army of Occupation in Germany. Even so, she would not agree to take this treatment, which did not seem to her to accord with her profession of poverty, until her confessor assured her that such was her duty.

Nevertheless she found means both of practicing poverty and of exercising her work for souls while undergoing the cure at this well known spa. For when she arrived at Cologne, she refused to take a cab from the station to her immediate destination, the house of her Sisters working in the parish of St. John the Baptist. This meant, as the Baedeker map shows, that she walked two thirds of the distance of the city lying between the old fortifications. It was, so one would judge, at least three or four miles, and she and the poor Sister who accompanied her were both completely exhausted by the time of their arrival. One must applaud; one cannot quite approve.

At the spa, when she got there, she would take next to nothing to eat, declaring that she needed very little food. This again was hard on her companion, who, feeling that she ought to do as Frances did, had an appetite clamoring for much more than she was getting. Fortunately three Sisters came in relays, so that each had only a week or so of this ascetic life. Therefore none was quite reduced to a skeleton.

As soon as Frances got a little better the doctor advised that she take a little exercise to regain her strength. He was thinking, of course, of a leisurely stroll through the woods, but Frances made this exercise an opportunity to visit the poor of the neighborhood. We may be sure that by some means or other she contrived to bring them some material help on these occasions. Still more did she bring spiritual comfort with her, winning all to whom she talked by the light evident on her face. In the one letter of hers written at this time that is preserved, there is not a single word about her physical condition. Instead, writing on the Friday before Pentecost, she offers only fervent exhortations to her community that all should strive to draw the richest spiritual benefit from the Feast. It was, as they all knew, the real birthday of their Congregation.

Upon Frances's discharge from the spa at Oeynhausen, she went to visit the prison at Minden. There, too, she might have a chance to bring some consolation. But her main purpose was that of making a kind of pilgrimage. Some years previously the Archbishop of Cologne had been incarcerated there for a while, during times of tension between Church and state. This was Clement August zu Droste-Vischering, and Frances was grateful to him, though she had never known him, because his courage had resulted in that religious revival in the Rhineland which had led her father to relax his prohibition against her undertaking the nursing of the sick poor. Frances gazed with veneration at the grim walls that had confined this valiant confessor of the faith. There was in truth very little that Frances ever did that was not in some way connected with the religion that so completely absorbed her.

Across the Atlantic

So FAR the work of Frances and the Sisters under her direction had been confined to the Rhineland. But this had merely been because she was dealing with immediate necessities, those closest at hand. She had never looked upon her work as distinctively German, much less as something to be restricted to one relatively small section of Germany. We have seen how she was prepared to transplant herself to Holland rather than surrender the principle of absolute poverty, and during the Kulturkampf that came after the Franco-Prussian War, she was again prepared to transplant herself, this time to the United States, where she already had obtained a firm foothold.

The American enterprise, however, was not deliberately designed, but appeared to come about by the merest chance. It originated, not with Frances herself, but through a lady of whom, until she actually met her, Frances had never heard.

This lady was a very remarkable person about whom a few preliminary words should be said. The well-to-do Virginian Thomas Worthington and his young wife Eleanor, because of their conscientious objection to Negro slavery, moved to Ohio, taking their slaves with them so that they could be manumitted at once, and there at Chillicothe on May 10, 1800, their daughter Sarah was born. Mr. Worthington became Governor of Ohio and may be described as the father of that state. He was a man of culture and charm, with a wide circle of friends, among them many of the most prominent people of the time. One of these was Senator Rufus King of New York, of Revolutionary War fame, whose son Edward married Sarah Worthington when she was only sixteen. They lived at Cincinnati until King's death in 1836, whereupon Sarah devoted herself to the education of her son Rufus, living at Cambridge, Massachusetts, while he was attending Harvard, after which she married William Peter, the highly cultured British Consul in Philadelphia.

A second widowhood brought her back to Cincinnati, where she was a social and intellectual leader at a time when Cincinnati prided itself upon being the center of culture and fashion in the West. As a result of her European travels, but more particularly because of what she had witnessed of the Catholic Church during a visit to the Holy Land, she herself accepted the Catholic faith in 1851. Her real life's work may be said to have commenced from that date.

Under the administration of John Baptist Purcell, elevated in 1833 to be Cincinnati's Archbishop after having served a short term as President of Mount St. Mary's College at Emmitsburg, Maryland, Catholicism in the new Western states was undergoing a spectacular advance. But though Catholic churches and mission stations increased, there was a crying need for the kind of work that only nuns can do. However, the Archbishop seemed to be content with the presence in Cincinnati of the Sisters of Charity, who had arrived there three years before he did, and with the Sisters of Notre Dame de Namur, whom he persuaded to go there in 1838.

Not so the redoubtable Sarah; with the zeal of a convert she took it upon herself to bring other orders there. And there are some indications that the Archbishop did not wholeheartedly approve of all her activities, feeling, with some justice, that this was his affair, not hers. It was, however, not very easy for so amiable a man to withstand Mrs. Peter, especially as it could not be denied that what she was seeking to effect were all, in themselves, good works.

Ohio was not a state to which went the most poverty-stricken of the immigrants who were now pouring in like a tidal wave from Europe. Those who settled in Cincinnati were, for the most part, solid German and Italian artisans, well capable of looking after themselves, though even among these there were many needy. As for the Irish, who were encouraged by the ecclesiastical policy of the time to congregate in cities, where their spiritual necessities could be cared for, though some of these, too, were artisans, the majority had been farmers and fishermen and so could usually hope at best for nothing but casual and unskilled jobs. Seeing their plight Mrs. Peter — at first without success, but with her persistence finally rewarded — brought over in 1858 a group of the Irish Sisters of Mercy from Kinsale to work among their fellow countrymen.

Another problem exercised Mrs. Peter's large heart: it was that of the many young women who, in so large a drift of population, fell into evil courses. Accordingly she had gone some years previously, to Angers in France, the headquarters of the Good Shepherd nuns, to try her powers of persuasion on Mother Euphrasia Pelletier. Her mission seemed a failure until, in 1857, a band of these Sisters also came to Cincinnati. Before her death twenty years later, Mrs. Peter had interested herself in the introduction of several other orders, of both men and women, ranging from the Redemptorists to the Religious of the Sacred Heart, the Little Sisters of the Poor to the Passionists.

These later activities of hers do not concern us here, except to say that Archbishop Purcell towards the end of his life was more or less won over to what he at first regarded as the good lady's uncalled-for disposition to run his diocese for him. But the poor Archbishop, a man harassed in many ways, could hardly reject the offers of so masterful a woman as Sarah was at fifty-seven, and indeed to the end of her life.

For she succeeded, after some initial discouragement, in obtaining the backing of several of the royalties of Europe and many of its nobility and, which, of course, counted still more, the commendation of Pope Pius IX. It was indeed the Pope who suggested to Mrs. Peter that she apply to Frances Schervier for Sisters to work among the Germans of Cincinnati.

At this time, 1857, however, Sarah Peter would not have gotten very far had she not fallen in at Vienna with a young lady of aristocratic connections, a Fräulein Augusta von Tietz; for she had just made application to an Austrian bishop for help and had been refused. But Fräulein von Tietz had attracted widespread interest by the fact of her conversion to Catholicism when she was eighteen, which resulted in her being cast off by her prominent family and devoting herself to works of charity. She had become a Franciscan tertiary, under the name of Sister Felicitas, but of course was living in the world as Frances herself had done for several years. She had gone on a collecting tour in the Rhineland, where she had made the acquaintance of Cardinal von Geissel, for the erection of a hospital in her native city of Danzig. It is virtually certain that, had it not been for Fräulein von Tietz's recommendation, the Cardinal would not have put Mrs. Peter in touch with Frances Schervier, nor, when Frances had promised to send Sisters to Cincinnati, tried to put her in touch with King Ludwig I of Bavaria. It was hoped that the King himself would help to finance the transportation of the Sisters to their new field of labor and that the *Ludwig-Missionsverein* would also assist this enterprise, as it had assisted so many missionary causes in a developing America. King Ludwig, however, would not even give Frances an audience; and the only help forthcoming was that of Baron von Overkamp, a well-connected priest of Munich, who undertook to see to it that the *Ludwig-Missionsverein* donated the money for the fares to the United States. Nor did his assistance end there; this society over the years made a number of invaluable contributions to the work of the Sisters in America.

The attitude of the King seems rather strange, for at least more courtesy might have been expected of him, especially towards the goddaughter of the late Emperor. But it may be that so many reports had been spread abroad of his munificence that people had often imposed upon him. It was a disappointment for Frances, whose pleasantest memories of Munich, therefore, were of the hospitality she received from the Bavarian School Sisters and of Baron von Overkamp's efforts on her behalf.

On her way back to Aachen, which she wished to reach in time to celebrate Easter, 1858, with her community, she had a near-accident of a serious kind. On the afternoon of Holy Saturday she reached Deutz, the town on the opposite bank of the Rhine from Cologne, now part of Cologne, just too late to catch the train. The drawbridge had already gone up, and if she were to reach Cologne in time for the train to Aachen she would have to find some other means of crossing the Rhine. Into a rowboat she went in her impulsive way. The rowboat was caught by the strong currents, which are often treacherous in the Rhine, and it came within an inch of being dashed to pieces on the piers of some new construction work that was going on. The boat in fact was badly enough damaged to oblige those in it to climb on the pier and wait there for another boat to take them across. Frances was well aware of her danger, but she kept calm, merely saying to her companion, Sister Raphaela, who was in charge of the house at St. John the Baptist's Church in Cologne, "Let us make an act of contrition!" When she reached Aachen late that night, quite exhausted and much shaken by her experience, she was able to bring good news: though the King had been unresponsive, the *Ludwig-Missionsverein** had come to the rescue.

Mrs. Peter, when she had obtained Frances's promise the previous year, had expected that a band of Sisters would go

---

* This society bore the King's own name and was founded in 1838. Ten years earlier the Emperor Francis I, Frances's godfather, had founded the *Leopoldinen-Stiftung*, naming it after his daughter Leopoldine. We shall hear more about both of these missionary societies.

with her when she sailed for the United States. In this she was behaving in her usual autocratic style, for though she must be presumed to have offered some financial assistance, it is also evident, from the appeal made to Munich, that it could not have been much. Later she placed her whole fortune at the Sisters' service, but at this stage she was, in effect, inviting them to leap in the dark. It is very remarkable that Frances had the courage to venture, unprovided for — even to the extent of lacking a house where the Sisters could live — to a city nearly 5,000 miles away where the manner of life and the language would be different, though Cincinnati had a large German element in its population.

Yet the choice of Cincinnati turned out to be in every way providential. New York was ruled out as a sink of iniquity. Boston and Philadelphia might have been regarded as morally preferable, but nobody had invited the Sisters to go there, and of the larger American cities none other except St. Louis at that time had a large German population. Mrs. Peter talked in her downright fashion of Cincinnati's claims, and she talked with such an intimate knowledge of the United States as a whole that she convinced Frances that Cincinnati was where she should make her start.

There was, however, at least one good reason for Frances's proceeding with more caution than Mrs. Peter wished. Hers was as yet only a diocesan congregation and it was essential that Cardinal von Geissel, as Ordinary, should first discover the disposition of Archbishop Purcell to the establishment under his jurisdiction of a group of Sisters coming from Aachen. Mrs. Peter could, and no doubt did, assure both the Cardinal and Frances that everything was going to be all right, that Archbishop Purcell was her good friend. Nevertheless both ecclesiastical courtesy and prudence demanded something more than Mrs. Peter's well-intentioned enthusiasm. Letters on this point had to pass between Cologne and Cincinnati, and it is to be supposed that the Archbishop, in his amiability, conveyed to the Cardinal a degree of welcome more warm than he really felt — for this is what subsequent events would indicate. On August 10, 1858, five Sisters, headed by Sister Augustine, with Sister Felicitas (not Augusta von Tietz, but another) as assistant, and augmented by a postulant, left for their great adventure in a foreign land.

At this point perhaps something might be said about Cincinnati itself, which Mr. Winston Churchill recently declared to be the most beautiful inland city in America. Even as early as 1841 the Queen City of the West must have had much to recommend it to have obtained from the plain-spoken Charles Dickens the praise he gave it in his *American Notes*. "I have not seen," he wrote, "a place that recommends itself so favorably and pleasantly at the first glance as this does; with its clean houses of red and white, its well-paved roads, and footways of bright tile. Nor does it become less prepossessing on a closer acquaintance. The streets are broad and airy, the shops extremely good, the private residences remarkable for their elegance and neatness." He further remarks on the "pretty villas with their well-kept gardens, inexpressibly refreshing and attractive" and the Cincinnati society which he calls "intelligent, courteous and agreeable."

One of the chief of these citizens was the first Nicholas Longworth, who lived in a fine colonial mansion on Pike Street built after the famous Latrobe's designs. As a means of counteracting the vice of drunkenness, Longworth had promoted the sale of Catawba wine — of the Rhine-wine variety — as much less harmful than whiskey or rum. He did very well with his vineyards and encouraged other vine-growers with liberal prizes. And Longfellow wrote a poem saying among other things:

> Catawba wine
> Has a taste more divine
> More dulcet, delicious and dreamy

than all other vintages, which was perhaps a bit excessive. Unfortunately a blight descended on the grapes, ending that enterprise.

Among Longworth's servants was a stalwart Negro named Harvey Young, who only a few years before had provided Harriet Beecher Stowe with the most celebrated episode of her *Uncle Tom's Cabin.* He was the real Eliza, for he had crossed the ice of the Ohio River from Kentucky, leaping from ice floe to ice floe, with the bloodhounds baying behind. When he reached Cincinnati he ran towards Pike Street and came in sight of Mr. Longworth near his home, who sized up the situation quickly and called, "Jump through that window into the cellar." Then a few minutes later when the pursuers came up, asking, "Say, boss! Seen a runaway slave?" Longworth said, "You will have to run faster than you're doing to catch the one I saw," and they raced on where he gestured to the hills. Harvey Young lived to a great old age as a servant in the Longworth household.

Frances Trollope, the mother of the famous novelist, should also be mentioned. She had established in Cincinnati in 1827 a department store, or "emporium," as she called it, which failed in 1831. Perhaps it was in expectation of astounding the natives — but also possibly because this accorded with a weird personal taste — that she had her bizarre bazaar erected in a combination of Moorish, Gothic and Egyptian styles. It was still standing when her son visited it in 1857. Since her departure it had served successively as a dancing school, church, military hospital, theatre, and "physico-medical institute" (whatever that may have been). Its proprietor told Anthony Trollope: "I believe, sir, no man or woman ever yet made a dollar in that building." Mrs. Trollope's own lack of success may partially account for her highly acute but jaundiced view of what she recorded in her best-selling *Domestic Manners of Americans.* It is worth mentioning, however, that her criticisms are directed not so much against Cincinnati as against the whole country. Her emporium was still one of the sights of Cincinnati when the Sisters arrived there; these young women from imperial Aachen must have gazed with bewildered awe on what she had left behind.

In short, Cincinnati had a good deal of liveliness and grace and opulent living among its richer inhabitants, who were not few; and the mass of its people were frugal and industrious, though not without some misery among them. But the need was rarely that of squalid poverty, such as was found then and later in the slums of New York. The Sisters who arrived in 1858 took on a task which was difficult for them because of their lack of English (though they mostly addressed themselves to Cincinnati's Germans), but it was not an impossibly difficult task. They could hardly have gone to a city better suited for the beginning of their American operations.

So much for the general social background. When we turn to the Catholic development of Cincinnati the picture becomes a little confused. Not long before this, when Archbishop (later Cardinal) Bedini visited the city, only to make general enquiries for the Holy See and with no official status — unless it can be asserted that the polite letter he bore to President Pierce put him in some sort of official category — there was so much Nativist agitation against him that he was almost lynched, and the church where he preached was destroyed. This was mostly the work of German secularists and Italian *Carbonari*, egged on by a handful of really "native" American groups of working men who imagined that they were imperiled by unfair economic competition from the immigrants. But all this blew over: it is perhaps enough for present purposes to say that when Archbishop Purcell arrived in 1833 there were only 16 churches and missions in the whole of Ohio, served by 14 priests, administering to 7,000 souls. When he died 15 years later, the state had been divided into four dioceses, with 500 churches and half a million Catholics.

Nor is this the whole story: Cincinnati had two Catholic papers, the *Wahrheitsfreund* for the Germans and the *Catholic Telegraph* for those whose language was English. This last-named paper was edited by Father Edward Purcell, the Archbishop's brother and his Chancellor, who must be admitted to have done wonderful things for the Catholic cause, although he also most innocently brought upon the arch-diocese a financial disaster without parallel in American Catholic history.

That unfortunate affair is mentioned here only because it seems to be the most likely explanation of a certain nervous-ness the Archbishop showed in accepting what he imagined would be responsibility for the support of the newcoming Sisters.

It is doubtful whether Mrs. Peter had any inkling of these financial uncertainties, and even had she been informed of them, it would not have occurred to her to mention the matter to Frances Schervier, for Sarah was a sanguine, force-ful woman, and she knew that Frances was not interested in investments — about which, indeed, she had what many will think an almost superstitious horror — but only in service to the poor. Had Frances suspected that the Archbishop had any reason to be less cordial than he seemed to be, she would never have put any of her Sisters under his jurisdiction. But she did not know, and her ignorance on this point, because it was so complete, was providential. A great field of fruitful work awaited her; of that she was sure, for that she was grateful to God. That was all that mattered.

Settlement in Cincinnati

A JOURNEY across the Atlantic 90 years ago was looked upon
as a hazardous undertaking. Young women from an inland
district of Europe — probably not one of whom had so much
as seen the sea — may well have imagined it even worse than
it was. And accustomed though they were to hardship, they
could hardly imagine what they would find in the steerage
section of the ship. Frances, who understood their tremors
and who shared them herself, felt that she should see them
safe on board and give them encouragement to the very last
moment.

The port of embarkation, as nearly always for the Sisters
who sailed for America, was Le Havre, for going from
Bremen would have involved another couple of days at sea.
And at Le Havre they encountered an admirable German
priest who served there for a number of years as chaplain for
his fellow countrymen among the immigrants. Frances struck
up what was to be a close lifelong friendship with him. He
was Father Lambert Bethman of the Congregation of the
Sacred Heart of Mary, and he served as a counselor to her
community and, when occasion served, as confessor to herself.
It was mainly due to his influence that she wrote the first of
her fragmentary autobiographies, lacking which we would
have the most meager information about her early life.

She, for her part, served him in a number of ways, both out of personal regard and because of the work he was doing. It was largely through the munificence of her poverty that she was able to accomplish as much as she did. Moreover, it was she who arranged for him to appear as a speaker at the German National Convention of 1862 to make an appeal for the people he was helping. Similarly she induced Father Peter Cahensly* three years later to make another appeal for funds.

The voyage across the Atlantic, which lasted from August 24th to September 8th, was extremely trying to the Sisters. The accommodations were very poor for steerage passengers on the *Fulton,* and so was the food, and nearly all the way across most people were seasick. Yet when the Sisters went on deck for fresh air, their habits caused astonishment and, in some instances, derision. Some passengers went so far as to line up before the Sisters while they were saying the rosary, and made the mocking response, "Holy Mary, Mother of God . . . "

Yet sick though they were, they found means of helping other passengers. One of these was a dying old man who, so it turned out, had been the tutor to Kossuth's children in Hungary. To become such, he must have lapsed from the Faith, but now he returned to it. There was no priest on board to give him the last sacraments; the best that the Sisters could do was to help him to make an act of contrition. Before his burial in the Atlantic the captain of the ship asked them to pray over his body, so as to give as much of the semblance of a Catholic ceremony as possible. In order that the other

* This zealous but not always tactful cleric later pressed so strongly the argument that the German-speaking enclaves in the United States should have priests and even bishops of their own nationality as seriously to offend the American hierarchy, whose efforts were being directed to Americanize the immigrants. The fact is mentioned here only to set against it another fact — that the Sisters of the Poor of St. Francis, though they began their work in the United States primarily for Germans, at no time, and not even in a largely German Cincinnati, restricted themselves in any way. Indeed, Frances successfully fought the attempts of the German Redemptorist church in New York to have the small hospital she founded in that parish confine its ministrations to the parishioners.

passengers should not know what had happened, this took place at three in the morning. The corpse lay on a table in the dining room, wrapped in a sailcloth winding sheet, weighted at head and feet, and around the table stood the Captain, the ship's doctor, a minister,* and three waiters. The Sisters knelt and recited the *Miserere,* a few Our Fathers, and the *De Profundis,* after which they sprinkled the body with holy water. Then they went on deck, followed by the six sailors who were carrying the corpse: these "with all possible respect lowered it slowly into the waves." This happened on September 6th while the first gray light of the summer dawn was breaking.

Two days later the ship came to its moorings and everybody disembarked at Castle Garden. The day of arrival was propitious, for it was the Nativity of the Blessed Virgin. In other ways, however, it was desolate, for nobody was there to meet them. They sat forlornly in the waiting room until the two Sisters who had gone to the "German" church returned with Father Isaac Hecker.†

The Sisters were bewildered and lonely and hungry. The officers of the ship were only concerned with getting off their passengers with the utmost dispatch and so would give them no breakfast. They had made do, as best they could, with a few peelings of the oranges they had brought with them which remained in the cabin of Kossuth's tutor. But shortly after Father Hecker arrived, came Father Edward Purcell, who tried to explain in English, eked out with a little French, that he had been sent by his brother the Archbishop to escort

---

* The Annals of the Cincinnati house record the presence of this minister. After all, this was not, strictly speaking, a Catholic funeral, nor had Kossuth's tutor made any formal return to the Faith but only a change in his interior dispositions.

† It must be supposed that they met him at the Redemptorists' church on East 3rd Street, for though Hecker had recently obtained permission from the Pope to withdraw from his former confrères and to found the Paulists, he had no house of his own as yet, only a site picked out on West Fifty-ninth Street, in those days a long way uptown. It is a pleasure to record this service rendered the unbefriended Sisters by this very remarkable man.

186

them to Cincinnati. His manner was most friendly, but he surprised them by advising them to remove the red cross from their habits, as this would be likely, in those days of Nativist bigotry, to get them insulted in the streets. Even their habits were a danger, but as they had nothing else to wear, they retained them, and no untoward event occurred as he led them to the Sisters of Charity * on Barclay Street.

The first thing they wanted to do was go to confession. When the first Sister went into the confessional at St. Peter's, she noticed that the priest said something which she did not understand, but she went on anyway. After the priest had vainly tried to interrupt her, both by word and gesture, he jumped to his feet and went out of the box and even out of the church itself. Then it suddenly dawned upon them that they were in an English-speaking country. A sympathetic, but amused, Sister of Charity promised to take them early next morning to the Redemptorists' church, where they might go to confession before Mass.

Other trials (though of a minor sort) had to be undergone. They had arrived after the substantial midday dinner, and for supper they were served only a few slices of cold meat and some slivers of tomato. They knew very well that if their hostesses had realized the situation, they would have provided something better, but out of delicacy they refrained from making any special requests.

Twenty-four hours later Father Purcell gathered them up and put them on the train for Cincinnati. The journey there, in those days, took a day and a half, so that they had plenty of time to look upon the, as yet, somewhat empty American landscape. Meals had to be hastily snatched at railway stations, and the Sisters, in the habits at which everybody stared,

* The New York Sisters of Charity wore then, as they still do, with a slight modification, a garb that enabled them to pass as widows or people of very strict life. The religious habit was at this time avoided by both men and women religious outside the confines of their own houses. This explains Father Purcell's nervousness at the thought of conducting a party of Franciscan Sisters up Broadway to Barclay Street.

insisted upon saying their long grace, with its mementoes for the dead and for benefactors, until Father Purcell burst upon them saying that the train was about to pull out. Then pushing into their mouths whatever was left on their plates, the Sisters took their seats again on a train whose engine was stoked mainly with logs. They were, however, edified by the bells they heard ringing at every town at which they stopped. They took these bells, in their simplicity, to be the Angelus, and congratulated themselves on having come to so very pious a country — until Father Purcell explained that these were only bells on the engines.

They found the mosquitoes very annoying. These insects preferred their warm European blood to that thinned by the American climate. At the first onslaught Sister Augustine said, in all seriousness, that the stings they endured at night had been inflicted by the Devil — no doubt to make them flee from their new charge. There was, nevertheless, one thing which they considered providential when they heard of it. They would have left for Cincinnati on the day of their arrival in New York had not Father Edward insisted that they have a day's rest first. Had they had their own way, they would have been in a train wreck in which a number of people had been injured and two killed.

At Cincinnati Mrs. Peter was waiting for them at the railway station. The news she had for them caused consternation. They had counted upon a house being available for them, one to which they might go immediately. Instead they were told that there was no house, but that they were to be temporarily lodged in a cottage on the grounds of the convent of the Good Shepherd Sisters. The Superior, however, offered this to them for a permanent home, saying that the plan met with the approval of the Archbishop and that she thought they might be able to accommodate a few patients there. This offer they had to decline; the house was too small to serve as a hospital and they foresaw that, with the best will in the world, friction was likely to arise from their close proximity to another community. Only because of the absolute need of an immediate roof over their heads did they accept the cottage in their emergency.

Here a mystery appears. A house had actually been offered them rent free. It was not a very suitable house, to be sure, for it was that of a former orphanage, dirty and in disrepair, but it was fairly large. The announcement of this had been made in the *Wahrheitsfreund*, the local German Catholic weekly, while they were on the high seas. Fräulein von Tietz, who had gone on in advance and who was parading as Sister Felicitas and, as such, was regarded as a member of the community, told them of it, as did Mrs. Peter. But they also had to break the news that because the Orphan Society, a lay organization, had not consulted the Archbishop in advance, he had expressed his disapproval at this precipitancy. The orphanage therefore remained unavailable.

That the Archbishop should have been irritated by what looked like the officiousness of people under his jurisdiction is understandable. What is not so easily understood is why, after sending his brother Edward to welcome the Sisters (unless Father Edward had acted on his own responsibility), he should receive them so coldly upon their arrival. The Sisters' own Annals express the very charitable opinion that he must have been trying to "test" them, though it is hard to see why he should have allowed a group of Sisters to travel 5,000 miles, to a country whose language and mode of life were unfamiliar, to subject them to such a test. Purcell was in fact a very genial Irishman, with amiability as one of his chief weaknesses. One cannot believe that he would have done anything as unkind as he did unless he was afraid that he would have to accept financial responsibility at a time when the whole financial structure of his archdiocese was, as he must have suspected, getting rather shaky. He did not realize that these Sisters intended to ask nothing from him, but proposed to support themselves and their poor by begging. But what they did need was a house, and though the providing of this would have cost him nothing, he had blocked the offer that had been made.

As the Archbishop himself did not like to perform disagreeable acts, he deputed Father Hengehold, the chief of the German speaking pastors of the city, a man who had already called on the Sisters, and showed great affability, to go back to them again and tell them that they were not wanted and should return to Germany.

Other factors may have operated. The Archbishop thought that Mrs. Peter was trying to rush him too fast and had taken too much upon herself. He may also have been displeased with Augusta von Tietz, who was not only using the name she had been given as a tertiary but was also wearing the Franciscan habit, which was very irregular. Moreover she assumed aristocratic airs, and while these may have been an asset in Europe, they did not commend themselves to America, least of all to what was then an area not far removed from the Frontier. It is not surprising that she came to be regarded as a pious eccentric, and in some quarters as an imposter. Quite possibly the Archbishop's suspicions of her made him rather wary of the Sisters coming from Germany. And these suspicions may have been aroused between the departure of his brother for New York and his return with the new community.

The exploits of the admirable Augusta von Tietz certainly did not help the Sisters. Though not a member of the Congregation, she took up her residence with them, and all were edified by her piety, though they saw to it that one so delicately nurtured had the most comfortable bed at their disposal. They were less edified by her self-assertiveness, for she could not refrain from pluming herself upon her superior education and her social status and she mildly irritated them (and perhaps mildly amused them too) by her claim that she understood the Franciscan idea better than they did. Before long she departed to found another Congregation and a hospital in Texas, after a similar venture of hers in Ohio had come to nothing. After that no more was heard about her doings. She may have been a saint, but she certainly did not have much discretion, and she was an embarrassment to Sisters who had enough difficulties without her adding to them.

To go back to Archbishop Purcell. On the day of their arrival he called upon them and when he saw how young they were, he expressed the opinion that they would probably be unable to overcome the difficulties that confronted them. He did not himself advise them to leave, but sent Father Hengehold later in the day with that message. The Archbishop said he would help them to collect the money for their fares, but as the Sisters needed the order of Cardinal von Geissel to depart, and also that of their Superior General, they decided to stay where they were. Desperately frightened and not knowing what to do, they gave themselves to prayer.

They began a novena to St. Joseph, with the result that on September 12th * the directors of the Orphan Society came offering them the use of the old orphanage building. In the meanwhile there had evidently been an interview between them and the Archbishop, and the Archbishop had been induced to change his mind, subject to reservations. The proposal was not without an eye to business. The Sisters were offered something which it would be difficult, if not impossible, to sell, rent free for six months. At the end of that time the Society hoped that the Sisters would buy it. Even if they did not, at least they could be counted upon to clean up a very dirty building and perhaps make some repairs. But the Orphan Society did also wish to be helpful, and performed a service not only by providing the orphanage as their abode but also by representing to the Archbishop how much the Sisters were needed in Cincinnati.

One must wonder a little that Sarah Peter had not prepared the ground a bit better. She had had plenty of time to do so.

* I follow here the American Annals. But Father Jeiler says that this happened on the eighth day of their novena, which would be the 19th.

And as she was a woman of ample means and was the one who was responsible for the Sisters going to Cincinnati, it might be thought that she should have realized that she had responsibility for seeing that they were properly housed. Perhaps the explanation is that she found the Archbishop too hard an obstacle to overcome. For all we know she may have been battling with him for months, getting neither a definite yea nor nay for an answer. As Sarah was not the kind of woman to take no for a final answer, she probably interpreted what he had said in her own sanguine sense. The upshot of all this may have been a suave episcopal, "Well, I have told them they may come; as to what happens then will depend upon circumstances." And of course Mrs. Peter may have been instrumental in persuading the Orphan Society to make their original offer — prematurely announced in the *Wahrheitsfreund* in its issue of August 26th as definitely settled — and again in suggesting to the officers of the Society that they approach the Archbishop, this time to request his approval.

The Archbishop was a kindly man and he came greatly to admire the Sisters, though every now and then during the years that immediately followed he would renew his suggestion that they withdraw — not because of any fears that they might be a tax on the archdiocese but because, being himself so very markedly Irish, he suspected that too German an emphasis was being laid upon their work. As to that, as soon as it was proved to him that he had misjudged this or that little matter, his favor was instantly restored.

The Sisters lost no time in moving into their new home, the old orphanage on Fourth Street, between Central Avenue and John Street, for they were in it two days after they were informed that the Archbishop had changed his mind, that is, on September 14th. It was a three-story structure, with a large yard thickly overgrown with weeds. The building itself, which they proposed turning into a hospital, was in a dilapidated condition and, as the Annals record, "Dirt and filth lay several inches deep upon the floors and everything was covered with black soot." The job of cleaning it was enough to daunt anybody, and of course could only be done a few rooms at a time.

About this we hear of something that sounds rather quaint. The German Sisters apparently had never heard of people going down on their hands and knees with scrubbing brushes, for their own convents in Germany had always been so clean that the use of a long-handled mop sufficed. These floors, so one would think, called for pickaxe and shovel. They themselves toiled every day until midnight, meanwhile keeping such little furniture as they had in the hallways. Fortunately Father Hengehold rounded up some of the women of his parish to help, and the first time that one of these was seen on her hands and knees, the Sisters thought she must have collapsed from fatigue and ran to give first aid. They themselves soon learned to work according to the American mode. Even so, they could hardly have put so grimy a place in anything like order had it not been for the kindly assistance they received from outside.

Other strange facts are recorded. Americans at this time were unaccustomed to seeing women walking the streets in a religious garb, for the Nativist agitation, though it had somewhat subsided, was by no means spent. The Sisters of Notre Dame rarely had occasion to leave their convent walls, which was even more true of the Good Shepherds. As for the Sisters of Mercy, they went on their charitable errands either in secular dress, or, when they wore their habits, in a closed carriage. But the Sisters of the Poor of St. Francis from the outset had to beg from door to door, or at the stalls of the market. Everybody stared at them, and some shouted insults, using words which the Sisters fortunately could not understand but whose tone was plainly offensive. By way of wearing down the prevailing prejudice, a number of the women and children of Father Hengehold's parish would make the begging rounds with them, something which also served to bring them into contact with possible benefactors. One of their most devoted helpers was a Mrs. Heuer who, a little later, became a Sister in another congregation; her husband became a Franciscan lay brother. The Sisters regarded their belated vocations as God's blessing upon a family that had been so humbly helpful with the hardest work.

There were benefactors of another kind. Thus one day they found on their doorstep a barrel of the finest flour, and another time a barrel of sugar. Though no indication was given as to who the donor might be, the Sisters eventually discovered that it was Father Purcell. He had purchased these useful gifts out of money that he now and then received from one or other of the European missionary societies. These were gratefully received, as was a present of two young pigs which were brought to the orphanage while the Sisters were all at Mass at the Cathedral. The only one at home was the postulant, and she, not knowing what else to do, thanked the man who had brought them — their little heads peeping out from under his arms — and shut the pigs in the dining-room! The postulant then hurried off to the Cathedral for a later Mass without leaving any warning. At breakfast, the Sisters could not understand what the squealing noise was until they found the young porkers scampering about the room. Then the bewildered intruders were put into a pigsty in the yard and flourished there until they had grown large enough to be eaten.

Among the most notable of their benefactors were Mr. Reuben Springer and his English-born wife. The way the Sisters first encountered him has a touch of humor. One day Mr. Springer called at the orphanage and asked to see the Superior, whom he asked if she needed any beds. She, taking him to be a peddler, supposed that he was attempting to make them buy what the Sisters could not afford and declined vigorously. The next morning Mrs. Peter, wishing to introduce the Sisters to some of the well-to-do families of the city, took Sister Augustine to call at a handsome house near the

194

Cathedral, and there, to her consternation, she recognized the peddler of the day before in their host, Mr. Reuben Springer! Then everybody laughed happily over the misunderstanding, and the Sisters accepted with joyful alacrity his generous gift of a dozen beds, completely outfitted with linen and blankets.

Other mistakes — not all of them so lucky — occurred. One day a Sister walked into a hardware store and, asked by the proprietor what she would like, thought him very generous and picked out from his stock a large number of articles, explaining, in one of the few English phrases she knew, "For a present." The man naturally concluded that *she* was going to give these articles as a present and that he would be paid. When she started to walk out with her heavily laden basket on her arm, he made her put everything back. This Sister, like the others, had grown so accustomed to being given things that she had lost sight of the depressing fact that most transactions are on a strictly business basis. The rest of the community was vastly entertained at recreation by her account of the mishap, and as the proprietor of the store had shown that he was distinctly annoyed by what he supposed was an attempt to "put something over" on him, they concluded that Americans had less of a sense of humor than Germans. They always enjoyed their own flounderings in the English language. Having picked up the American colloquialism "folks," they would ask at the door of somebody upon whom they had called whether the "foxes" were in. Most of their sources of supply were found in their street or market begging. Only now and then did they encounter a Mr. and Mrs. Springer.

These were, of course, rich people and did what rich people should do, not only towards the Sisters, but for many another worthy cause, religious and civic. A friend of another sort, who appeared a little later, might be mentioned here. This was Henry Richards who, after graduating from Kenyon College, was ordained in 1842 to the Episcopalian ministry, serving in Columbus, Ohio. Ten years later he became a Catholic and, as his wife and children were, for a while, estranged by this step, he took a position in New York and, after his family had joined him in the Church, settled with them in Jersey City. There among his circle of friends were the Ripleys of Brook Farm, John A. McMaster, the editor of the *Freeman's Journal*, Father Hecker, and no less a person than the tremendous and tumultuous Orestes Brownson. Mr. Richards took it upon himself to meet every ship bringing recruits to America for the Sisters of the Poor of St. Francis; to escort them to his home and provide them with a good meal; and to put them on the train for Cincinnati or, in later years, to conduct them to whichever house in the East was their assignment. It was an invaluable service, and such kindnesses much more than offset the stupid insults the good German Sisters often had to encounter in a land to which they had come only to offer their charity.

But to return to the hospital. Long before the cleaning of the dirty orphanage had been completed, the first patient was received. This happened on September 21st; but since no bed was available, the condition had to be imposed that the patient bring her own bed along, together with whatever else she needed. The Sisters were all the more glad to receive her because she had been living with a Protestant man outside of wedlock. She returned to the practice of her religion and died five days later. Her case was of great encouragement, for they could believe they had saved a soul as well as having given alleviation to physical distress.

The second patient came on September 22nd. She was a Protestant and in her case also it had to be stipulated that she provide her own bed. She was in too weak a state to receive religious instruction and died after a few days. But the Sisters noted her sighs of repentance and the patience with which she bore her afflictions. They thought that these would suffice for her salvation.

These two cases throw a strong light on the principles that animated the Sisters. They did not wait until everything was ready; if a premature and inconvenient appeal was made they promptly answered it. And they demonstrated from the outset that no distinction whatever was to be drawn between the "deserving" and the "undeserving"; all that mattered was need. If there was spiritual poverty as well as material poverty, that was all the more reason for their hastening to the rescue. Young and not very experienced though these Sisters were, they had already been stamped with the spirit of Frances Schervier.

To illustrate the point further, in 1861 at least three Freemasons were admitted to the hospital, though Masons in the America of that time — whatever may be true now — were full of a violent antagonism to the Church. One of these Masonic patients was a Jew, a Mr. Sturm, who had become a Protestant. The Catholic books the Sisters gave him to read had to be handled very secretly, because his fellow Masons often visited him and kept their eyes peeled for any sign of proselytism. It was, however, not so difficult for him to attend Mass, as that was celebrated early in the morning, or to say the rosary, as he could keep the beads under his blankets. He became a Catholic and so did another Masonic patient. Since Mr. Sturm feared the wrath of his lodge, he appealed to Mrs. Peter to protect him. This she did, when he had recovered, by sending him to the well-known Jesuit missionary, Father Weninger, a special friend of the Sisters, with the result that Mr. Sturm entered the Jesuit college at St. Louis and was later admitted into the Society.

If these conversions were remarkable, even more so in some ways was another, for it presented a problem, somewhat similar to that of the young postulant who, in 1852, had brought a message from heaven that Frances should resign her office. Father Stehle of St. Joseph's parish asked the Sisters to take in a woman who was apparently an ecstatic, with her "spells" lasting regularly from Thursday afternoon until three the following afternoon, the day and hour when Christ died. During this period she neither ate nor drank and was supposed to have the stigmata. Until Easter Sunday she was altogether emaciated, but then she suddenly appeared to be in perfect health. What could one think about such a case? The ordinary procedure would have been to consult the Archbishop, but since he was still looked upon as rather unfriendly, the Sisters were probably afraid of bringing these matters to his attention. That the Sisters regarded the woman as an imposter, or at least under a delusion, is shown by the fact that she was not encouraged to go to Holy Communion at Easter, though this was not positively forbidden by the Sisters or their chaplain. Instead they asked a Mrs. Groninger — one of their many lay helpers — to make a novena for the woman's recovery, and we may be sure that they themselves prayed. At the novena's end the trances entirely ceased; the patient announced that she was cured "of her delusions"; and she went home. Though the Sisters had several times later to treat this same patient in their hospital, she never again manifested any pseudo-mystical states. It is the kind of case often encountered in religious history; not often is the solution so complete.

It was under such conditions that the work of the Sisters was begun in Cincinnati. Catholic missionaries take it for granted that they will encounter difficulties and are prepared for active opposition; but rarely can it have happened that the difficulties were so great as this band of Sisters had to contend with, especially as they were not sure just how they stood with their Ordinary. But they went quietly along, doing the appointed job, a handful of six at first, counting the postulant. They had to maintain themselves and their poor by begging, always uncertain whether this would supply what was necessary, as the city had so many anti-Catholic elements. But they accepted their lot — was not an absolute poverty, a total dependence upon God their cardinal principle? — and they proceeded to lay the foundations of an immense success.

American Consolidation

WHAT TURNED out to be a substantial source of revenue for the Sisters was the giving of concerts, which became an annual affair. This happened more or less by accident. A Tyrolese family of singers — for the Trapps had their fore-runners — had been giving performances in various parts of the United States, and when they reached Cincinnati they heard of the work being done by the Sisters. Immediately Herr Hauser, the head of this family, came forward with an offer to sing for the benefit of the struggling hospital. The *Wahrheitsfreund*, in its issue for December 23rd, 1858, an-nounced that on the following January 4th at the Tyrolese House this concert would be given and that the tickets would be 25 cents each. As a sum of 800 dollars was cleared, after allowing for incidental expenses and a nominal fee for those who took part, the audience must have numbered 4,000 people. It is clear that Cincinnati contained a large popula-tion of music lovers. Though probably not all the selections were of the most "classical" sort, for concessions had to be made in this respect, that such a concert could be given at all, though never again by the Hausers, tells us a good deal about the kind of Germans and Italians inhabiting the city.

We also learn how the work at the old orphanage was distributed. The first group were soon augmented by other

Sisters sent out from Aachen, but even so the band was pitifully small for what they had to undertake. Sisters Felicitas, Genevieve, Hildegard, Placida, and Michaela were those who usually went out begging. Sister Augustine, the Superior, aided by the postulant, looked after the sick. Sister Isidora did the laundry and general housework, and Sister Joachim attended to the kitchen. Some convalescents from the men's ward were a welcome help in the work at the hospital, and there were always a number of good women who offered their services in various ways.

The orphanage had been given rent free for only six months and served the purpose of getting the Sisters started. But when the Orphan Society offered to sell, the Sisters lost little time in declining. The building was not really very well suited for their needs, and Sister Augustine had made up her mind to build as soon as she had collected the necessary funds and had secured a suitable site. They knew that the residents of the locality in which they were had a prejudice against having a hospital so close to their homes and had tolerated them only because it was understood that they would not stay there permanently.

A site was now offered to them by the Archbishop, and the Sisters clapped their hands with joy when they heard of it. Father Hengehold was commissioned to take them there, and he said, "Look, Sisters, the place is on the outskirts of the city, and though there is an omnibus going there, it will cost us five cents each." Father Hengehold's good children — for that was how he had come to style them — answered that they would walk to save the fare, an instance of Franciscan poverty that edified him.

But though they were poor in spirit, and physically poor, they also had ample prudence. As soon as they saw the place — Mount Adams, with, in those days, rough and steeply graded roads — they saw that it would not do. Builders' trucks could get to the summit only with difficulty; still harder would it be for the begging Sisters to toil up that hill with their heavily laden baskets (for at that time they had no wagon), or for the sick poor to crawl to their doors. At once they had to say that they **were sorry but they** would have to look elsewhere.

The Archbishop had offered them something which, because of its inaccessibility, was not at that time worth much. Other people, hearing that they were in the market, offered to sell them tracts of land still worse — in one instance it was hardly more than a dumping ground and as such would have provided no firm foundations. But at last they heard of some lots near St. Joseph's Church that could be purchased for $3,000, providing the first payment was made on March 8th. But when that day arrived they were still $200 short of what they needed, in spite of all the efforts they had made. When the owners of the property arrived to close the deal Sister Augustine was in the greatest confusion. All she could think of was to send a Sister quickly to some of their benefactors nearby to see if she could not borrow the money, but the Sister came back confessing that she had not been able to obtain anything. Poor Sister Augustine was wringing her hands in mortification when the postulant handed her a letter which she said had been brought by a lady in black who carried it from Mrs. Springer. In it was the exact sum needed, $200.

It was a general alms, not specifically intended for the purchase of the site, about which Mrs. Springer had as yet heard nothing, for the negotiations had been conducted with the utmost secrecy. The money therefore came to them as though borne by an angel of God. Now the Sisters had their first permanent home in Cincinnati — or rather the place where they could put it up, the block on Betts and Linn Streets. They could not have obtained it at all — or, having obtained it, built there — except for the fact that there were few residences at that time in the neighborhood and therefore no possibility of any objection being raised to a hospital because of the supposititious danger of contagion.

There was a real need of a German hospital in Cincinnati, for most of the people of that race, being all of them new-comers, understood little or no English, and so could not explain their ailments to English-speaking doctors and nurses in the city institution, nor, in many instances, were they able to afford the fees asked there. So though this hospital was not intended solely for German use it bore at first the name of *Maria Hilf Krankenhaus*, and not until later became known as St. Mary's. When first erected, it had only 90 beds, but even so was quantitatively — and even more qualitatively — a great advance over the makeshift arrangement at the old orphanage.

How to finance the building of the hospital was a problem. The Sisters had had difficulty in purchasing the site, and though, after that was effected, they could appeal for dona-tions, what came in was far from sufficient to cover the cost of the building. They were therefore obliged to proceed in a blind faith that Providence would supply their needs. The method was heroic and is one fraught with so many risks that no American bishop of our time would give his consent to a work of such magnitude being undertaken in such a way. The Sisters were made to understand clearly that, if at the end of any week they were unable to pay the workmen, the work would stop at once. So also with the building materials; for though they got a little more leeway there, it was not much more. Nevertheless the work begun under such condi-tions never did stop; somehow or other the money was always found.

The American Annals (which were not compiled until the 1880's, though from documents exactly contemporary with the events) say that unfortunately no record can be found as to who made the necessary large donations of money and materials. But it was in the memory of the Sisters that it was often a question of touch-and-go, that there were many weeks when it seemed that the obligations could not possibly be met, but that every time somebody came forward to cover the bills or meet the pay roll. It is fairly safe to guess that the Springers were among these benefactors, they and Mrs. Peter. In all probability they kept their eyes peeled, considering themselves as those to be drawn on in an emergency, but, for the rest, leaving the necessary contributions to be made by a host of less affluent people.

There are indications that the bulk of the money for St. Mary's came in relatively small amounts. We are told that many gifts of $50 or so were made by people who themselves appeared to be needy; that even washerwomen brought in that amount, or double. The only return they asked was that the Sisters would pray for them. And we know that the architect (who also acted as contractor) gave his services gratis and that he even persuaded some of the workmen to pay back a certain proportion of their wages each week to the building fund. Even so, these men had to get their wages, or they could not go on working. It was in this hazardous fashion that St. Mary's Hospital went up.

When the structure was completed, the good women of Cincinnati came forward again to scrape the floor boards and to wash them clean. There was none of the luxury that one finds in most modern hospitals, but a solid and serviceable building was produced. During the period of its construction it was the main concern of the Catholics of the city, and as non-Catholics had already discovered that they would be received there when they were sick, some of them also contributed.

The *Ludwig-Missionsverein* of Munich and the *Leopold-inen-Stiftung* of Vienna several times sent donations towards the erection of the building and afterwards towards its maintenance. So much we know from the records that exist, but as these records are only fragmentary, in all probability the missionary societies sent more than appears, though we hear of at least a couple of thousand gulden.* The Sisters' audacious trust in the Lord was rewarded.

* This was the former currency used in Austria, worth about 50 cents.

A new question arose. A hospital in those days often had rather primitive equipment, nothing of the expensive apparatus that would be considered indispensable today, probably hardly more than surgical instruments and a pharmacy. But beds and dressing tables and new kitchen utensils were needed for an institution now so much enlarged. Just who paid for all this does not appear, though as Mr. Springer had previously given twelve beds and was a man of munificent generosity, it is hardly to be imagined that he failed to do his share now. One rather pathetic detail does appear: in her love of religious poverty, Sister Augustine had felt that wooden steps must be used at the entrance of the new hospital, but when the "name day" of the young Superior was nearly due, on August 28th, the Sisters decided to surprise her with a present. Accordingly they secretly collected a number of donations from friends, whom they pledged to silence, and on the feast day Sister Augustine was presented with the money necessary for stone steps, by the daughter of Mr. and Mrs. Heuer, generous benefactors of the Sisters.

The first name day of Sister Augustine had fallen while they were at sea. At that time there was no opportunity in a cramped cabin of doing much, so that it was decided that they would wait until their arrival at Cincinnati for carrying out the ceremonies in style. But in what a style! Only the front rooms of the first floor of the old orphanage had been cleaned of the worst of their grime, when Sister Augustine was ensconced in a chair, on the back of which a red ribbon had been wrapped, with (as a carpet was lacking) a bit of cheap oilcloth put at her feet and a pot of flowers on each side of her. Then the Sisters sang a hymn in honor of our Lady, after which they tendered Sister Augustine their felicitations. The Annals read: "Truly nowhere on the face of God's earth could a spot be found where were harbored such fullness of soul and such satiety of heartfelt content and happiness as in the little community of Sisters on the occasion of this celebration."

Sister Augustine had accomplished wonders, but overwork and the American climate impaired her health, as it impaired that of many of the Sisters brought up in the milder Rhineland, so soon after this time she was recalled to Aachen, along with Sister Gabriela. On October 4, 1859, Frances wrote to her: "Oh Sister, I am often anxious for you, when I behold you in your difficult position, so far away from the Motherhouse, without due foundation in the spiritual life. How often would my grave concern for you have caused me sleepless nights, had I not, in humble acknowledgment of my insufficiency, cast myself prayerfully and in tears at the feet and on the heart of our Divine Redeemer, recommending most earnestly to Him, the most benign and solicitous Shepherd, yourself and your little band. I never experienced an anxiety and distress like that which I feel concerning this small branch of our Congregation transplanted to a soil so far away . . . Our Lord, always the truest helper in all difficulties, heard my prayer. With His assistance I have found the Sister on whose shoulders I can place the cross of the office of Provincial * Superior, and now I can realize my plans concerning America. From the moment her functions begin, you, my good Sister, will be relieved of your heavy burden, and will retire to the ranks of a simple Sister living under obedience." She instructed Sister Augustine to keep this news to herself for the present, and quietly to put the affairs of the house in order pending the formal appointment of her successor, who turned out to be her second-in-command, Sister Felicitas.

In writing to Sister Felicitas Frances condoles with her because of the cross she must now bear. "I have begged," she said, "our dear Lord to give you much courage and strength to endure and also love of suffering . . . Therefore courage and confidence, dear Sister; let us be crossbearers for love of our Divine Saviour . . . I pray for you every day with all my heart and confidently hope that with all your strength you

---

* Though Frances herself uses the term "Provincial," which the head of the American enterprise was in effect, strictly speaking she was only Frances's Vicar; the Sisters of the Poor of St. Francis did not have any provinces during Frances's life-time.

will respond to the divine Grace. Pray for me too, dear Sister. Now you can understand somewhat my difficult position, yet I rejoice that the Lord has permitted me to carry a small portion of the cross."

The burden was indeed heavy. A hospital of 90 beds could not be entirely supported by begging from house to house or in the markets. Fortunately the second concert proved even more popular and profitable than the first, and a bazaar held in June, 1860, brought in the astonishing sum of $10,000. Yet as even this was far from enough to meet the pressing needs, a picnic up the river was organized. This, however, was not much of a success, for after deducting the hire of the steamer, and the refreshments of the junketers, less than $300 was realized. The statistics of the year show that 509 patients were cared for in St. Mary's, 426 of them Catholics and 83 Protestants. Though no payment was demanded from anybody, 20 of the Protestants did pay for their care — at the rate of three dollars a week! In all this brought in $232, with $719 paid by such Catholics as could afford it. The total income for 1860 (the big bazaar belonged to the previous year) came to $6839.43, and the expenditure was $6832. The number of patients in the hospital at the end of the year was 92, two more than it could really accommodate, and the community by that time consisted of 15 Sisters. One is simply staggered by these figures, and one can only conclude that they do not take into account the provisions that came in as a result of begging but only monetary contributions.

It had become obvious by this time that other means of making ends meet had to be discovered. Delicacy forbade a continual appeal to the few wealthy benefactors the Sisters had; moreover repeated requests might have resulted in tiring those who had been giving. Cincinnati was a sponge which by now had been squeezed almost dry. That it was far from being a Catholic city is shown by the fact that at this time it had 86 meeting houses of various denominations, 113 lodges of different kinds — but all of them more or less antagonistic to the Church and usually the centers of what remained of Nativist activity — whereas there were only 21 Catholic churches.

The environs of the city were first approached, but it was really hardly possible for the Sisters to carry back large baskets of supplies over several miles (for they still did not have any wagon for this purpose); so they were elated when they were invited to go to Minster, about a hundred miles due north of Cincinnati, near the Indiana border. There in Father Andrew Kunkel of the Congregation of the Precious Blood, they found a warm-hearted friend who recommended them to the Germans of the locality.

He took the Sisters under his wing. Accompanied by lay brothers of the Congregation, they called upon the farmers who, almost to a man, were generous in gifts of money and provisions. The Sisters were simply laden down with what they were given. Not only that; Father Kunkel told them that they must come at harvest time every year and regard Mercer County as the storehouse of the hospital. They took him at his word, and sometimes went in spring as well. When they did so, as canals were the main means of transportation, the barges took a long time to reach Cincinnati; it was often July before their "loot" arrived. Smoked meat was the main contribution, but as we also hear of a large quantity of eggs, there must have been some means of preserving them on the barges with ice. When they reached Cincinnati, a number of wagons were required to bring these stores to the hospital. Even to this day, the Minster collection is made annually.

Still further did the Sisters have to go in search of alms for the support of their work, to Milwaukee, to Montreal, to Maine, and in later years, even to Cuba, seeking in these instances donations of money rather than of provisions, which obviously they could not have borne back. Such collections had to be conducted with considerable finesse, for they could be carried out only with the written permission of the bishop of the diocese, and individual pastors could (and sometimes did) throw obstacles in the Sisters' way, being often harassed enough financially without outsiders coming in.

Furthermore, these collecting tours lay under the handicap of the Sisters' very imperfect knowledge of English. And as the appearance in the streets of women wearing a religious garb — something rarely seen in America at that time — excited astonishment and occasionally even untoward incidents, the Catholic authorities were in some instances afraid of anti-Catholic demonstrations from the Nativists who were rampant until the Civil War gave them something else to think about; there was therefore an understandable reluctance to add to their troubles by having Sisters wandering from house to house. Thus when they called on Bishop Fitzpatrick of Boston in 1861 they found him out, but his Vicar-General absolutely forbade any begging in the diocese, and when, at the suggestion of the Sisters of Notre Dame, they went on to Lowell, the pastor to whom they applied for permission to collect in his parish, not only refused but upbraided them harshly for thinking of such a thing when his people were suffering privations. However, the pastor of the Franciscan church, to which no less than 5,000 tertiaries were attached, while he would not allow a house-to-house solicitation, took up a good collection for them on Sunday.

At Burlington, Vermont, they fell in with Catherine Hooley, who lived in New York State and was there only on a visit. She was greatly impressed when she heard the Bishop recommend the alms-gathering of the Sisters and especially when he mentioned that he had offered to take up a collection for them, but they had replied that it would be more in accord with the spirit of their vocation to go from door to door. A year and a half later Miss Hooley felt drawn to apply for admission to the community, and on being accepted as Sister Alcantara she became an outstanding member of the Congregation for more than 50 years of religious life. Soon after her acceptance she was followed by her sister Mary, in religion Sister Camilla, who died four years later. These two vocations the collectors felt to be a much richer return than the very welcome money they had gathered on their trip to Vermont.

But if, of necessity, they went afield looking for support, so also they began to give help outside of Cincinnati. Bishop Carrell, almost as soon as St. Mary's was in operation, wished to have a similar institution for Covington, on the Kentucky side of the Ohio river. As this was almost within Cincinnati itself the request could hardly be refused. Indeed Mrs. Peter had already begun to urge "her Sisters," as she called them, to undertake some new work, and Mrs. Peter was the kind of lady who was hard to resist. Her argument that all this was for the salvation of souls was fully granted; the difficulty was to find enough Sisters to do what she wanted. Sister Felicitas was obliged to fall back, time after time, on the argument that the American activities were entirely subordinate to the Motherhouse at Aachen. Our good Sarah looked upon this as an evasion; she never really understood the obstacles but was forever trying to push the Sisters into undertakings which, at that stage, were quite beyond their resources. They did in fact owe a great deal to her, as they fully acknowledged, and she was to do still more for them in the years that lay ahead. But she did now and then prove a trial —especially after she established them in her house — though probably they, with their German ways, also proved something of a trial to her. It is much to the credit of both parties that they succeeded in remaining in most cordial relations to the end.

There was another side of the matter that Mrs. Peter could not be expected to understand. It appears in an undated letter from Frances to Sister Felicitas, apparently about 1863, when she wrote: "The Most Reverend Archbishop [Purcell] said only that, when we wish to make foundations in *his* diocese, we must obtain his approbation; there was no mention made of establishments in other dioceses; for those we need simply present the matter to him or, as I told you, let the bishop of the other diocese make his request [to the Archbishop]. I regard this as a mere formality by which he, the Archbishop, shows that he is shepherd over the house from which the foundation is made. I told him that on our part just such a representation is made to the Cardinal in Cologne, so that he knows where his children are." She added, however, very significantly: "It seems to me that for the present he does not wish us to make further establishments in *his* diocese, for he thinks that thereby the Sisters of Mercy — the Irish Sisters — might be restricted in their work."

If, as appears to be the case from several small incidents, Archbishop Purcell was unconsciously not very favorably disposed towards Germans, a longer view of the matter might have suggested to him that all foreign communities in the United States would inevitably become Americanized in time by the infiltration of American vocations. Indeed this had begun to happen to the Sisters of the Poor of St. Francis as early as 1862, through what appeared to be the merest accident. Then the admission of the sisters Lizzie and Annie Feeny was the harbinger of a new age, little though this was suspected.

Sisters Dominica and Hildegard were commissioned to go to Chillicothe on a begging campaign, but their English was so unintelligible to the ticket clerk that he gave them passes to Chicago instead. One would have supposed that they would soon have discovered the mistake, as Chicago is nearly four times further away from Cincinnati than Chillicothe, the town to which they wished to go. The great difference in the fare should itself have been sufficient warning. But no, in their simplicity they went aboard and stayed on the Chicago train.

When they got to Chicago Sister Dominica thought the best thing they could do was to call on a Jesuit she knew there, to explain what had happened and to ask his advice. While they were there Miss Lizzie Feeny arrived and was introduced, and the Jesuit suggested that she take the Sisters around in his parish to see what could be collected. This girl already felt a strong inclination for the religious life but was undecided as to what order she should join. Then, while they were making their rounds, a Voice from heaven seemed to speak to her inner being saying, "You must bcome one of these." So she did, despite the opposition of her family to her joining what was at that time still, quite naturally, a purely German community. Her elder sister also felt the same compulsion. Thirty years later, as Sisters Magdalen and Martha, they delighted to tell of their experience; it seemed to verge on the miraculous. And it had all come about because of a ticket clerk's error.

Nor did the matter quite end there. The pious Feeny sisters had pious friends. Though these heard no Voice speak to them with dramatic suddenness — that was not necessary in their case — the fact that their friends were in a convent in Cincinnati drew them there too. Though for some time to come the Congregation retained its German complexion — chiefly because it had to be constantly recruited from Aachen — it might have been foreseen that this would not always be the case, so far as America was concerned.

As American postulants of Irish extraction were being received, the kindly German Sisters decided to make them feel more at home, by reciting the common prayers in English and by making English, in fact, so far as possible, the language of the house. But then there came a regulation from Frances that may be misjudged. Though she was quite devoid of any nationalistic prejudice she ordered that no English-speaking novice was to be professed until she had learned German well enough for practical purposes, at the same time evening the balance by regulating that the German Sisters should try to learn English in order to help them in their work.

The object of this was sound enough: as the Sisters of the Poor of St. Francis were at that time a predominantly German Congregation, Frances believed that only through German could its spirit be thoroughly learned. But Archbishop Purcell, far from being edified, was distinctly annoyed. He had always shown special affability towards the Irish novices, giving them a gold piece at their profession and humorously telling them to "treat" the other Sisters. Now he got the impression that the Sisters, by clinging to their German ideas, would be of little service in the United States. On August 28, 1866, he sent for Sister Dominica and was very sharp in his speech. He had the idea that English was to be virtually prohibited, which was not at all the case. But persisting in his own misunderstanding of the matter, he felt that the newly introduced regulations would disgust the English-speaking members of the community with their life.

The difficulties were eventually composed; it was explained to the Archbishop that the regulations were not so sweeping as he had imagined at first, and what their purpose was. As time went on — though this was after Frances Schervier's death — the recruits from Germany gradually diminished and finally ceased altogether. Now even those of German ancestry who are admitted in this country, probably more often than not do not know the language spoken by their forebears. The Congregation in America has become entirely American in feeling, and the present Superior General is an American. The regulations about learning German have been long since abrogated. The process would, in any event, have been inevitable; actually it may be said to have begun on that day in 1862 when "Chillicothe" sounded like "Chicago" on a German tongue.

19

*

During Three Wars

WHEN IN 1861 Frances was reelected Superior, as always very much against her wishes, she assembled all the Sisters on the Feast of the Holy Trinity and read a carefully prepared address. After some reflections on the mystery being celebrated, she said that she was not at all grateful at having been chosen as Mother again and then proceeded to speak about some new and more distinctly defined lines of operation. "The present state of affairs," she said, "is such that the welfare of the Congregation demands [from me] almost complete application to its concerns alone. Hence I have decided to entrust the First Assistant with the office of Superior of the Motherhouse, and in all household affairs the Sisters will go to her, even when I am at home. All Sisters charged with any office, from the Second Assistant and the Procurator to the youngest in service, will refer all domestic concerns to her. To her as my First Assistant and lawful representative I delegate also the conducting of the ordinary spiritual exercises, not only during my absence but also whenever I am prevented from attending. The supervision of the Congregation as a whole I shall nevertheless dutifully retain."

She went on to explain the object she had in mind: she was like a pilot at the helm: as such she could not concern herself with the needs of the passengers or the internal management of the ship; otherwise disaster might come. She added: "Should it seem that by this arrangement I wish to withdraw myself more from you, remember that only by this means can I be free for those affairs which concern us most intimately and are most important and most sanctifying for us. You know, for example, how absolutely necessary is the revision of our Statutes; the expansion of our Congregation demands a more definite internal organization. This is the first task I have set for myself. It is a work that requires many and fervent prayers, and this I ask in particular of you, dear Sisters." She told how the Sisters could help most effectually — by being obedient; thus they could enable her to fulfill her responsibilities towards them: "Your submission in the manner I desire to the Sister whom I have appointed Superior of the house will enable me to carry out my duties with ease and joy."

On October 4th came Frances's name-day celebration. Some of the Sisters had gone the previous August to the name-day celebration of Mother Clara Fey, and this was carried out with little ceremonies which so commended themselves to those present that the Sisters wished to introduce them when Frances's turn came. It had been customary on the eve of St. Francis's Day for Frances to sit on a seat on a dais in the chapter-room, when each of the professed, bearing a candle in her hand, would offer congratulations. Frances disliked even as much as that, saying that it made her feel like Westhoff — this was the most notorious of the criminals she had accompanied to the scaffold! So she announced that if they proposed anything like that, she would leave the Motherhouse on her name-day.

A compromise was effected. A statue of St. Francis was placed in the middle of the refectory and its pedestal was decorated with leaves and flowers, with candles burning before it. Evergreens were draped along the walls, mingled with colored paper. A hymn to St. Francis was sung before supper, and afterwards a few specially composed poems in honor of that Saint and of St. Anthony were recited. But the Sisters had taken the very broad hint that the slightest allusion to Frances herself would displease her. Or they thought they had, but some such allusions were made, so that when Frances at the end of the meal rose in her place and rapped for attention, she remarked, "Our holy Father Francis, on account of failing strength and of the wounds in his feet, allowed himself to be carried by a donkey from place to place, so that he could speak to the people. And whenever the people in joy and veneration for St. Francis threw flowers at him, some petals naturally fell on the donkey, especially if the winds were blowing, though the animal in no way deserved them. Now St. Francis has made me his donkey, in order that I may bring him, or rather his spirit, from one place to the other. Today many leaves fell on the donkey. In general you did well; such a celebration pleases me. But there was still too much wind. Therefore, dear Sisters, less wind in future!" Everybody was delighted by the whimsy of that little speech; it even pleased Frances herself, for over and over in the years to come she used to describe herself as God's little donkey.

Several other events of these years should be noted briefly. Our friend Herr Kuehlwetter, who had not so very long before threatened to use the police to prevent the Sisters from begging from door to door, now turned to Frances when a plan of his had not turned out as well as expected. The plan — an excellent one in its way — concerned running a cheap municipal restaurant where the poor could buy meals at nominal prices. He bought the entire equipment of his establishment in Berlin and imported its personnel from that city, the result being what might have been looked for, that the expenses greatly exceeded the receipts. Now at his wit's end he appealed to Frances to take charge of the institution on Jacobstrasse, leaving everything to her, down to the keeping of the accounts about which he had previously been so fussy. The charity kitchens the Sisters had maintained in various parishes of Aachen were discontinued so that the whole effort might be concentrated in a single enterprise. Again every recreation of the Sisters was devoted to the paring of potatoes, the peeling of onions, and the scraping of carrots; but though a great saving was effected, too much had already been sunk in expensive equipment, so that Herr Kuehlwetter never quite got out of the red. The bureaucratic gentleman, however, expressed himself as well satisfied with the reduction of losses.

About the same time a training home was founded in Aachen similar to those that had been set up elsewhere. Some of Clara Fey's young girls had grown into young women, and it did not appear desirable to keep them with children. First one of these young women and then four were received into the Motherhouse, and eventually a large group, for whom a new building was constructed. They were trained in domestic science, especially sewing, washing, and needlework, careful attention being given at the same time to their thorough instruction in doctrine and decorum. There was no difficulty in finding positions for such girls with good families. This work continued at the Motherhouse until 1875.

Similarly Frances accepted, though with reluctance, because of her still scanty resources, the management of the hospital for incurables in Cologne. Two factors overcame her disinclination. One was that the institution was placed under the patronage of the Immaculate Conception; the other was that she did not have the heart to refuse what Cardinal von Geissel asked as a personal favor. "We *must*," she wrote, "undertake the management of St. Mary's Hospital . . . We have to engage in more work than seems good for us. But I hope the Lord knows the weakness of our shoulders and will sustain us by His strength, when our own infirmity and spiritual insufficiency prove an obstacle. You see, I live by hope and confidence." When the hospital opened, a hymn that Frances had composed for the occasion was sung.

She had not needed the same pressing when the *Marien-Stiftung*, another institution for the training of domestic servants, was offered her at Erfurt. This was near the home of her beloved St. Elizabeth of Hungary. Moreover Queen Augusta of Prussia herself asked her to go there, and the Queen had put Frances under an obligation by intervening when local authorities threatened to stop the begging practiced by the Sisters. But indeed the Queen was, or was eventually to become, a personal friend of Frances's. She had several times visited the Motherhouse while still only Princess of Prussia, and she was already addressing Frances as "my dear little Mother." The Queen showed by some of the letters she wrote subsequently to Frances that, though not, at least openly, a Catholic (for that would have been impossible to her at that time), she had so much of the Catholic spirit that she might have put many professing Catholics to shame. The time was soon to come when she was to draw upon Frances's services, and she did what she could to protect her in the 1870's during the storm of the Kulturkampf.

From Erfurt Frances had brought back a precious relic, a silver cup used by St. Elizabeth. Though not until 1867 was she able to carry it in procession filled with roses during the septennial exposition of relics, she took an enthusiastic part in the exposition of these relics in 1860. Few churches in Europe are so full of relics as the Aachenerdom. They are so many that they have to be classified as major and minor, and among the major relics are the swaddling clothes worn by our Lord in the manger, the loin cloth He wore on the cross, the robe of the Blessed Virgin, and the sheet on which St. John the Baptist's body was placed after his beheading. While it is not an article of faith to believe in the authenticity of these (or any other) relics, they have what would seem to be the best of attestations, for they go back to the time of Charlemagne, who received them from the Pope, and even to the time of St. Helena, the mother of the Emperor Constantine. Where else, unless to Rome itself, would such things be more likely to find their way than to the imperial city?

To anticipate a little at this point in chronology, in 1867

Frances reports that these relics had effected some miraculous cures among the Sisters. She wrote that Sister Thecla was cured of her serious malady after touching the shroud of our Lord. She goes into some details: Sister Thecla can now stand and walk, and her vomiting has ceased. With every hour she is improving. Then (and here we may see Frances's good sense operating) she says that two other sick Sisters have also greatly improved after touching these relics — though not in a manner to be regarded, in her opinion, as miraculous. The Sisters of the Poor of St. Francis were appointed to sew these relics into silken coverings at the end of the exposition, after which they were locked away in silver-gilt caskets for another seven years.*

No relic of St. Joseph was among them, but St. Joseph, of all the saints, received most veneration from Frances, after the Blessed Virgin and St. Francis. On January 21, 1863, the first of the Nine Wednesdays in honor of our Lord's foster father, the Sisters, upon entering the refectory, saw before the picture of St. Joseph hanging there a candle burning and a pot of flowers. During the dinner Frances knelt before this picture, eating her sparse meal on the floor. Afterwards she informed the community that on each of the rest of the Nine Wednesdays a Sister in perpetual vows would be permitted to take her dinner in the same way, beginning with the Superior of the house, and then the oldest Sister, thus going in order down the line. Each would also spend the entire day in prayer and recollection, a practice which is still maintained in all the houses of the Congregation.

This devotion to St. Joseph, universal though it is among Catholics, is mentioned as an illustration of the special spirit of prayer animating the Congregation. When Frances was elected again as Superior in 1862, she tried to avoid the office and to join the Recluses. In a letter dated June 30th that year, she wrote to a Franciscan father: "It has pleased the

---

* The relics were put in their charge for safekeeping during the First World War.

Lord not to release me, as I had so ardently desired. I was not deemed worthy of the better part of our Saviour; I am to remain a Martha, it seems. Five years [her term of office] is a long time; according to my presentiments I shall not outlive them. But as the Lord disposes; it is not for me to argue with Him . . . If it is His pleasure to use a worthless instrument to attain His adorable designs, His wisdom and power thereby shine forth so much the brighter."

In America the Recluses had been established in 1861, largely at the urging of Mrs. Peter, who herself wished to retire from the world, elderly woman though she was, and give the rest of her days to contemplation. She had written to Father Hecker in May: "My child * is the only tie that binds me to Cincinnati. Yet is not fifty-eight too late a period in life to begin a new thing? If there were a well-established community of Carmelites near at hand, I should be strongly tempted to apply for admission, for I experience a growing inclination for the contemplative life, perhaps natural at my age." As the Carmelites were not available, she conceived the idea of establishing the Recluses at Cincinnati, of making over her own house to them (which was later enlarged for the purpose), retaining only a couple of rooms for herself, and of guaranteeing their support.

Frances accepted the offer and sent Recluses to America. But she managed to stave off Sarah's actual admission, for she knew that a desire for contemplation does not necessarily prove a contemplative vocation. Sarah was not only too old but too individualistic. Thus, she undertook to watch for regular hours during the Perpetual Adoration of the Blessed Sacrament (which was not with exposition until 1938); but even though she had been on her knees only 10 minutes, if somebody came in and whispered that her son Rufus had

* This was Rufus King, who was now in his forties and prominent as a lawyer (in which capacity he rendered many services gratis to the Sisters), and to some extent as a politician. His mother never ceased working for his conversion, but not always with due discretion. He remained friendly to Catholics but never entered the Church.

called, she would at once go off to receive him in her beautifully furnished parlor. This usually meant at least an hour of argument with him on the subject of religion.

She was not the kind of a woman to be pinned down; in short she was quite unfitted for the following of a religious rule of any kind. Moreover the autocratic old lady was inclined to be a bit interfering, every now and then going to the kitchen to give the cook directions. There may have been some justification for this, for we hear of Sister Michaela sometimes standing with a prayer book in her hand, totally absorbed and oblivious to the fact that the soup was burned or the fire out! But even Sister Stylita, who replaced her, did not escape Mrs. Peter's habit of ordering people about.

One fancies that it must have been at Mrs. Peter's instigations that one of the Recluses had written to Frances suggesting that, as they lived apart as contemplatives, they should not have even the external activities of housework. For Frances had to tell them plainly in reply: "The domestic duties to which you must attend should not be a hindrance or cause of disturbance to you; these too are a sacrifice to God, as is everything He wishes of us." On the other hand Mrs. Peter had written to Frances objecting to the long probation demanded of any Sister before she was allowed to become a Recluse, and to their complete seclusion. She had argued, with the *tradere contemplata* idea in mind, that much good might be accomplished if the Recluses were permitted to converse, if only through a grille, with visitors. Mrs. Peter, in short, wanted a rewriting of the Constitutions so that Frances was obliged to explain patiently: "I can now tell you truly that our Lord Himself has established our Clarisses.* I have not the power to change the matter. It would be its ruin, yes, its destruction. Nevertheless, if after this explanation, the regulations should not please you because they do not coincide with your own views, you will

---

* As the term "Clarisses" might suggest some connection with the Poor Clares, where none exists, it has long since been abandoned.

not, my esteemed Mrs. Peter, displease us in any way if you send our Clarisses back to *Maria Hilf*." Very gently but very decisively Frances had put her foot down, and the masterful Sarah yielded at once.

We have seen how when in 1848 Frances had surrendered her penitents to the Good Shepherd Sisters, she had heard an interior Voice telling her, "I will send you other penitents." But though the Recluses when started were joined by a girl whom Frances had rescued from evil courses, those later assigned to the group — they were always assigned, though never against their inclination, though they were sometimes called back against their will — were all perpetually professed Sisters, not one of whom could be described as a penitent, except in the sense that all Christians should have a penitential spirit. They were in fact the select members of the community — that is, the spiritually select — for those of marked ability in some special field could never be spared, any more than was Frances herself.

Now, however, there did seem to be a chance of founding another group made up of penitents, or those more nearly resembling what we commonly understand by the word. It was one of Mrs. Peter's ideas, and it appealed to Frances. One of the converts of Sarah was a worldly-minded — though not, I believe, strictly speaking, a bad — young woman. And it was proposed (with the approval of Frances and Archbishop Purcell) that she and a few other women of somewhat the same kind should be settled in a house the Sisters had opened at Hessen-Cassel in Allen County, Indiana. They were (unlike the Recluses) not to wear the brown habit but one of ashen grey. Nor were they to be entirely separated from the other Sisters in the House, but were to have their meals and recreation periods among them. But they were to live a life even more austere than the rest, rising in the middle of the night for Office and giving themselves solely to prayer. Though this group was to be known as the Penitents of St. Margaret of Cortona, the "Magdalen" of Franciscan saints, it was supposed to be restricted to virgins possessed of an extraordinary spirit of penance, and only in exceptional instances to be open to those who had notoriously strayed from the paths of virtue. Such women were actually never admitted. The main purpose of the group was to devote themselves to prayers for the souls in Purgatory.

Perhaps something might have come of the undertaking had the house at Hessen-Cassel prospered. Frances herself, while on her first visit to the United States in 1863, installed the Sisters there, with her own hands making their straw-filled mattresses. The Sisters who were assigned to begging had little time for this activity, as they found that they were expected to run the house of Bishop Luers of Fort Wayne, something outside their province. They got practically nothing to eat, and the cold, so the Annals tell us, was so extreme in winter that "when the table was wiped, the cloth froze under their hands. The dough placed under the stove often froze so that instead of bread pancakes had to be made. It was so cold in church that the Precious Blood from the Consecration to the Communion became hardened into ice, and the celebrant had to give the chalice a hard knock to loosen it from the sides." On top of all this the farm that the postulants of the Penitents of St. Margaret had to work was a mile away from the house, and their postulancy was to last five years. It is hardly to be wondered at that they soon became discouraged.

Nor was this the full tale of their woes. It was the custom of the local farmers to help one another when special work had to be done. The Penitents, as it happened, received no help themselves, and yet they were called upon to give it, also they were expected to feed those working in the fields. One cannot help suspecting that there was some exaggeration in all this — or that the American farmers were practicing a rather malicious humor on these young women.

Even so, the physical tribulations might have been endured had not spiritual consolations often been lacking. Every third

Sunday the pastor of Hessen-Cassel had to go on another mission, and then he was absent all the rest of the week. At such times one of the Sisters had to ring the bell at the hour for High Mass, and when the people arrived, the Sisters recited the Mass, so that the congregation might unite themselves in spirit with the Holy Sacrifice. But in the end it was a bit too much for them. In 1865 when the state of affairs had been explained to Frances, she ordered a withdrawal from the place, and not very long afterwards the Penitents of St. Margaret of Cortona, none of whom had as yet had time to finish the novitiate, were disbanded. The undertaking had been only an experiment, and it had failed.

Shortly before the first visit Frances made to the United States, which was in 1863, Cincinnati reached out to the Atlantic coast. This also came about through the instrumentality of Mrs. Peter. On a visit to New York the previous year she had become acquainted with Father Anthony Cauvin, the pastor of Our Lady of Grace Church at Hoboken, New Jersey. After some correspondence between himself and Mrs. Peter on the one side and Sister Felicitas on the other, it was agreed that a beginning should be made there with four Sisters and a postulant, who were settled in a small rented house on Meadow Street. Hoboken, in those days, had the character of a suburb of New York and, as such, was preferred to the great and supposedly very wicked city. When less than 12 months later a foundation was made in Jersey City, this was largely to prevent the Sisters at Hoboken from feeling completely isolated. Both houses served, incidentally, as *pieds à terre* for new recruits from Germany, who were always glad of a few days of rest after the horrors of a long ocean voyage.

The day before Frances left Aachen for America, she took part in the Corpus Christi procession, not only out of devotion but to fortify herself for a journey which she confessed that she, even more than others, dreaded. Her brother Henry Schervier took the little group of Sisters to the railway station and at Le Havre Father Bethman saw them on board, offering some bottles of Cognac and good French wine, as he knew that these would be useful in seasickness. "Oh no, Father," said Frances. "This is very kind of you but we already packed a couple of bottles of red wine and shall need no more." But Sister Afra, who had brought them, discovered that they had been broken on the railway journey, just at the moment when, in the adjoining room in the hotel Couronne d'Or, Frances was refusing Father Bethmann's gift. He laughed when he heard of it and said, "Now, Mother, you will have to take what I have brought!" Lucky it was that this was so, for Frances was so ill on the ship that little sips of Cognac were almost all that she could keep down.

The first stage of their journey was to Southampton, from which port they were to take a German steamer. As they found that they would have to stay there all that afternoon and night before it arrived, they went to a hotel, where their religious habit caused a good deal of comment. But a gentleman who saw them there, addressing them in French, advised them to leave at once — possibly because that hotel did not have the best of reputations — and found them lodgings with two Catholic ladies. He turned out to be the local Catholic priest, and they looked upon him as a kind of guardian angel. All that afternoon they rested quietly with their hostesses and slept so well at night that they awoke at what was for them the unwontedly late hour of seven. Writing from Southampton on the morning of June 10th, Frances tells her brother and his wife that every member of her party, except the postulant, had been sick during the short crossing and that she herself had been the first to be overcome, "although I boasted, and I thought I had, the constitution of a happy sailor." The two kind ladies who had taken them in had made them almost feel "as if we were in a convent." They had attended the eight o'clock Mass, at which they had received Holy Communion. They were then waiting for the ship to sail at eleven.

The voyage in the steerage was terrible. But the Sisters,

forewarned about the poor food, had brought various dainties with them. One day Frances exclaimed, "I feel the need of giving something to somebody!" The words had hardly left her mouth when she saw a woman who, because of having been assigned to the late table, got very little to eat and was almost crying with hunger. Frances at once gave her some of the food she had with her. Similarly she protected a woman who was made the butt of coarse and clumsy ridicule by some of the passengers because of her enormous appetite. She had been heard to remark that dumplings were her favorite dish, so one day when they were served, she found her plate heaped high with these things by the so-called humorists. She rushed out in tears and came on deck. There Frances, who had not been able to go to the dining room and was trying to get a little fresh air, offered her some of the plums and oranges she had in her cabin. They may not have satisfied the woman's appetite but they consoled her.

Sister Felicitas and some of the other Sisters were waiting for Frances at New York. All were so overcome with their joy that they wept, and all that Sister Felicitas, her Vicar in America, could say was, "Mother, dear Mother." An hour later she was at the convent at Hoboken for a day's rest, during which she had the familiar sensation of still feeling the ship rolling under her feet.

It did not take her long to discover how trying the American summer could be. For on June 24th, the day after she landed, she wrote to the Sisters at Aachen, "Here in Hoboken the heat is very afflicting; in Cincinnati it will be still worse." Then, perhaps because she felt some compunction at making even this slight complaint, she added in a sportive vein: "In any case, it is nothing in comparison with that of purgatory, which we deserve." * For her, as we shall soon see, the summer climate of America was no joking matter.

---

* Often in her letters of this period her handwriting changes, sometimes in the middle of a long letter, but sometimes not until the last page. Then the neat small script would become sprawling, suggesting haste but, more

After the thirty-six hours' journey to Cincinnati, where she arrived early in the morning of June 26th, almost dead with fatigue from the torrid heat of the American summer, she went straight to Mass, as this had just begun. Afterwards to celebrate her safe arrival the *Te Deum* was sung and the Benediction of the Blessed Sacrament given. It was noticed that though a prie-dieu had been placed for her in the center aisle near the communion rail, she would not use it but knelt instead in the front pew. It was also noticed that after breakfast, in a refectory made bright with flowers, when she was welcomed with songs and poems, all her tiredness seemed to have disappeared. She greeted the Sisters in the recreation room afterwards, renewing the affection she felt for those new American novices and postulants whom she was meeting for the first time. Over thousands of miles she had already impressed herself upon them and was in their eyes a kind of legendary figure.

Frances came in the middle of the Civil War, and something will be said in a moment about the activities of her Sisters as nurses. But first we might glance at several more general concerns of hers. The most important of these was a fiasco, or close to being one, though her engaging in it was to the credit of her heart, if not, perhaps, of her judgment, though that cannot be seriously blamed. While she was usually very careful to avoid any undertaking that fell outside the lines of the vocation she recognized to be distinctively hers, she was not a rigid doctrinaire, and in her kindness of heart, distrusting what she did, Frances consented to take charge of the domestic necessities of the college and seminary of the diocese conducted by the Franciscan friars at Teutopolis. The Sisters were assisted by the Franciscan lay brothers; even so their acceptance of the charge proved to be a mistake.

probably, extreme fatigue. Even her signature now was often abbreviated to "*E. getr. M. Frz*", meaning: "Your faithful Mother Frances." And rather than take up a new page for a postscript, she writes along the margins of her letters or in their corners.

It is true that the Franciscan Fathers tried to recompense them by supplying them with recruits. Thus Father Matthias, the Superior, preached a sermon in which he said, among other things: "You maidens of Teutopolis . . . the Reverend Mother is now among you and will receive you at once." But no bevy of maidens rushed forward at this appeal. The Sisters eventually had to withdraw from a work which they saw more clearly every day not to be theirs. They remained, however, long enough to initiate a new group of brothers into the duties to be done.

Frances's main business in the United States was that of making visitations among the houses of her Congregation, that she could so become acquainted with all phases of the Sisters' activities. Their regular work remained what it was — the care of the sick poor in hospitals and their homes — but this for the moment seemed secondary to the clamor of war. The part the Sisters played will soon be related.

But before coming to that it should be said that the American climate undermined a constitution never very strong. Not long before her journey to the United States Frances had suffered from inflammation of the lungs and asthmatic attacks, and though she seemed to have recovered after a stay at the orphan asylum her friend Clara Fey conducted near Düsseldorf, where she found rest, pure air, and a milk diet very beneficial, in America the asthma came back worse than ever. Her many journeys were also trying, especially the one she took to see to the establishment of her Sisters at Teutopolis, when she had to make, from the nearest railway station, a two-hour journey over a very rough road. The driver, by way of encouraging them, told them that when traversing that road the previous week a boy had fallen out of the farm wagon and had broken his arm. "So you Sisters had better hold on tight," he added. Frances, seeing how the chairs in the wagon were slipping and bumping about, thought it safer to sit on the floor.

And now for the American Civil War, in so far as it affected the Sisters. St. Mary's Hospital had at the start as chief doctor a genial little "Pennsylvania Dutchman" whose German very much amused the Sisters, accustomed though they were to hearing the Plattdeutsch of Aachen. They were all delighted when he was received into the Church on his deathbed. He was succeeded by a Doctor Blackman, a man more of the new school. During the war he was put in charge of a river boat, the *Superior*, and a train of three-story hospital barges on the Ohio River. With Mrs. Peter, very much in her element, and five Sisters he went from point to point to receive wounded men and convey them to the military hospitals on land. Everywhere they found the soldiers in a miserable condition, the wounded often lying, quite uncared for, in the open.

Throughout all this time Mrs. Peter was a tower of strength. She had so assured a social position that she freely reprimanded the inefficiency and waste and venality everywhere rampant. The sharpness of her tongue was so resented by a sergeant that he reported her as a Southern spy. She went at once to General Willich, to whom this malicious report had been made, and demanded an investigation as to the treatment that the wounded Southern prisoners were receiving. She left on the gallant General's arm. As though to make her triumph complete, the accusing sergeant was stricken a few days later with smallpox. Then Sarah herself nursed him, bathing his sores and feeding him as though he were a baby, while tears of compunction ran down his cheeks.

The Sisters who served at the Marine Hospital at the corner of Sixth and Lock Streets, Cincinnati, were anything but well received, owing to anti-Catholic prejudice. There systematic control had been entirely lacking, so that anything that the patients could pay for — including unlimited quantities of hard liquor — was smuggled in to them. It was for this reason, among others, that Dr. Blackman induced the doctors there to put the men under the charge of the Sisters. At once they began to complain — if of nothing else that they were now served sausages instead of steak for breakfast! They had in fact been entirely spoiled by the "patriotic" ladies who hitherto had looked after them and who had considered nothing too good for such heroes. So feeling that they could accomplish little in that atmosphere, Dr. Blackman arranged that the Sisters be transferred to another hospital; but there too they found that they were unwelcome, the subordinate officers this time being the chief troublemakers. They once went so far as to search a large basket of soiled linen that was about to be taken to St. Mary's to be washed, as though the Sisters had stolen something or were trying to pry out military secrets. In the end Sister Felicitas simply had to announce to the officers in charge that as soon as other nurses could be secured she would have to withdraw the Sisters. It was not a very pretty picture, but the fact is that, though the war killed the Nativist movement as such, it did not remove the bigotry that was widespread in America at that period. That the Sisters were Germans as well as Catholics was quite enough to bring upon them the basest ingratitude for their selfless services.

Cincinnati was a key point throughout the war, and one that was rather dangerously exposed. On at least one occasion a cavalry division of Confederates encircled it at night but decided not to attack. Nevertheless, such an attack might come, should the Southern forces find an opportunity of driving up from Kentucky. There were constant rumors that this was about to happen. So Frances wrote with a faintly detached humor: "Great excitement and ceaseless drumming in the city. The enemy is approaching. Here and there railroads were torn up and train connections are impossible. A few days ago a thick cloud of dust arose; the enemy was thought to be advancing. But excitement changed to general merriment when the cause of the dust became known — a large drove of mules were being driven into Cincinnati to be used in the war!"

She wrote in a more sober vein on July 15th, when she told

the Sisters at Aachen that the stores were closed and that soldiers were mustered to repel an assault from a Southern army thought to be only 50 miles away. She adds: "Some time ago they advanced even closer and Archbishop Purcell requested the prayers of our Recluses. I encouraged them to pray also, and they complied with great earnestness. The good Archbishop ascribes it to their pious prayers that the city was spared. We have not the least fear. So reckless and courageous a spirit predominates here, that one makes light of everything." By this time it had become evident to all observers that, however long the stubborn Confederates might prolong the war, they could not possibly win it.

The Sisters of the Poor of St. Francis in Cincinnati at the end of 1863 had 23 Sisters in perpetual vows, 17 others temporarily professed, 18 novices, and 18 postulants. At St. Mary's that year nearly 500 patients were treated. Statistically that may not sound very impressive; but to anyone who knows something of the conditions of that time, it was already evident that a sound foundation had been laid.

One slightly comical fact may be recorded before we come to another of much more importance. Until the arrival of Frances the Sisters had thought that the use of mosquito nets was contrary to holy poverty, and so had submitted to being bitten all night. Frances, with eminent good sense, decided that they should have these nets, as the loss of sleep diminished their efficiency. The important fact is that, before departing for Germany, she appointed a new Vicar for the United States in Sister Dominica. This she did in a speech delivered on the Feast of the Assumption (August 15th) in which, with the most graceful consideration, she said she was doing this to give Sister Felicitas a chance to get a much needed rest. She added that she knew that the Sister would be glad to take the lowest place in the community at Cincinnati, but she was going to take her back to Aachen. The fact is that the humid heat of the Ohio Valley told on all these Sisters who had come from the mild Rhineland. All that Sister Felicitas could say was a tremulously grateful, "Mother!" To all these Sisters superiorship was a burden, and though office of any kind is a burden that many people hanker after, what emerges very distinctly is that no single instance is known in which any of the Sisters of the Poor of St. Francis accepted superiorship except in a sacrificial spirit.

Frances no doubt condoled with her new Vicar immediately after this address, as she did later by letter. Yet not all was penitential; there was also a good deal of human grace. Thus Frances, writing to Sister Dominica on the ship on September 2nd, tells her to "have a coffee," which means a little party. Though the world does not conceive of this, there is a fair amount of mild fun in a convent.

Because of the effects of the Civil War in America, Frances departed temporarily from her principles to the extent of allowing the establishment of orphanages, or at least foundling homes. She forbade this at St. Mary's for the good reason that the crying of infants might disturb the patients there. She did, however, permit this when a separate house was secured for the children, and also at Covington, Hoboken, and at Brooklyn, when foundations were made in those places. These mostly took babies deserted by their mothers who had been deserted in their turn by soldiers. An emergency of this sort broke down all rules. But she thought of it only as a measure to meet an emergency; it was to be given up as soon as possible. In the few instances when older children were taken in, Frances insisted that they attend the ordinary schools; she remained quite adamant in her resolution that the education of such children was not part of the Sisters' vocation.

Soon after Frances's return to Aachen two other wars, of less virulence than that between the Northern and Southern states of America, involved Germany. And in both of these, Frances and her Sisters served as nurses, giving their aid impartially to the wounded of both sides. She was not concerned with the rights or wrongs of the quarrel and probably did not so much as suspect that these wars were part of a carefully thought out plan on the part of Bismarck, one that led eventually to Prussia's attack on France and the establishment of the German Empire. Nor of course did it cross her mind that all this would bring about the Kulturkampf, against which she played a quietly valiant part.

The war of 1864 was over the Schleswig-Holstein strip of Denmark. Just why this war needed to be fought at all is not very apparent, for Prussia was so overwhelmingly powerful that she could have forced her neighbor to yield after going through the farce of "arbitration." But of course Bismarck wished to display the military might of Prussia and so was determined on war. By way of concealing his next move he brought in Austria, marked down as Prussia's next victim, as an ally.

It was in the Austrian hospitals (because they were Catholic) that the Sisters mostly served, and Frances was summoned there at the personal appeal of Queen Augusta, soon to be the first Empress of Germany, and she could not have refused to respond at once to this eminently good and pious woman — even supposing that she had not been actuated by compassion. In Berlin Frances was received by the Queen with the utmost graciousness, getting from her 100 thalers for the wounded and some gold pieces; and she noticed that Augusta and the King were scraping lint for the bandages that would be needed. The Minister of War during this visit, when Frances and her companion stayed with the Borromean Sisters, assigned them for duty with the Third Field Hospital near the seat of war at Rendsburg.

Regarding this it may be sufficient to quote one of Frances's letters to the Motherhouse: "Yesterday I went with Count Galen all through Flensburg to find an abode for the Sisters. As yet the hospitals are in a sad condition. There is scarcely room for the wounded, much less for nurses. We remained half a day in a Prussian hospital, in a large room full of wounded soldiers, whose beds were the only places we could sit on to rest after our fatiguing tour of exploration.

. . . At last after many failures we succeeded in renting a room in the neighborhood, from which we go out to the sick. Today Count Galen took two of our Sisters to Schleswig, where we have five Sisters in all to minister to the wounded Austrians. The excellent Austrian commander, a polite, religious gentleman, at first quartered the Sisters in the city, but afterwards removed them to the hospital. I pity the poor Austrians with all my heart . . . Among them are many really good and simple-hearted people. With them one feels that one is with Catholics . . . Here we have constant opportunity to practice interior and exterior self-denial and mortification. But we are in good spirits. Last night we slept on straw, on the floor. When the young Sisters awoke once in a while they laughed."

Frances could stay with them only long enough to get them well started in their work. But before she left she took off her own scapular, which was marked with the red cross, and gave it to Sister Tabitha, the Sister who was left in charge, and who was not entitled to this badge of distinction, as she was not yet in perpetual vows, taking her unmarked scapular in exchange. And Frances wore Sister Tabitha's scapular and Sister Tabitha Frances's until the Sisters returned to Aachen. Then they made an exchange again.

At the conclusion of the war there came from the young Emperor Francis Joseph, who had succeeded his uncle Francis I, the godfather of Frances, a beautiful chalice in recognition of the services the Sisters had given. Its base was decorated with the letters F.J., interwoven with the imperial crown in enamel. From the Prussian government came a request that the name of every Sister who had served be sent in so that each could be given a medal. This list Frances declined to supply, saying that no individual Sister be mentioned, as all had served in the name of the community. She was herself decorated, however, with the Cross of Merit, which she accepted not for herself but for the whole Congregation.

The chief reward was that in an almost completely Protestant section of what is now Northern Germany, at Flensburg just over the present Danish border, a Catholic center was established and is still flourishing. While there during the war, Frances had written: "There is no Catholic church either here, or in Schleswig or Rendsburg, and we cannot visit our Lord in the Blessed Sacrament. But in spirit we transfer ourselves as far as St. Clare's in Aachen." Mass for the Austrian soldiers had been permitted of course, but after they had departed, the government prohibited this; only through the influence of Queen Augusta was this prohibition withdrawn. Frances had been somewhat dubious about the advisability of establishing a branch house so far away, but she had said, "As soon as I should become convinced that it was the will of God that one should be established there, I would immediately reverse my decision." Her decision was reversed as soon as it became evident that the only way this part of Germany would be allowed a Catholic church was if she set up a permanent hospital in that place.

Two years later there broke out between the former allies, Prussia and Austria, what is usually called the "Seven Weeks' War." Bismarck had carefully planned the whole thing in order to destroy even the shadowy authority of the imperial house of Hapsburg and give Northern Germany a new imperial house in the Hohenzollerns. The Austrians and their allies were overwhelmed at Sadowa in spite of several costly mistakes made by some Prussian commanders. But the war was virtually over after Sadowa, fought on July 1st, and when the Prussians were outside Vienna an armistice was concluded on the 21st, followed by a peace dictated by Bismarck.

Frances would have gladly given her aid — and to both sides — had not the issue, to everyone's surprise, been decided so quickly, but she did dispatch 20 Sisters as nurses. She was greatly distressed at the fratricidal strife and a week before its sudden conclusion wrote: "The war is taking on entirely the aspects of a religious war, and it may easily happen that the cause of Holy Church will demand martyrs." Rather

234

hopefully she thinks that some of these might be drawn from her Congregation. In this there was a good deal of discernment (as well as some slight exaggeration), for seven years later Bismarck did begin the persecution known as the Kulturkampf. At the moment, however, Bismarck did not wish to carry out that side of his policy. He was concerned first to effect the unification of the scattered German states under their own Emperor.

Between these two German wars Frances, whose health had been seriously affected during her visit to the United States, had in 1865 so serious an attack of asthma that her cousin, Dr. Gerard Schervier, thought she should be anointed. At once she improved, though she was still weak, and on April 7th, when 21 postulants received the habit, she received the new novices in her room for a few minutes. For a complete rest she went to Coblenz, where on the occasion of the twenty-fifth anniversary of the incorporation of the Rhineland with Prussia, Queen Augusta visited her friend, "the dear little mother." In a letter written on May 11th, to a Franciscan Father, Frances tells him: "Great as was my fear of dying during one of my asthmatic spells, I am not afraid of consumption. It gives a person opportunity to prepare for death." The family disease, however, never manifested itself in her; as for asthma it is a disease which often makes its victims feel themselves to be on the point of death, but of which hardly anybody actually dies. Frances, though not robust, must not be thought of as an invalid.

20

★

The Large Heart

THIS MIGHT be a good place to interrupt for a while the general narrative of events to give some consideration to the character of Frances Schervier, though by now its main lines should be apparent. There will be an opportunity here to touch on incidents not introduced before, but no formal commentary on her virtues, such as is always prepared in order to help demonstrate the heroism of any man or woman who is being considered for beatification.

First for her appearance, as we know it from the few photographs we have of her. In the family group, taken sometime before 1855, we can see what struck everybody who knew her — deeply set eyes glowing in a rather pallid face and a wide mouth which, though not usually accounted a beautiful feature, makes Frances attractive by showing a strong character which yet is very sensitive, very kind. There is something else in her remarkable eyes, a sense that she lived always *sub specie aeternitatis,* in unbroken consciousness of the Divine. Her whole bearing gave beholders the impression that she was animated solely by the love of God. This overcame her often, notably when at Christmas she read to the community the first chapter of St. John's Gospel. At the words, "The Word was made flesh," she always burst into tears.

Apart from this portrait, the only other that we have — except for one later in which she figures in a crowd and the picture taken of her wasted body as it lay in its coffin — is one taken at New York in August of 1863. Several poor pictures have been subsequently based upon it, and one good one. Sister Dominica prevailed upon Frances to allow this photograph to be taken, but only on the strict understanding that copies be limited to the houses in America. Even so, Frances, who did not like sitting for her portrait, wrote from Hoboken to Sister Dominica on August 28th, just before she sailed for Germany, "You dear naughty Sister, you have played a fine trick on me!"

That trick was nothing to the one that followed. Sister Dominica, despite her promise, could not forbear sending a copy of the photograph to the Superior at Bonn, enjoining her to keep it out of Mother Frances's sight. Frances, arriving at Bonn unexpectedly one day, saw the picture and was much surprised and not very pleased. But what might have been expected happened. In due course all the branch houses received a copy in secret; the only house left without one being the Motherhouse at Aachen. We, however, must be glad of this trick, for without it we should lack any very clear idea as to just how Frances looked. The picture showed her just as she was, because it was taken before the days of "artistic" photographers who so often try to turn their subjects into something that avoids a real likeness, making over their sitters according to their own hearts' desire. This photograph is as factual and candid as a "Holbein."

Strongly and deeply though she was apt to be moved, no one could have been less of a sentimentalist than Frances, or more cool-headed and practical. Was there a particularly loathsome case of nursing to be attended to, then she claimed that duty for herself. And in any case of nursing she neglected no smallest detail. Thus when visiting Bonn, she went one night to nurse a sick woman, who later sent to thank the local Superior — not having the slightest suspicion that she had had the attendance of that Superior's superior — and told her that her nurse had thought of everything, even the preparing of her husband's breakfast before he went to work, though this was after a long weary night of watching. As for the soiled bandages of cancer patients, Frances would, as a rule, allow nobody to handle them but herself, when they had to be taken to the hospital for washing. "No, no!" she would exclaim, half sportively, "You are not worthy to do this. First work for perfection!" She made assistance in this task a kind of reward for special zeal in the performance of duties.

Though it can hardly be said that her joy in Franciscanism equaled that of St. Francis — rather she was sedately serene — she did have some gaiety. Often she used to say: "Above all I rejoice and prize as the greatest grace that I am a child of the Holy Catholic Church; the next thing that gives me joy is being a child of holy Father Francis." If that joy will not be recognized by some people as clearly as they can see it in the Assisian, this is only because too often a prettified St. Francis has been presented to the world, not the man of the astounding experience of the stigmata but merely the one who picked flowers and patted animals. None of us would want to lose that charming side of the Saint, but it would be doing him the gravest injustice to imagine that this is the most important thing about him.

Frances Schervier drew her joy from the same source that St. Francis drew his, from love of Christ, in her case shown through corporal works of mercy. "Whenever," she said, "I give food and drink to Our Lord in His poor, I always feel an increase of sensible love for our Divine Saviour; this compensates me abundantly for the little sacrifices which this exercise of charity imposes on me. Oh, how pure and sweet was this love!" It had filled her while she was still a small child; she may be described as having been a Franciscan almost before she had heard of St. Francis.

She lost no opportunity for even the little services that are commonly neglected as not very important. Thus, meeting some people in a railway station who were heavily burdened with baggage, she hurried forward to carry a couple of their packages to their destination in the city. Similarly she would go a long way out of her way — and when she was busy — to direct a girl who was a stranger to the place she wanted to go, again insisting on carrying her baggage. Nor did she, though she was in a religious habit, hesitate offering such attentions to feeble old men, if it was only to help them cross the street. But if necessary she would do much more — as when she helped a one-legged man to make his way home, with his arm leaning on her shoulder. She had cared very little for what are called appearances. Her safe cloister was her own kind and pure heart.

In the cloister her joy and kindness were even more visible. She condoled with a sick Sister who was unable to attend the saying of the Office, explaining that this was a sacrifice for which God would reward her in heaven. Then she confided: "Often I feel so sorry for you that I lower my own voice [in choir], so that you may not suffer so keenly." (Could anything be more delicately considerate?) She went on: "In fact, I must always moderate my voice during the recitation of the Office, lest I pray too loud and drown out the others . . . I should like to call again and again the praise and glory of our God in a voice so loud that all men might hear it." There were times, especially during the great feasts of the Church, when she was unable to restrain this mode of expressing her joy; then she almost shouted the words of the psalms and canticles. On the other hand, on All Souls' Day, she would pray in the chapel almost the entire time, saying, "Today I cannot work; I can only pray."

To love Christ with a whole heart she had to be poor, like Christ, and one of the poor herself. Poverty was to be in everything — food and furniture and clothing, and also in the chapels of her convents. "[This] must be their chief ornament. By this we shall be known to be true children of St. Francis, who demanded that everything be removed that would dim or wipe away in the least degree the features of poverty."

In this there was not merely physical poverty but that poverty of spirit which, if it be lacking, makes everything of no value, the poverty which comes from interior wealth. "Poverty without charity, humility without charity, penance without charity," she was wont to say, "none of these is of any avail before God." All were crowned by joy.

Her sense of humor was sly and droll rather than exuberant. But now and then she reminds us of that indefatigable humorist St. Philip Neri. One day walking with a companion in clear mild weather along the river bank of Cologne she insisted that they keep their umbrellas up. "Let it be so," she remarked drily. "People think us fools already! Give them a good laugh." She was fond of describing herself as "God's little donkey," fit for nothing but hard work.

Her love of sparrows — and few people would think them the most attractive of birds — reminds one of St. Francis's special fondness for larks. The sparrows, like the larks, were clad in brown, and so seemed to her rather Franciscan. She had loved flowers and poetry from childhood, and she continued to love them all her life, though she eventually gave up the making of verses. She also clung to such local customs as the "blessing of St. John's wine" on the feast of the apostle, when whatever was in the cellars of any of her houses was thankfully dedicated as God's good gift, though she herself hardly ever tasted it, and then only when it was almost drowned in water.

Before coming to some instances of her boundless, and often seemingly rash, charity, let it be noted in what spirit it was exercised. Thus, writing to Sister Vincentia at Cincinnati on September 25th, 1871, she says: "I well understand that there is need of relinquishing for America a few more trusty Sisters; we shall do our utmost, dear Sister. One thing I ask of you: send me a list of those Sisters whom you deem most suitable for there. I will then try and make a selection and do all I can to obtain the consent of the Sister Councillors. Let us make sacrifices in a heroic, sensible way." That conjunction of words — heroic and sensible — is very characteristic of Frances.

Yet when we come to her manifold generosities we are positively staggered. Her charities, one would have thought, would have been great enough, had they been confined to her chosen field, work among the sick poor. But she always stood towards everybody with open hands, rejoicing in any opportunity for giving, especially if this could be done in secret. Father Jeiler estimates that towards the support of religious projects with which her Congregation had no connection at least 100,000 marks passed through her hands. The very fact that wealthy benefactors in later years — those who were aware of her unselfishness — brought her large sums to dispose of made her all the more inclined to donate the money in many instances to enterprises for which she was in no way responsible, rather than use it herself, pressing though her needs always were.

A favorite charity of hers was to help students for the priesthood at the archdiocesan seminary or the University of Bonn. Her delicacy of feeling here was as great as her charity. Thus when a young man called to see a Sister he knew, hoping that she would pave the way for him to Mother Frances, and found that the Sister was not at home, Frances went to pains to have him hunted out; she then did for him what she had done for several other young men in a situation of financial stringency. And a secular priest who wished to enter a religious order but who was unable to do so because his mother was dependent on him was relieved of all cares by Frances's promising to look after his mother so long as she lived.

Then, too, she had a particularly tender feeling towards families who had seen better days and had fallen into difficulties. She knew how hard the goad of poverty presses in such cases, for people of this sort are humiliated and have not yet learned the stratagems with which others of the poor contrive to avoid some of their discomforts. As such people cannot bring themselves to beg, especially as their needs, if presented, might seem exorbitantly high, she used to go in search of them. Father Jeiler tells of a case that had come under his notice when she sent no less a sum than 6,000 thalers to a family of this kind. In this case a priest was her emissary; more often it was one of the Sisters. Then she would say, "Sister, take this bag of money to the So-and-so's. I shall not be able to eat a mouthful of dinner until I know that this has been done." This was a class of the poor of whom even the generous among the well-to-do rarely think. Just because they may still have a few good clothes and some remnants of good furniture, the world finds it hard to believe that their larders may be empty.

Her delicacy towards people more obviously of the poor was equally as great. She found that a man being nursed by the Sisters of a branch house was in need of a watch. At once she told a Sister, "So as not to embarrass him, put it quietly on his table, so that St. Anthony shall let him find it in the morning." And when one of the inmates of a home she maintained for the aged expressed a wish for some trout, she ordered, "Bring them to good Henry, and may he enjoy them!" That he was not a Catholic did not in the least diminish her promptitude; nor even did the fact that he was rather feeble-minded and might therefore be merely venting an idle whim. On the eve of St. Francis's Day, she made a custom of having the poor admitted en masse. Crowds of them would come, to congratulate her on her nameday, but also to pour out their troubles. None of them departed without alms. Jeiler says that on one of these days the Procurator told him that over 1,000 marks had been distributed.

What gave her the greatest pleasure was in assisting other branches of the Franciscans, or in helping them to get founded. She aided a community at Olpe in Westphalia that was doing a work somewhat similar to her own, another in

Belgium, and a third, headed by Mother Teresa Bonzel, that now has two provinces in the United States. To the Poor Clares she was most devoted, and when in 1853 she visited their convent at Tongres in Belgium, she would have prostrated herself at the feet of the Abbess had this been permitted. Instead she was drawn to her feet and embraced and treated while their guest like one of themselves. They knew that she was a Poor Clare in all her feelings.

Perhaps the most remarkable instance of this kind of activity was the aid she gave John Philip Hoever, when, after the death of his wife, he associated himself with a small group of friends, forming a kind of novitiate, to which Frances supplied the necessary food.

This group at the outset lacked, as Frances never had, certainty as to what should be their distinctive work. Frances prayed with great fervor that they might be directed towards it, until one night in a dream the Divine Child appeared to her in swaddling clothes. This she took to be an indication as to what Brother John's work was to be, so the next morning she sent him a baby boy. The Brothers were at Mass in their parish church at the time, and greatly surprised were they, upon their return home, to find this infant lying in John Hoever's bed. But they at once recognized that this was the sign of their vocation, and the following year (1858) they received ecclesiastical approbation under the title of the Poor Brothers of St. Francis. When two years later they bought a large house for an orphanage, Frances advised a girl who was about to join her own Congregation to give her dowry of 9,000 thalers to the Brothers instead of to the Sisters. It was through Frances's efforts in their behalf that in 1866 they migrated to the United States, and two years later established themselves in Cincinnati.

This mention of a possible dowry leads me to say that some of the Sisters brought larger or smaller sums with them into the community. These Frances did not refuse, but she left the money at the novice's disposal — uninvested — until her perpetual profession, when it was immediately used in some good cause. Nobody was ever barred because she could bring nothing, and at least one girl was rejected because she talked a bit too complacently about the wealth the Sisters would acquire with her. Until then Frances had been on the point of accepting this applicant; but she decided that this concern about money was not one of the attributes she looked for. Money was acceptable only if poverty of spirit accompanied it, for there alone was true riches.

Her reverence for priests reminds us of St. Francis. But with her it is extended even to a priest's lifeless body, as when she took from the morgue that of a Belgian priest killed in a railway accident to give it fitting burial.

Toward the friars of the First Order Frances showed such veneration that the least among the lay brothers was treated by her with the greatest possible deference. When the Saxon Province, which had been officially (but not quite) obliterated under Napoleon and then by the government of Saxony, was restored, she aided them to settle at Düsseldorf and Burtscheid, near Aachen. It was the appeal of this community, when it founded a college at Teutopolis in Illinois, which made so strong an appeal to her sympathies that, against her better judgment, she allowed some of her Sisters, for a while, to take charge of the domestic arrangements of the institution.

Much of the same story can be told of what she did for the Jesuits and Redemptorists, and if her help here was on a smaller scale, this was because these orders were in a better position to help themselves. It may, however, be said with truth that nobody ever appealed to Frances in vain. If at the moment she happened to lack any means for giving, she prayed until the means were forthcoming. And when she did not actually supply money herself, she found means of unearthing benefactors for them elsewhere, though people in her position might well be pardoned had they kept such benefactors for their own needs.

It might also be mentioned that she felt an intense interest in Jews. This was no doubt increased when, in 1870, she made the acquaintance in France of Herman Cohen, once almost as much celebrated for his infidelity as for his musical gifts, but by that time a priest. But this interest — rather this compassionate sympathy — did not originate with Father Cohen. Of the over 100 women whom she received into the Motherhouse for a course of instruction before they were received into the Church, a good third were Jewesses. To one of these converts of hers she wrote: "You have entered the sanctuary of the Church. You now belong to the one flock of Christ and are a member of that sacred body of which Christ is the head. Now I can greet you as a sister, as a dear sister in the Lord. Mary, the holy, the immaculate is our Mother . . . Who can comprehend the graces, the bliss, you, the highly favored, have received? I can give thanks only in mute admiration. Today I cannot speak to you of anything else; the day, the time is too sacred."

Frances's friendship with Clara Fey and with Clara's two priest brothers has been often mentioned. A little gift she made Clara may seem trifling but eventually it had wide effects. It was only a miniature Bambino for a Christmas crib. But one of the Sisters of Clara's convent learned how to reproduce it, first in a small size and then a large. We hear in 1894 of 10 big packing cases of these figures being sent out, some containing a complete full-sized crib and others with the diminutive figures which Frances had started.

Clara's brother Andrew was the director of her educational enterprises. He was naturally frequently brought in contact with Frances, and of her generosity he says that it was "incomparable in great things and small. One could not visit her without having to accept something. How often she compelled me to accept large sums for the relief of poor families, even at times when she was oppressed with debt. One had to be very careful not to mention the wants of others in conversation with her." He goes on to tell of saying something about a girl he knew who wished to enter a contemplative order but who could not do so because of lacking the necessary dowry of 3,000 thalers. That very day the girl received the required sum from Frances.

Each founder of a religious congregation has some distinguishing virtue, almost peculiarly his own. Of Frances Schervier it need not be asserted that her charity exceeded all others (for charity, being an interior disposition, is not for me to assess). But perhaps I may be permitted to say that I have never heard of a more free-handed person. Others, being much more affluent, may have given more, but surely none can ever have given so munificently from such scanty resources. If that is the standard — as it should be — I can think of nobody who is her equal.

To say that she had courage — and we have seen how dramatically it sometimes displayed itself — is hardly more than to say that she had virtue. For the wise Dr. Johnson, while rightly denying that courage is the whole of virtue, also denied that any virtue can be safe without it. Usually Frances's courage came out in forms less startling than some of those we have witnessed; her generosity in giving, her whole life was supremely courageous. But more soberly she recommends fortitude to those who had followed her: "Never allow yourselves, dear Sisters, to be cast down by adversity or elated by prosperity. It is one of the characteristics of faith to keep the soul humble when things go well and firm when they go wrong." With this we come again upon her prevalent tone of quiet serenity.

Of her simplicity two examples may be cited. One has an element of quaintness about it that makes it all the more engaging. When Cardinal von Geissel blessed St. Mary's Hospital in Cologne in 1864, he attended the reception held afterwards and passed among the guests affably offering his snuff-box to the men present. One of these men refused the offer, saying, "I do not use snuff!" but in a tone so offensive as to be a rebuff to a friendly gesture. Frances, feeling that his action might be resented by the other guests, went up to the Cardinal and said: "Will Your Eminence permit me to take a pinch of snuff for the Sisters?" Probably she only pretended to take it, for she would not have known how to use snuff. But her action served its purpose by restoring good humor in gales of laughter.

Again, while dyeing Easter eggs during Holy Week, she said to the Sister helping her: "How fortunate we are in being able to gladden the hearts of others. But first let us kneel down and say an Our Father that we do it with a pure intention." That she should have done so on an occasion like this makes it evident that her actions were not classified into categories of varying values; they were all done for the glory of God.

Her austerity of life has been often noticed in these pages. What should be also remarked is that when this led her, as it sometimes did — especially in the early days of her Superiorship — to be too strict towards others, she would privately do penance for this fault. In an instruction given to the assembled Superiors of her branch houses delivered on Pentecost Tuesday, 1869, she told them: "If you correct passionately, that would be very harmful and profit nothing with the Sisters. Do not think you must reprove and punish every fault, always standing with the stick, blaming faults of the Sisters and thereby committing greater faults yourself." She was by that time a seasoned hand in her Superiorship.

Sometimes her penitence for overseverity — rarely though this occurred in later years — may have been so embarrassing as to be virtually the infliction of a new punishment. Similarly some of Frances's ascetic practices are not in accord with the modern theory of asceticism, which lays the emphasis upon interior mortification and not upon physical discomforts. To have mixed bitter gall with her food on Fridays, especially as she ate so little, savors of the rigors of the Desert. Still, even in our own time there are people who wear hair shirts and sleep on the bare boards of the floor, so that it is hardly becoming to those of us who make life as easy as possible for ourselves to offer anything but admiration to one who took her religion in a more drastic style. Nevertheless it is hard to see why one who suffered so much from her various ailments needed to have added to them of her own accord. She herself, writing to one of the Sisters — an asthmatic — about her own asthma, said: "Heat and cold, wind and rain exert a great influence on you and me, and are for us the best of mortifications. They are special graces from above. By their means we can perform great and continual works of penance which are the more meritorious because they are performed secretly, and nobody has even the least suspicion of them."

She might have let it go at that, or, had she wanted more, have accepted as the most salutary of penances what Gerard Manley Hopkins has called "The bitter taste of me." But no, in all sorts of small ways she had to add external acts of penance. Thus when, coming in very tired one evening, the Sister serving at supper gave her a boiled egg as well as the soup that the others got, she said, "If you want me to eat the soup please take away the egg." On another occasion when a postulant, who was later Sister Eucheria, set before Frances, after she had returned from a long journey, a plate of soup better than the other Sisters were getting, Frances exchanged bowls with the server, laughing (one is glad to record) mischievously as she did this.

Though Frances was perhaps inclined to be more punctilious than a good many other Superiors — for she declared that fidelity to duty and love of God are synonymous — so strongly did she feel about rash judgments that she used to declare that, in her experience, most souls who lapsed into tepidity began with censoriousness. The dictum was one of profound psychological truth. Again she used to say: "Combat a temptation to rash judgment as resolutely as you would a temptation against chastity." And in a circular letter written in 1866 on the Feasts of Our Lady of Victories and St. Francis (which happened to fall together that year, as they did when she made her First Communion), she said: "Let us take no scandal; let us not judge. It is not enough not to give scandal; we should take none, if possible. Let us close our eyes, in case we are not Superiors, to the disedifying conduct of others, and, I repeat it, judge not. Our Lord will not pass judgment on us for the conduct of others but for our own actions."

Upon obedience, Frances laid a very special emphasis. She herself could, as a rule, practice it only by accepting the cross of office, for this was so much against all her inclinations that it was a kind of act of obedience to those who had elected her. Once, when she seemed more than usually reluctant to take up her burden, she submitted as soon as the Archbishop had made his wishes known. And whenever she had occasion to stay for a day or two as a guest with another community, it was remarked that though she was under no obligation in the matter, she would not do the smallest thing out of the ordinary — such as seeing a visitor or making a visit herself — without asking permission to do so, as though she was the most newly arrived novice there. A long catena of her sayings on this point could be compiled: but these four or five will suffice:

Often recall that you have chosen the religious state to live a crucified life, in penance, humility, and total submission to obedience.

If a Sister does not regard as holy and exalted the duty with which she is charged, no matter of what kind, whether great or small, she is not suited to our Congregation.

If we would know whether we truly love God, let us ask ourselves whether we fulfill all our duties faithfully and fervently for the love of Him who assigns them to us.

In a certain sense, faithful religious can be called martyrs, for by fidelity to their vocation they give testimony to the holiness of the law of God and to the power of His grace every day and every hour of their lives.

With any Sister who complained of the hardness of her lot she had scant patience. "Well, you chose it that way," she told one who said that she (probably only momentarily) found things difficult.

To these quotations one more should be added. It comes from a circular letter dated from the Motherhouse on the Feast of the Espousals of the Blessed Virgin, January 23, 1863:

Whoever cannot submit herself wholly to obedience must either leave voluntarily or be dismissed. Hence I urge such to leave at once, without waiting to be sent away. No long procedure is necessary; the affair can soon be arranged. Every well-ordered Congregation not only may, but must, expel unruly, dissatisfied members. I say expel, for such have already by their interior rebellion severed themselves from the body of the Congregation.

How literal Frances could be in her demand for obedience is shown by her treatment of the Sister whose duty it was to provide the habits for the novices. Because she feared that she would not be able to finish her work in time, she asked permission to work until ten that night. Not having finished her work at ten she ventured to go on until eleven, and Frances with her own hands undid all that had been sewn during that unauthorized hour.

If that sounds rather severe, it should be noted that, now and then obedience had to be inculcated, not only by precept but by special example. Frances usually tempered her principles with characteristic kindness. Each Sister felt herself to be the apple of the Superior's eye, and therefore served all the more eagerly in love. But as for anybody's being allowed to feel that a long illness had made her an encumbrance in the community, she had to be assured that the patient endurance of her sufferings was itself prayer, and that "Their couch of pain was their workshop and altar, the place of their employment and sacrifice." She was exceptionally solicitous for them all in any sickness. As for those who were dying, it was her custom, instead of kneeling at the bedside and praying, to stand at the head, with her little shawl wrapped around her shoulders, and to say aloud pious ejaculations, one after another, which increased in beauty and fervor. Perhaps she had in mind that this was how Father Istas used to pray beside her bed when she was suffering from typhoid fever many years before.

In spite of her talk about summarily dismissing the dissatisfied, she realized that sometimes dissatisfaction may be justified and that, even when it is not, concessions may have to be made to human temperament. To one unhappy Sister she wrote on June 12, 1876, only a short while before her own death: "If you cannot continue where you are, tell your Superior to send you to the Motherhouse, for I cannot permit you to pine away physically and morally."

But perhaps the shortest and clearest way of illustrating her combination of firmness and mildness — with mildness always predominating — is to repeat a story that Father Jeiler tells. When Frances heard of an altercation between two Sisters, she was so distressed that in the refectory at dinner she intoned the *Miserere* to make amends for their fault. She supposed that this would bring both Sisters to her, asking pardon. When this did not happen, she went to the one whom she considered mainly to blame and said, "I was so disturbed on your account that I was resolved to sleep on the floor tonight in reparation. But go and ask pardon and then come back to me." The Sister was herself by this time very upset and returned in tears, whereupon Frances to comfort her gave her a nice pear! This sudden transition from the stick to the stick of candy is very characteristic of Frances. The Sisters had to be very bad children indeed not to get a lollipop after a scolding. Frances was, in fact, inclined to be indulgent towards the Sisters, especially in those little homely ways which women often appreciate more than larger concessions.

Regarding Frances's interior life we know very little except the fragmentary account she wrote of her early years. Even that was most reticent and reserved and would not have been undertaken at all except under obedience to her confessor. This alone, she felt, saved it from being a breach of humility.

251

Though in early life Frances sometimes appeared to be self-willed, actually she took the position she did because she believed that it was in obedience to God. Her lifelong submission to the Divine Will was of course the essence of humility, manifested over and over again in the most signal fashion.

It was in humility that she renounced — not once but many times — her longing for the contemplative life. Yet she undertook no duty until she had first lifted her heart to heaven, so that all might be done in the spirit of prayer. One private practice of hers we are told about: until her asthma weakened her, she watched in prayer in the chapel every Thursday until the stroke of midnight brought Friday. But though her spiritual director Father Bonaventure Wessendorf says that she attained a high degree of mental prayer, he imparts no more information than that; so that we have to infer the rest from what we know of her customary actions.

Frances was often very prompt in decision, but whenever time permitted she would pray a long time and consult others before doing anything of importance. Yet in an emergency she relied, not on her personal judgment, but upon interior illumination; and though she did make a few mistakes — not because of this reliance but because her kind heart found it very hard to refuse an appeal for help — ordinarily she proceeded, in spite of her natural impulsiveness and audacity, with the utmost caution and prudence.

Her spiritual insight was sometimes rather startling. Thus when Sister Eutropia Thielen applied to enter the Congregation, Frances asked: "Why do you wish this?" She got the answer, "That I may serve God and be perfect." "But," Frances enquired, "are you willing to be humiliated and despised, to live poor and obedient?" Catherine (as she was then) thought a moment before returning hesitantly: "Mother, by the grace of God I think I may be able to do that." Frances's face brightened: "Yes, my child," she said, "by the grace of God. I see you have a vocation. Had you said, 'Oh, yes, I can do that,' I should not have accepted you.

Of ourselves we can do none of these things. No, only by the grace of God." We also hear of many occasions when she read a troubled Sister's mind, greatly to that Sister's surprise. But things of another sort also occurred, of which this may be taken as a sample. One day she told a Sister to go and visit her father at once. When the Sister remarked that there was no need for this, as her father was very well, Frances made the rejoinder, "You had better not delay beyond tomorrow or the day after." The man was dead a few days later. Whether this was due to the possession of what is called "second sight" or real prophecy cannot be confidently determined. But we are assured that the pure in heart shall see God, and according to all experience, spiritual insight is one of the results of holiness.

This holiness impressed itself upon all the priests who knew her. Still more did it impress itself upon the Sisters. But when one of them ventured to remark one day at recreation, "Mother, you will be canonized some day," Frances replied with the light jest, "Many things will happen before that."

Second Visit to America

AT PENTECOST, 1867, Frances was elected again. This was the occasion to which reference has already been made, when office had virtually to be forced upon her. She deferred to the wishes of the new Archbishop of Cologne, Paul Melchers, but she would allow nobody to congratulate her on what she had undertaken only in a spirit of sacrifice. Her feelings about the burden of office came out in a letter she wrote on November 16th, 1876, to Sister Vincentia, the American Vicar: "Let us then continue to endure and remain beneath the cross as our dear Lord wills. The desire to be released from it is not sinful, if it be subordinated to the will of God. Let us surrender ourselves entirely to Him, so that He may dispose of us according to His good will and pleasure." In much the same terms, but even more strongly, she had written on November 9th, 1869, to Sister Blanca, when appointing her novice mistress at Cincinnati: "It is easy for a subject to sanctify herself, but hard, very hard for a Superior, because with her own sanctification is connected also that of the souls confided to her. But whenever obedience imposes an office, one should accept it with cheerful disposition, firm confidence in God, and an absolute distrust of one's own powers . . . That this is hard, very hard, especially when the office entails heavy responsibilities, is but natural; if this were not the case, it would be no good sign." It is a broad general rule that the person best fitted for office is the one who says, *Nolo episcopari.* But here there is a good deal more than the decent modesty normally requisite; we see a profound humility.

There was always with Frances an additional reason operating: her constant wish to retire to the contemplative life. But as God so clearly willed her to be a Martha instead of a Mary, she gladly submitted. Just as many of the most exalted mystics have been people of immense external activity, so also those whose vocation is to the active life, sometimes have a degree of union with God that makes one feel that they also should be placed among the mystics. Frances, by becoming a Martha, became a Mary too. What mattered in her case, as in every case, was readiness to conform completely to the Divine Will.

By this time she was able to count among her branch houses in Germany those at Bonn, Cologne (where there were three) Deutz, Mülheim, Kalk, Siegburg, Mainz, Minden, Coblenz, Ratigen, Kaiserswerth, Crefeld, Eschweiler, Euskirchen, Stolberg, Erfurt, and Flensburg. Similarly the work in the United States had grown, with Cincinnati steadily increasing in strength and with branch houses in the Middle West (about which more in a moment), with a cluster of them in and around New York City. But though some American recruits were gained, it was still necessary to send Sisters from Germany. At the end of 1864 there were in America 26 Sisters perpetually professed and wearing the red cross on their scapulars, 27 Sisters in their first vows, 21 novices and 20 postulants. The following year the corresponding figures were 26, 27, 24 and 30. However, the year 1866 shows a considerable advance, for though the professed Sisters had not greatly increased in numbers, there were 42 novices.

The most notable change in the American scene was in the small hospital which Frances had at last been prevailed upon to conduct in New York City. It was in the Redemptorist

255

parish on East 3rd Street. There difficulties had been created by the attempts made by several among the good Fathers to turn the place into something for the exclusive use of their own flock — a proceeding flatly at variance with the principles of Frances, who absolutely refused to admit any distinction on the ground of race or color or creed. It was an old difficulty in a new form; apparently it was very hard to make people understand how strictly Frances had limited the scope of her work, on the one hand, and how indefinitely she had extended it, on the other.

The Redemptorists' parish was predominantly German. Perhaps not unnaturally, the English-speaking pastors of the city disapproved of Sisters who came to beg in their parishes for activities from which their own parishioners would derive no benefit. This being the situation, Frances purchased elsewhere in New York a plot of ground for $45,000, intending to build there, free from all hampering limitations. Her strongest card, however, was that she allowed it to be understood that unless she were permitted faithfully to conform to the Constitutions of her Congregation she would withdraw all her Sisters. The fact that she had land for a new hospital — the fact too that whereas in 1865 only 44 patients had been cared for at St. Francis's Hospital,* in 1866 the number had risen to 485, and in 1867 to 593 — was a means of inducing the few individual Redemptorists who had been rather too insistent in their demands to be amenable to a compromise. Under the new arrangement, the hospital was declared to be open to anybody, and the Sisters, while being invested with the proprietorship, agreed that the Redemptorists should be acknowledged as the founders of the institution and that their parishioners should be given special consideration. As for the plot of land that had been bought for another hospital, that was disposed of at a substantial profit.

* This institution is not to be confused with the St. Francis Hospital in the Bronx. When this new hospital was dedicated in March, 1906, the institution on Fifth Street became known as St. Francis Home for the Aged. It was closed in March, 1951.

Frances had always had the greatest admiration for the Redemptorists, and she still had. But she knew her own mind, and the precise limits of her distinctive vocation. She was as overjoyed as the Fathers on 3rd Street that a *modus vivendi* had been reached and that what had threatened to be a heavy storm had blown itself safely out, and all misunderstandings were removed.

An ecclesiastical difficulty of another kind arose about the same time in Germany, when a question was raised by the Franciscan Fathers as to whether the more recently admitted members of the Congregation had ever been received as tertiaries or were entitled to wear the habit. It was pointed out that latterly the vestings had been conducted by Canon Kloth, and as he was not himself a Franciscan, there was reason to ask whether they were valid. To allay all doubts, whatever might be technically lacking was supplied by a Franciscan Father, and both in Germany and the United States the practice was introduced of having those who were about to receive the habit at the hands of the Bishop or his representative be first incorporated into the Third Order by a friar. Some years later the Holy See ruled that Bishops were empowered to perform all that was required in the case of communities subject to them. On such occasions Franciscans might or might not be present — usually one of them *did* assist; but the jurisdiction over the Sisters was episcopal not Franciscan, thought it need not be said that they did not value their Franciscan connection any the less.

The main reason for Frances's second visit to the United States was to acquaint herself on the spot with whatever problems might have arisen, to see how matters were developing, and to renew the acquaintance of the Sisters she already knew, as well as to make the acquaintance of those whom she had not yet met. Such a visit has a tremendous revivifying force, especially when conducted by such a person as Frances Schervier.

Another reason, however, was that in the fall of 1866 Sister

Dominica, the Vicar for America had died. Regarding this Frances wrote that year on St. Michael's Day to the Sisters: "What shall I say? The message you sent me has inflicted a deep wound on my heart; indeed, I scarcely know how anything could have affected me more keenly . . . Truly, it was an Isaac who had to be slain. As much as you long for me, even so, and more, do I desire to be with you. I will endeavor to come in a short time . . . See in Sister Antonia your temporary Superior. Obey her with willingness and in a childlike spirit, according to the example of our holy Father Francis, who could say of himself that he would obey as willingly a novice of one day — if such were given him as a superior — as he would the oldest member of the Order. On the other hand, let Sister Antonia remember that, as Superior, she must be the servant of all. And then be comforted, dear Sister Antonia; you will not have to bear the cross long . . . I mentioned the death of our dear Sister Baptista. At that time we did not know of our loss in America. And yet for the past two weeks I have had a premonition of it. Yes, I even spoke of it."

A week or so later Frances wrote to the Sisters again, saying that a new Vicar for America had been appointed, adding: "Receive the Sister whom I am sending you as though I myself . . . came to you . . . Make no conjectures as to the Sister chosen for you, but receive in the spirit of faith the one designated for you as the representative of our Divine Master, with childlike and reverential submission." In a postscript she adds: "My guardian angel urged me to tell you that you should exercise tender care for the good Sister whom I am sending you, as the climate will be strange for her." The new Vicar turned out to be Sister Paula, one of the two daughters of the Frau Nellessen who had given the furnishing for the altar in the house beyond St. James's Gate in 1846. She had served as First Assistant to Frances since the death of Catherine Daverkosen and was therefore a most precious gift. For America she proved to be a most happy selection. Even so, Frances felt that she should visit the United States herself.

On Easter Sunday, April 12, 1868, two days before Frances departed for the United States, she assembled the Sisters in the Motherhouse and addressed them in burning words based on the last discourse of our Lord to His disciples. Especially were they urged to the practice of sisterly affection. The next day, when she said farewell to the sick Sisters, the parting was harrowing, for several of them were in such a condition that they could not hope to see Frances again. Especially was this true of Sister Cupertina, who in her childlike simplicity said it seemed hard for her to lose the help she would get from Mother Frances at the hour of death. "Still," she went on, "I am ready to make even this sacrifice and will ask my guardian angel to give you notice as soon as it happens." And this really did come about, for Frances was moved to think of poor Cupertina at the very hour, as investigation subsequently showed, that she passed from this world.

On May 6th, the Feast of the Patronage of St. Joseph, the *Ville de Paris* arrived at New York; and waiting there for Frances and her two companion Sisters, were Sister Paula, the Superiors of the houses in the East, of which there were now five, and several other Sisters. She was conducted at once to the new convent at Hoboken, where all the Sisters of the East were waiting in the chapel to celebrate her safe arrival. There they chanted the *Laudate Dominum omnes gentes*, after which Frances knelt before the altar to offer a prayer of thanksgiving and, turning to the Sisters she blessed them. In the recreation room afterwards the Sisters vented their joy by singing a song of welcome that had been specially composed. One hears much of these songs and poems; they were probably rarely artistic gems but rather the kind of family versifying common enough at birthdays and other events. Good simple hearts — all they aimed at was making the warmth of their affection known!

The visitation of the Eastern houses began the Sunday after Frances's arrival with Hoboken, where there was a great contrast between the quarters occupied then and those of 1863.

They had, besides a real convent, a well-ordered hospital and a special department for the care of children, a charge that had come to them after the Civil War and was still a necessity.

In the infirmary was an Irish-American postulant who, in anticipation of Mother Frances's arrival, had tried to learn some German — enough to answer a few simple questions. When the moment arrived her German deserted her, but not her Irish impulsiveness. She sprang out of bed, to throw herself at Frances's feet, until suddenly abashed, she permitted herself to be led back to bed. In the conversation that followed, Frances showed that she understood the Irish temperament, and how best to confirm the postulant's vocation. The girl was thrilled to be told, through the interpreting Sister, "I love the Green Island." A lifelong devotion was instantly created, and the Annals record that as Sister Beatrix, our former postulant often received help from Frances, after her death, and had never invoked her in vain, as she testified in 1898.

After affairs in the hospital in New York City had been disposed of, Brooklyn received Frances's attention. The house there had been opened in 1864, just after Frances's previous visit to the United States, and had passed through periods of great trial. First the children the Sisters took in, as a war emergency, contracted a very contagious eye disease, and when the orphanage was closed — from the beginning it had been understood that this would happen as soon as possible — the displeasure was almost universal among a people who could not understand that orphanages definitely fell outside the scope of the work of the Congregation. But in 1867 the hospital at Brooklyn had treated 198 patients, and in March of the year of Frances's arrival three adjoining houses had been purchased, making possible a much wider field of operations. This fact served to reconcile Brooklyn to the departure of the children.

Jersey City and Newark, the most recently established

house in the East, were also visited. Here Bishop Bayley, a Roosevelt on his mother's side and the nephew of Mother Seton, destined to be an Archbishop of Baltimore, heartily seconded the efforts being made by Monsignor George Doane and Father Bernard McQuaid (later Bishop of Rochester) on the Sisters' behalf. Father McQuaid, upon their arrival, led loud cheers in public and exclaimed, "Happy day for Newark! St. John at the Lateran Gate! This is the grandest day that Newark has ever seen!" Monsignor Doane used to say that Frances Schervier was one of the uncanonized saints. She, for her part, remarked to the Newark Sisters, when the Monsignor visited her in the Bishop's company, "What must heaven be if earth contains such excellent persons!" In such an atmosphere the success of the Newark enterprise was assured.

The center of American operation, however, remained Cincinnati, and there Frances, accompanied by Sister Paula and another Sister, arrived on May 23rd, very tired, of course, after their long train journey, but to be greeted with jubilation. This was very delightful, but a little rest would have been welcome, which could not be, as the very next day the new hospital at Covington was to be dedicated, and to it Mrs. Peter wanted to take Frances in her carriage, driven by her colored coachman "Coony," in which she never failed, except in the very worst weather, to take a morning drive. Such ceremonies are always very exhausting, even when, as in this instance, they gave a sense of satisfaction over work well done. Hitherto the Sisters had been quartered in a little house on Seventh Street; now on Eleventh Street they obtained a much larger and more suitable building.

With Bishop Carrell, Frances talked in French, and in his presence she was presented with the deed to the property. It was a pleasure to her to hear that much of the needed money had been collected by some of the most prominent men of the city and that they had not felt it beneath their dignity to go begging from door to door, basket in hand. Something of the spirit of the Sisters had taken possession of their minds. But the project owed most of all to Father Conrad Rotter, who had asked the Bishop to appoint a temporary substitute to his parish so that he might devote himself entirely to the gathering of funds for the hospital.

Covington was still, in one of its departments, a foundling home. And when late one evening a man brought a colored child there, Frances had it baptized at once, as it was ill, and herself became its godmother, giving it the name of Francis. While on her visitation at Covington, Mother Frances showed great interest in this child, often warming its little face with her breath and, when she could not go to it herself, would say to Sister Emilia the Superior, "Dear Sister, would you kindly look once more to see how little Francis is." But two days later baby Francis died. Frances wrote from Covington to Sister Fidelis in Germany, "In our hospital here are many dear little sick children, who will soon be among the angels. It would do your heart good if you could tend these little ones, some black, others white."

The work at St. Mary's had grown, so that it was always crowded to capacity and sometimes beyond. Yet financial difficulties had increased since the war. The possibilities of begging had fallen off in Cincinnati, and few American bishops were disposed, as in the past, to permit the Sisters to solicit alms in their dioceses because of the hard times. Several Sisters had been obliged during the previous year to go as far afield as Cuba asking money from the well-to-do for the support of their work, being introduced to Cuba by the Religious of the Sacred Heart at Seventh Street, New York City. This excursion had been very successful, but even with that and with loads of provisions regularly brought in from the Minster farmers under the care of the Precious Blood Fathers, it was hard to make both ends meet. But the Archbishop had ordained that the customary offerings in Cincinnati during the Holy Year of 1865 were to be given to the hospital, and these amounted to $1730. And the Sisters were glad that the annual concert brought in as much as $710, as clear profit, though this was less than had been sometimes obtained in the past. Yet they had to say sadly that 10 times as much would hardly suffice for their needs. Fortunately, just before Frances's arrival, the concert of that year, as reported by the *Wahrheitsfreund*, netted $3,000, with Mozart Hall filled to capacity; and this must have meant that the price of the tickets had been raised to a dollar.

For some time past the more delicate among the Sisters and the postulants — those unsuited to the hard work of trundling heavy baskets of food from the markets — had tried to help in another way: by the making of vestments and artificial flowers for the altar. In order to train them, Sister Norberta had been sent in 1863 to take lessons in embroidery from the Sisters of the Poor Child Jesus at Aachen. Now this enterprise was proving the main means of support, for a ready market was found for their handiwork at good prices.

The arrival of Frances gave new zest to all that was being undertaken, and in particular was the signal for the founding of a society named after St. Elizabeth of Hungary, to which any woman, married or single, Catholic or Protestant, might belong, for everybody knew by now that the work of the Sisters was for the benefit of all, without distinction of race or creed. The officers were installed at a meeting held on June 7th, and when the President introduced Mother Frances, the Foundress and Superior General of the Sisters of the Poor of St. Francis, a solemn hush fell on the assembly. This society guaranteed a regular income from its members, derived from dues which were, in effect, an early form of hospitalization insurance. Frances was so grateful that she promised to send them, when she returned home, a replica of the silver cup she possessed that had once belonged to St. Elizabeth, a cup from which the Saint had herself drunk and had given drink to the sick.

Busy though Frances was with her round of visitations, she nevertheless found time to help other communities. Especially was this true of the Poor Brothers of St. Francis, which she had been largely instrumental in founding. After the Sisters had been obliged to withdraw from the charge of the domestic arrangements of the college at Teutopolis, Frances had got the Brothers to replace them there, until they too decided that the work was of a character that did not properly belong to their institute. Therefore Brother Bernardine went to see her in Cincinnati, and through her assistance they were able to secure a house in the city, and thus were able to return to their original work, which consisted in providing orphanages for young boys.

A problem of a different and more important sort had to be solved. In 1865 the Sisters had taken charge of a hospital at Columbus, one that had formerly been part of the medical college there. That it was given up would indicate that it must have been replaced by something much better; even so, the Sisters were troubled in conscience in accepting a building that seemed to them much too grand to accord with the Franciscan spirit of poverty. But Frances, when she was taken to see it, reassured them on that point, after she had recovered from her astonishment, arguing that as the structure had been put up before the Sisters had accepted it, they could not be held responsible. Moreover, the furnishings of the house were poor, and as the people of Columbus were not accustomed to almsgiving, there were at that time many privations to be suffered — more than enough to make up for the stateliness of the exterior of the hospital.

Another offer, one from Cleveland, had to be refused, as it involved the running of an orphanage. So also was the offer of a hospital at St. Louis, when it became known that the pastor intended it to be reserved for the people of his parish. In the same city and elsewhere the Sisters were begged to staff schools; they had the greatest difficulty in making people accept the fact that all such activities were at variance with the spirit of the Congregation, and indeed its written Constitutions.

Even good Mrs. Peter did not always grasp this point, or at any rate believed that exceptions could be made. It was through her friend, Mrs. Sherman, the wife of the famous Civil War General, that a vocational school was offered in Washington. It called for a great deal of tact to make such refusals, especially as the Sisters were under heavy obligations to Mrs. Peter. Not only had she given her own residence to the Sisters, she was also tireless in rendering them personal services at considerable inconvenience to herself. For example, before a suitable material was available in this country, she made a special journey to Washington in the hope of persuading the government not to enforce the heavy tax demanded on a bale of cloth for the Sisters' habits. Though in this she failed, the Sisters were none the less grateful to her for her efforts on their behalf. As our Sarah was not only very kind but inclined to be domineering, it was not at all easy to resist her. It speaks volumes for the forbearance on both sides that the friendship between Mrs. Peter and the Sisters remained undamaged. The situation was briefly indicated in a letter that Frances wrote her brother and sister-in-law from Cincinnati on July 9th: "There are already ten houses of our Congregation here in America, and one must maintain a really firm position . . . in order to be spared from making new foundations."

Exceptions, however, were now and then made, but only with a limited period of service in mind. The chief of these was the Sisters' willingness to open orphanages during and immediately following the Civil War. But when Bishop Juncker of Alton fell seriously ill, a request was granted that the Sisters nurse him in his house. This was because he was an old friend, with whom they had maintained cordial relations even though they had felt obliged to withdraw from the Franciscan college at Teutopolis, which also served as the diocesan seminary. Those sent to look after him were dispensed from the regulations of the Third Order Rule that enjoined frequent abstinence, for they had the excuse of their heavy night duties. Moreover there was little served in the Bishop's house except meat foods. He himself was in almost constant delirium, and on one occasion he took the two Sisters waiting on him to be a bridal couple and bade them kneel for his blessing, to their great mirth. A month or so later the Bishop was released from his sufferings and the Sisters from their duties.

This of course was a special case, but the Sisters made it a practice to answer an emergency call whenever it was within their power to do so. Thus, when at the end of 1867, Archbishop Purcell asked Sister Paula to send some Sisters to Memphis, Tennessee, to nurse those stricken with yellow fever, every member of the community begged to be chosen for this highly dangerous duty. Those selected found, however, upon their arrival that the situation was a good deal less serious than had at first been reported, so that after caring for such people as were ill and finding no new cases developing, they returned to Cincinnati. That the epidemic was not as bad as had been supposed in no way detracts from the prompt and universal heroism of those who had offered themselves.

That they were called upon in this way may have been because the Archbishop knew of what they had done in Cincinnati during the cholera epidemic of the previous year. At first the pestilence was not very alarming, so that the Sisters were able in secret to care for the few cases they had to deal with. But as August wore on people were dying like flies, with 68 deaths reported on the 13th and 86 on the 14th. But from then on the ravages lessened until, on the last day of the month, there were only seven deaths. Though this was not the dreadful Asiatic cholera, from which few ever recover, it exhibited similar symptoms and was, as the figures just cited show, serious enough.

Frances was herself stricken with this type of cholera, but hers was not a bad attack and she got well in a day or two. America did its worst work upon her by its climate. Since her previous visit she had suffered a great deal from asthma, so much so that one of the Sisters had written from Aachen to Cincinnati: "An American lady told us that the Indians have an excellent remedy for asthma. Our dear Mother, who would willingly make every effort to preserve herself for us, wishes you to enquire earnestly about this remedy, and if it be at all possible to procure it, to send it or bring it with you." As to whether this was done we have no record; in any event the remedy probably had no value. Perhaps it was one peddled by a sharper, with a bogus Indian grunting beside him, guaranteeing that a bottle of the mixture would cure anything from asthma to fallen arches.

These asthmatic attacks often lasted from 24 to 36 hours before subsiding, and they were dreadful to behold. Thus Sister Felicitas, writing to Sister Paula on March 31st, 1865, said that Doctor Schervier had declared that his cousin would recover when better weather arrived, but went on: "This . . . does not, however, relieve us of all anxiety for our dear Mother; she is already so weakened and run down from the many years [she] has taken so little nourishment, that we can hardly understand how her life, under such unusual trials and exertions, is prolonged without some higher sustenance for upholding it. We are already accustomed to rely upon almost miraculous preservation of her precious life; but when serious illness threatens, one fears anyway." It was all the more self-sacrificing for Frances to come again to an America which, as she knew from previous experience, would be a very bad place for her health.

It was very like Frances, before she left at the end of August, 1868, to seek out a young man of good family from Aachen — a Clement Marsorati — who had migrated to the United States against his parents' wishes and had lost his faith here. She brought her spiritual batteries upon him so successfully that he returned to his religious duties; but as she may have been a little doubtful as to his constancy — or perhaps had been asked to do this by his family — she persuaded him to go back with her to Germany, where she had the joy of returning him safely to his anxious father and mother. It was rather wonderful that the travelers got to Germany at all, for the steamer on which they were making the crossing collided with a large sailing vessel, so that for a few minutes it seemed as though one of the great sea tragedies was about to occur. But not much harm was done to either ship, and Frances's steamer reached Le Havre safely on September 8th, the tenth anniversary of the day the first group of the Sisters of the Poor of St. Francis had landed in New York. Frances's brother Henry was waiting to escort her to Aachen and with her the young man she had rescued.

A couple of months after her arrival Frances was asked to undertake in Cologne what she had so long accepted in Aachen — the charge of the women prisoners in the city jail. But she found that there were so many hampering restrictions that she had to explain to Herr Blum, the chief of the royal government in the city, why she felt obliged to give a conditional refusal. That same evening she received a telegram from Queen Augusta, asking her to call on her at Coblenz.

By way of preparing for this she visited Archbishop Melchers who gave her many details of the deplorable state of affairs among the women prisoners and said that it was he who had petitioned the government to look into the matter. It was he also who had approached the Queen. In Coblenz Frances promised Augusta that she would withdraw her refusal if the Queen really wished her to shoulder this somewhat thankless task. Accordingly on November 18th, she notified the government of her acceptance, should certain concessions be made, as, backed by Her Majesty, she thought would be the case. But the Prussian government would not budge, so Frances did not feel that under the circumstances her Sisters would be of much use.

What Frances's relations were with Queen Augusta comes out in a letter Augusta wrote addressed to "dear little Mother

Frances" on May 31st, 1869. The Queen told her friend: "You and I have done what we could, therefore we may calmly leave the result to God, Whose wisdom effects what is best in all things, even if we do not attain the success we thought ourselves justified in hoping for. It is His affair: let His holy will be praised in all things, even when the sacrifice is painful to us; and in this case the pain is a real one. But what did not succeed now, may succeed later. The point is always to walk before God in humility and fidelity and to await His pleasure." One would imagine that letter to have been written by a Catholic, and one of great piety. It was an open secret that the Queen's sympathies were Catholic and that a Catholic priest acted as her adviser. It may even be that secretly she held a faith which her position made it impossible for her to profess openly.

*

A Cure at Lourdes

IT IS A WONDER that Frances was able to accomplish so much,
handicapped as she was by poor health — or it would be a
wonder were it not common knowledge that much of the best
work is done in the world by semi-invalids. She was seldom
well, and yet always occupied. The worst of it all was that
the austerities she practiced were anything but an aid to vigor.

Yet she had a very good excuse for mitigating her penances
when on October 25th, 1869, Archbishop Melchers visited the
Motherhouse at Aachen and ordered that since some of the
Sisters were delicate they should have a more nourishing diet.
Taking exactly the same line that his predecessor had done a
few years before, he dispensed those engaged during the
night and those engaged in specially hard work from the
frequent fasts enjoined by the Rule of the Franciscan Third
Order. To Frances he made a special appeal; as he knew of
her asceticism, he said he hoped she would be more careful
of herself in future.

Frances accepted the dispensations — for other Sisters. She
would not avail herself of them, saying calmly: "I must give a
good example, even if I should die a few years earlier." The
most that she would permit herself when she was weak or exhausted was a sliver or two of an apple or a glass of water

into which a few drops of wine had been poured. But it would seem that she was often unable to eat much. We hear of a prolonged asthmatic attack in the January after the Archbishop's visit, when she was left so prostrated that for a month she could take nothing but water that had been poured over toast. And she was not much better when, after a visit to Coblenz, she had to leave in stormy weather. The Sisters, after much argument, prevailed upon her to take a cab to the railway station. But on the way there she burst into tears, declaring that she suffered more from allowing this exception to her private rule than she would have done from the most fatiguing walk. On an earlier occasion she had stopped the cab after a few blocks, paid the driver, and gone on by foot. She wished to be herself of the very poor, and they could not afford cabs. After that the Sisters never again tried to make her ride in a carriage.

That Frances's attack in January — apparently the worst and most prolonged that she had had to endure — sprang, as asthma often does, at least in part from an emotional root, is indicated by the statement of Father Jeiler, who visited her at the time. He said that "the least mental exertion caused attacks of suffocation, especially at night." She felt almost as though she were sharing the Agony of Gethsemane, for she believed, in her weakened condition, that she was forsaken of God — a notion that only served to bring on a new asthmatic spasm. She was also worrying about not being able to attend to her duties, and this too made her worse. Father Jeiler, who said that asthma was nothing new to him, confessed that he had never seen anything so dreadful as Frances's condition. It appeared to be that of a dying person. This time there was well-grounded fear that she might actually die.

The whole community, as well as a number of friends, were praying for Frances night and day, and in April the asthma left her, almost entirely — which may have been due to the prayers or the arrival of fine weather, or both. But Frances was by now so exhausted that Dr. Schervier insisted that she complete the good work that had been accomplished by seeking a change of climate.

As with everything, Frances had regarded her illness with indifferent detachment. "Thank God," she said, "I am entirely at peace interiorly; just as in nature, when the wind is still, not a leaf stirs. God sent this illness; let Him cure me or let me die." This was the reverse of a fatalistic attitude, for while accepting what God willed for her, she made use of all the medical advice available; though she must have doubted whether it could accomplish much. However, she did see that she was of little use to the community she governed unless she recovered her health. As the Sisters would not hear of her resigning, she wished very much to be cured.

She had long wanted to make a pilgrimage to Lourdes, and she had little difficulty in getting Dr. Schervier to agree that the little town in the foothills of the Pyrenees would be a good place for her, though he probably was dubious as to how well she could stand so long a journey. A benefactress of the Congregation, Fräulein Alwine Kamper of Cologne, offered to accompany her and to defray all the expenses, so problems of ways and means were completely removed.

Frances would not permit any of the Sisters to go with her to Lourdes. In fact, except for the small group that took her to the railway station, where they met Fräulein Kamper, the Sisters did not know what was afoot. It seemed to one not saturated with faith a desperate venture; not feeling any too sure that they would ever see their beloved Mother again they could but commend the travelers to the protection of St. Joseph.

She did, as it happened, almost die en route. For though all went well as far as Paris, where they had to change to a different railway line, the journey from Bordeaux saw her getting worse and worse almost every mile. Fräulein Kamper believed Frances too ill to proceed, but Frances insisted on pushing on to the last stage of her pilgrimage and was in such a condition when she reached Lourdes that she had to be lifted from the train and carried, like many other pilgrims, to a hotel on a stretcher.

There, since she was a rather celebrated person, the Superior General of a religous congregation, she was visited by the man made renowned by the controversy over Bernadette's visions. He was the chief priest of Lourdes, Father Marie Dominique Peyramale, a giant of a man, with a large heart and a rather sharp tongue. At first he had been disposed to think Bernadette an imposter or a fool and on one occasion had threatened to sweep her out of his house with a broom. But he had been won over by her transparent candor and innocence and became the doughtiest of her champions.

He had become almost too doughty in the opinion of the ecclesiastical authorites, for though they were brought to a belief in the authenticity of the apparitions Bernadette had seen — as these had been attested by countless miracles — they thought that the overwhelming Father Peyramale was trying to set himself up as Pope of Lourdes. The result was that everything was taken out of his hands, and instead of the beautiful edifice he had envisioned as a shrine, one of those sugary confections so characteristic of French Catholic taste at the time was substituted. The basilica that had been built was not too bad, for it incorporated some of Father Peyramale's ideas, but it might have been a great deal better. His glory, which nothing can ever diminish, was the tender heart under his gruffness which had discerned what a treasure he had found in the poor girl for whom he had obtained a refuge from the notoriety she hated and feared in a convent at Nevers. He remained Bernadette's most intimate friend.

When he called upon Frances he said in his blunt fashion that he was surprised that a nun should have traveled such a distance in order to seek the prolongation of her life. Frances smiled, instantly recognizing a very genuine person. She said, "I have done this because in my present condition I cannot attend to my duties as superior." Father Peyramale seized the point, and when she added, "I want to get well or die," he answered curtly, *"Guerissez,"* that is, "Get well." A moment later he somewhat amplified this. "You must pray to the Blessed Virgin either to cure you or let you die, because, as you know, a sick Superior General is good for nothing." Again Frances smiled at thoughts that so perfectly reflected her own. That she wished to get well for a community which she knew still needed her is shown by her having made the 1200-mile journey (counting the rather roundabout route) from Aachen to Lourdes.

She was so weak that she had to be carried to the grotto at Massabielle on a stretcher. It was there that 12 years before the Blessed Virgin had appeared to Bernadette many times, saying most mysteriously, "I am the Immaculate Conception." It had been one of the foulest spots in the wide world, a dumping ground, where Bernadette's father, when out of work, had been glad to be employed to take the soiled bandages from the hospital for burning. And Bernadette's somewhat shiftless family had lived in a dank deserted prison, for want of any other shelter. Yet out of such squalor had risen this resplendent lily. All that she asked at this time was that her name be forgotten and that she be allowed to live unnoticed in her convent.

Of the water of the spring that had suddenly appeared at Massabielle where no water was before, Frances drank that first day, immediately feeling physically stronger and spiritually refreshed. The next day she was able to walk to the grotto and visited the basilica, spending most of her time there, praying fervently and noting with joy the fervor of the pilgrims. One of the very rare photographs taken of her shows her wandering about rather casually, evidently very much at home. Since there were not so many pilgrims on that day Frances is easily to be picked out, standing by herself, half facing the camera. Yet the picture is clearly not "posed," not one of Frances with the grotto simply as a background. Rather it appears to be a picture of the grotto, into which Frances had strolled by accident. It must have called for some skillful strategy on the part of Fraulein Kamper to get this snapshot, and one with so excellent a likeness, for Frances had a great repugnance to such things. Probably it was done without her being aware of it until too late.

One day she had a bath at the spring, the same spring in which the Bouhouhorts baby had been dipped, when on the point of death, by his mother and was immediately cured. He lived to be present as a very old man at St. Peter's in Rome when Bernadette was canonized. Frances at once felt the effect of the water, and yet was not instantaneously cured of her asthma. It was not until 12 days later that she knew herself to be quite free of this disease. Another of the miracles of Our Lady of Lourdes had been performed.

Frances doubtless would have liked to have met Bernadette. Nevers, however, was not very near Lourdes, but almost in the exact center of France, and Frances understood perfectly how the child in refuge there wished to avoid meeting strangers, who would of course want her to tell all about what had happened to her. So she carefully avoided intruding herself. But she did get to know the Sisters of Bernadette's congregation in their house at Lourdes. One fancies that they may have been slightly tiresome; Father Peyramale was not only a more reliable authority but, in his way, a very remarkable person. In any event Frances had not gone to Lourdes to meet people, however interesting, but to be cured; and cured she was, of an ailment that can usually be said to be incurable. That was enough.

Before she left she wished to signalize her gratitude in some more than ordinary manner. Therefore in the presence of a priest she consecrated herself and her Congregation to the Blessed Virgin (as though they had not been so consecrated already!) and made three promises that had almost the character of vows. The first was to miss no opportunity of promoting devotion to Our Lady of Lourdes. The second was that the following prayer be inserted in the daily devotions of the Sisters: "Holy Mary, be thou this day my Mother and the Mother of our entire Congregation. Be our Mistress, and we will be thy servants. Remain our most benign Mother, and we will be thy faithful children." To these she added a third promise which may strike some people as a little odd: she promised never to refuse assistance asked by a Jew, and she would do all that lay in her power to bring about the conversion of Jews.

This, however, was not really anything very new. She had made it a principle to help all those in need, whatever their creed or race might be; and she had long had a special interest in Jews — a very Catholic interest. It was heightened by a friendship formed at this time with Father Herman Cohen,* whose life was dedicated to reclaiming the lost sheep of the house of Israel. It may also have been heightened by the fact that Frances's cure had been effected by a Jewess, Mary the Mother of Jesus, another Jew. By way of marking this more definitely Frances, on her journey back to Aachen, spent a day with the Daughters of Sion in Paris, a religious community made up mostly of converted Jewesses and founded by Père Alphonse Ratisbonne, himself a Jew. Frances remembered that the Christian revelation was super-imposed upon the revelation to the Jews, which it fulfilled, and that however much the Jews may have failed in their awe-inspiring mission, they still remain, in a sense, the Chosen People. Such ideas were not implanted in her mind by any particular person but flowed from her perception of the Christian idea; it proves her grasp of that idea. Frances did not often show any startling novelty of thought, and still less of expression. But what do these matter when she had so Christian a heart?

* His religious name as a Carmelite was Père Augustin du Saint Sacrement.

★

The Triumph of Prussia

THE BISMARCKIAN policy — with the wars that followed one another in such quick succession — culminated in 1870 with the Franco-Prussian War, by which all the states of Germany came to be unified under the Hohenzollern Emperor. The wars were, of course, an implementation of that policy and were entirely successful, somewhat to the surprise of the rest of the world, which thought the France of that day invincible, but of course not at all to the surprise of the statesmen and commanders of Prussia.

The Rhineland had been for about thirty years a part of Prussia politically, and yet it was very alien from the stiff and arrogant Prussian spirit. The easygoing Catholic Rhinelanders were more akin to the distant Bavarians, or to the Austrians. Yet so pervasive is what is called patriotism that Rhinelanders, for the most part, responded as did the genuine Prussians to the demands made upon them. It was their "Prussianization" on the anvil of war that largely served to account for the relative lack of resistance they put up when Bismarck, after having given Prussia the hegemony of Germany, proceeded to try to round out his gains by subjecting the Church to the Empire.

We shall hear more about this last move a little later. Since it was as yet veiled from sight (as Bismarck veiled all his moves until the last moment, a moment always chosen by himself), at this stage we are concerned only with the services the Sisters of the Poor of St. Francis rendered during the war of 1870, as they had rendered them during the wars of 1864 and 1866.

To Frances the conflict was particularly painful, not only because her mission in life was mercy, the salvaging of the unfortunate, whereas war is destructive, but because this war represented a strife in herself. She was both French and German in blood; in fact, under the example of her French mother she had become more French than German in habit of thought and sentiment. She had grown up in the kindlier Germany, which at that time was often sleepy and cloudy — though there was nothing sleepy or cloudy about her, for her charity was wide-eyed and alert. On the other hand, if she showed (as she did) a good deal of German efficiency, she used it for ends vastly different from those aimed at by the efficient German bureaucrats and military officers. As one not given to the expression of generalized opinions — especially about matters which she treated as altogether outside her province — she prepared at once to give the services of the Sisters as nurses.

By way of preparing for the immediate task, as soon as war threatened, Frances allowed a number of novices to make their profession, for in many instances this had been postponed because of her illness and her absence in France. Similarly the postulancy was shortened for many, and the habit conferred. Frances knew that she would need the largest contingent she could muster.

The Knights of Malta were the first organization to ask the Sisters to nurse the wounded in the military hospitals. They were soon followed by the Patriotic Ladies' Association, which was under the patronage of Queen Augusta, and probably acted under her prompting. This association engaged the services of the Sisters for a hospital at Coblenz, and after the battle of Spicherer Heights they were also summoned to Saarbrücken. From every side appeals came to Frances for nurses, far more than she could possibly supply, though she did her best.

Although considerable and steady progress had been made in the United States, the houses there, perhaps because of the rapidity of their increase, had continually to be recruited from Germany, as at this stage the American postulants were not coming in in sufficient numbers. The statistics of 1870 show that on this side of the Atlantic there were 48 Sisters in perpetual vows, 67 in temporary vows, and 54 novices. There were presumably a good many postulants as well but their number was no longer recorded in the American Annals. In short, the Vicariate of the United States was flourishing, although it largely depended as yet upon Germany.

Crossings of the Atlantic in time of war were not without their dangers. There was no longer any possibility of using the convenient Le Havre. Instead German steamers had to be taken from Bremen, and those sailing from America were obliged to follow a course far to the North and then come down the East coast of Scotland to an English port, hoping somehow to get to a Germany that the more powerful French fleet was blockading. However, no mishap occurred; whatever the difficulties, a road between Germany and the United States was, after a fashion, kept open.

One hundred and twenty-five of the Sisters were engaged in this war effort — a large number considering that this was still a small Congregation, occupied with many other activities, most of which could not be even temporarily abandoned. What it meant was that already overtaxed Sisters had to work twice as hard as before.

It fell to the lot of Frances to work mainly for sick and wounded French prisoners, for whom concentration camps were established at both Cologne and Aachen. On October 26, 1870, she wrote to a Franciscan friend: "Now is a time for prayer and sacrifice. Yesterday I was at Cologne, where thousands of French soldiers are ill of typhus and dysentery.

Their misery is beyond description. One feels that the war is a punishment by God, which, however, will be the salvation of numbers; for I think that many who would never have thought of it otherwise, now receive the holy sacraments and die reconciled to God." To the same friend she wrote again at the end of December: "What a dreadful time we are having here! It seems as though the evil spirit had been granted special powers to achieve his diabolical ends. Now is a time of watchfulness and prayer. The work here is scarcely to be mastered. But this is also a part of the trials of war, and we will strive to appease the justice of God by patient suffering."

For the sake of these prisoners, but with others also in mind, she spent a very large sum — 18,000 marks — in having religious pamphlets and catechisms printed. It must be remembered that she never kept substantial reserve funds and when, as sometimes happened, she was urged to have some care for the future, she only answered smilingly: "The good God will take care of everything, and He who provides for the little birds of the air will certainly not forsake those who have left all for love of Him." Her printer was rather alarmed, no doubt wondering whether he would be paid, but she told him to proceed. "Divine Providence," she assured him, "will look after this." And Divine Providence did.

War in those days still had some amenities. Or perhaps it was because for the third time the plan of a *Blitzkrieg* had proved to be so well based that the Prussians felt that they could afford to be generous. In early August two great victories were won over the armies of Marshal MacMahon, and on September 1st, Napoleon III, the French Emperor, surrendered with what was left of his forces at Sedan. It was the virtual end of the war, almost as soon as it had begun, though a kind of resistance continued until after the siege of Paris. The early sweeping victories of Prussia meant that unending columns of French prisoners were taken to Germany, and among these were groups of French officers who were brought to Aachen. It was granted that their wives should have safe-conducts there, where they lived in lodgings so as to be able to visit their husbands. To these French ladies Frances was very kind. She arranged that they should come to the Motherhouse three times a week to sew, not only for their husbands but for the other French prisoners there. The Motherhouse was, in fact, turned into a kind of club for them. As the war was already virtually over, not even the most suspicious Prussian officer could regard these French-women as being dangerous as spies, even had any of them wished to act in that capacity.

Frances invited these ladies and their children to a Christmas party. She then introduced them to something that was quite new to them — something that had been almost unheard of in England until the German Prince Albert introduced it there — a Christmas tree. Though this has since become throughout the English-speaking world a distinctive — perhaps too much *the* distinctive — feature of Christmas the French had hardly so much as heard of such a thing. The wives and children of the French officers were charmed especially as upon the tree hung a gift for each of the children. It is all the more pleasant to record this because the war was the greatest shock the French had received up to that time. They went down almost as ingloriously before the iron armies prepared by Bismarck as they did in 1941 before Hitler. On January 18, 1871, William I was proclaimed the Emperor of Germany in the Hall of Mirrors at Versailles. Napoleon III was deposed, and two years later he died in his retreat at Chiselhurst in England.

For Frances there came out of this war a hospital, when a temporary military infirmary at Düsseldorf was opened, with some extensions, as a permanent institution in charge of the Sisters. They already had a home for invalids in that city; now in a single year they established there not only a hospital but, under the title of St. Ann's, a home for the training of domestic servants in housework and in sewing. This latter was a work that had long characterized the Congregation, and on

December 26, 1873, it formally accepted the charge of a similar establishment — similar to the extent of being a servants' hostel — existing in Aachen. Under the stress of war the Sisters, without abandoning their other activities, found themselves pressed more and more in the direction of conducting hospitals, always hospitals for the poor, to which the more well-to-do were not admitted except under very special circumstances.

On December 31, 1871, the Empress Augusta, who had been so long Frances's friend, wrote to her enclosing the decoration of the Cross of Merit, "with which His August Highness has honored German women and maidens distinguished for their deeds during the late war, and directs you to preserve it as a lasting memorial of ministrations during a period of renown, and of the gratitude which I, the German Empire's Empress and Prussia's Queen, owe them, and which to express was a pleasure to me." This Frances could not do other than accept, in the name of the 125 Sisters who had served so valiantly, averaging among them three thousand patients a day. But what went before this should also be mentioned, because it reveals Frances's attitude towards the honors of this world.

On July 10, 1871, she had written to Count Egon von Hoensbroesch regarding some forms he had sent her to fill in and return to Prince von Press, the Inspector General of Volunteer Nursing, on which she had been asked to give the names of each of the Sisters engaged in the nursing service, so that a suitable recognition be given to them individually.

Frances's feeling about such things after the war with Denmark had apparently been forgotten, but she took precisely the same line again, declining to fill up the forms and saying that in her opinion such a recognition would not be in accord with the spirit of Catholic religious communities. What was done concerned not so much the personal merit of the individual Sisters as the Congregation. Therefore she wrote:

"Their ministrations in military hospitals, much as they may have been in accord with their own desire and the spirit in which they were educated, were nevertheless not the result of their own volition but of their Superiors' order and arrangement. Everything done by individual Sisters on the fields of battle and in military hospitals in pursuance of their vocation would have been accomplished just as well by other members of the community, whom the Superiors were obliged to keep at home for the service of the poor, sick etc. in their neighborhood." She added that she could say without rashness that those who did serve as nurses often overtaxed their strength, but that all the members of the Congregation would have done the same had they been called upon to do so. And she explained further: "Those German women and maidens, who generously devoted themselves to the service of the wounded without belonging to a religious community, selected the place for and the nature of their ministrations by their own free choice, and their achievements redound to their own personal, individual merit, for which they deserve acknowledgment. But not a single member of a religious community was engaged anywhere by self-appointment and independently of her Superiors." Frances does, however, say towards the end of her long letter to the Count: "If they deserve recognition, it belongs not to individuals, but to the community as such." This hint was acted upon a little later by the Empress, who did not give Frances the chance to refuse when sending her the Cross of Merit. By this method the whole Congregation was recognized, not only those who had actually served but those who would have served had they been assigned to this duty. It seems extraordinary that, after this, the government should have proceeded to the persecution of the *Kulturkampf*.

Following the war there were two urgent emergency calls of the kind to which Frances never failed to respond. At Hellenthal, in the district of Schleiden, there broke out an epidemic of smallpox of a very virulent type. Immediately

Frances sent there Sister Agnes, who had recently returned from the smallpox hospital at Düsseldorf, together with a younger Sister. They lodged in a house all of whose inhabitants had been swept away by the pest, but though they had no fears for themselves, they were never allowed to cross another threshold, when they went from house to house begging. The little they received was handed to them from behind a door ajar, so terrified was everybody of infection. When anybody died, it was hard to find people brave enough to prepare the body for burial. In at least one instance the Sisters had to attend to this themselves and then put the coffin out in the street where it would have to be picked up.

After a month of incredibly hard work and worse privations, the epidemic subsided. But when the Sisters proposed to leave, since they were no longer needed, the Burgomaster, speaking for all those in the little town, begged them to remain a few days longer, "as a protection against the disease," as he put it. This was the closest they got to receiving thanks for what they had done.

The same two Sisters shortly afterwards received a summons to go to Wallenberg, a nearby village where typhoid was raging. It was so bad that in one house seven members of a family died. Again there was a deep dread of admitting the Sisters, or anybody else, lest they should spread the pest. In the widespread panic everything was so neglected that the Sisters were obliged to turn farm hands and give fodder to the cattle in the barns and milk the protesting cows. But far from repining, they rejoiced that they were able to do something to alleviate human misery.

In this same year, 1871, Frances did what she could by way of celebrating the Papal Jubilee of Pius IX. She sent him a present of a rug and of a *zucchetta*, the white skullcap a pope wears. They were carried to Rome by a priest from Aachen, and with them went an address in French composed by Frances herself. She explained that the rug, which was made by stitching together a number of pieces of silk, represented "a symbol of the mutual charity in which [the Sisters] desire to grow and persevere as true children of the One, Holy, Catholic Church, and as loyal subjects of our glorious Supreme Pastor."

One imagines that this rug was no great work of art, but Pius accepted it in his usual affable style, and he gave Frances's messenger the *zucchetta* he was wearing at the moment. She was of course delighted. She had hoped for this and had even ventured to tell her emissary that, should the Pope ask what return he could make, that it be suggested he do what he actually did. Women — even very holy women — usually have artful ways of obtaining what they want.

The Kulturkampf

FRANCES SCHERVIER had grown up in a society which was accustomed to having the state interfere every now and then with the operations of the Church. After the rather summary way such matters had been often dealt with during Napoleonic times, Catholics could, indeed, consider themselves as relatively free, for secular intrusions were only intermittent, though they did occur, as when Archbishop zu Droste-Vischering had been imprisoned in 1837 for refusal to comply with some of the state's arbitrary requirements. The Prussian ideal was that the Church should be reduced to being an instrument or a department of political administration, in which capacity it would of course have been very useful to the government. Even governments professedly antagonistic to religion are rarely so foolish as to attempt to uproot the Church; they would be perfectly satisfied if they could detach it from the Roman obedience and make it obedient to themselves. After the Franco-Prussian War this idea took a more definite hold in the atmosphere of megalomania that was induced. The German states had been unified with the King of Prussia as Emperor; it seemed necessary to complete the process by making the Church subservient to secular authority. It seemed intolerable to the mind of Bismarck, and still more to some of the men around him, that Germans should be permitted to acknowledge the jurisdiction of the Pope.

The issue was not of course placed publicly in these unequivocal terms. But that was what was behind the ensuing events. And the definition of papal infallibility in 1870 seemed to such secularists a challenge they could not ignore and were now more than strong enough to meet. The decree of infallibility found some measure of opposition in almost all parts of the Catholic world — though this was usually on account of doubt as to its opportuneness rather than to any doubt of the content of the decrees, which almost everywhere was accepted once it had been promulgated. But in Germany the opposition was more determined and was led by a group of exceptionally gifted men, the chief of whom was Dr. Döllinger,* who broke with the Church in preference to accepting a doctrine which they considered had been foisted upon them. These formed themselves into what was known as the Old Catholic Church.

This Church still exists in various countries, though it is everywhere negligible. But in the beginning it created some stir in Germany, and not only priests but nuns fell away — most of them only for a time. As far as these nuns were concerned, Archbishop Melchers entrusted their reclamation to Frances Schervier, and with very good results. But for a while Bismarck strongly backed the so-called Old Catholics, in the belief (one that was quite sound) that such a body severed from the Papacy would be national rather than Catholic. He was counting upon Catholics leaving the Church *en masse;* had they done so his plans for integrating religion with the political regime would not have caused undue friction.

There, however, Bismarck soon saw that he had miscalculated badly. He made some attempt to reassert his position

---

* To Döllinger's credit it must be said that he refused an alliance with the Dutch Jansenists, though he was willing to accept alliances elsewhere, and that (probably) he died reconciled with the Catholic Church.

when the Holy See demanded that all Old Catholics who were teachers of religion in state institutions be dismissed, for this could be represented as interference on the part of the Holy See with secular sovereignty. He retaliated by not only refusing these demands but by abolishing the special section that had previously existed in the Prussian ministry of public worship that dealt with Catholic affairs. When he saw that this was going to be ineffectual, that the weakness of the Old Catholic Church was that it consisted of leaders but had few followers, he turned to other courses.

In 1873 the notorious "May Laws" were passed in the Prussian *Landtag*, with still more oppressive laws in 1874 and 1875. The autonomy of the Catholic Church was revoked; bishops were to be nominated by the government; priests could not be appointed to a benefice unless they had followed a state-approved course of studies; the clergy had to give implicit obedience to all the secular laws (which included the laws directed against themselves); priests were not to make "political" statements from the pulpit; education was to be state-supervised; certain religious orders were to be expelled; marriage was to be made a secular affair; birth and death were no longer to be registered by the clergy; and a special court was set up to try such members of the clergy who refused to conform, with power to withhold the former state grants and even to remove them from their posts. It all reminds one of the totalitarian process now going on; its failure should be instructive to totalitarians of our own day. The only real difference was that though the Prussian laws were drastic, the authorities refrained from Hitler's vilification or the absurd charges we have seen brought against even such a man as Cardinal Mindszenty. Still less did the Kulturkampf stoop to extracting bogus confessions by the use of tortures or drugs.

That the attempt of regimentation of Catholicism broke down about 15 years after it was begun,* and that its failure

---

* In a sense the Kulturkampf may be reckoned as beginning with Bismarck's assumption of office in 1862 — and indeed there had been friction between State and Church long before that. But when the May Laws were passed in 1873 war was declared on the Catholic Church.

became apparent some years before then, need not concern us, except to say that this was from the outset inevitable in the face of the constancy of the Catholics of Germany. Frances Schervier did not live to see Bismarck's defeat, though, relying upon God, she was sure that ultimately he would fail. What may be admitted is that Bismarck, from his own point of view, had some justification. He had to break a number of opposing elements. Against him stood the more conservative members of the *Junker* class, who, though Protestant, took the line that the authority of God is higher than that of the state. And the strong Catholic elements in Germany — in Bavaria, in Western Poland, and in the Rhineland, for instance, had formed what, after 1858, was known as the Center Party. It was not actively anti-imperial, though it would have preferred to see the imperial title retained by Austria. But it was a threat to Bismarck's general policy, so by way of eliminating it, he struck at the Church, using all kinds of disparate groups for his purpose.

The German hierarchy, of course, protested against the May Laws and urged passive resistance on the part of the Catholic population. The clergy ignored the summonses sent them to appear before the state courts or, when they did appear, refused to pay the fines imposed. The Archbishops of Cologne and Posen were arrested, as was also the Bishop of Trier. But it was all to no good. Bismarck, looking back on his blunder later in life, said frequently that he had been pressed further than he had ever intended to go, especially by Dr. Falk, the Minister for Public Worship, and that the laws had deliberately been made more severe than their execution was going to be. He had looked merely for some concessions on the part of the Catholic Church, and with these he would have been content. Though he probably spoke what was upon the whole, the truth, he was also trying to minimize his defeat.

Frances was fortunate in managing to found a branch house at Frankfurt-am-Main just before the May Laws went into effect. But the separate novitiate house established in

1875, which she had long perceived to be a crying necessity, had to be abandoned almost at once because of the laws that gave the state supervision of all educational institutions — and a novitiate was regarded as such. What Bismarck (or rather Dr. Falk) was aiming at was to bring all Catholic organizations under the control of the state. It is what all the enemies of the Church consciously or unconsciously aim at, for, naturally, in that supine position the Church would be innocuous — indeed it would be rather a convenient instrument of the state. Frances would very willingly have died to prevent that happening to her Congregation.

As events proved, she was able to weather the storm, though at several moments she was far from sure that she would be able to do so. To provide against possible contingencies she purchased a house at Enghein in Belgium and built another near Verviers which would serve as a novitiate. But in this case, either Frances was not very expert at noticing all the details on the blueprints, or the architect took it upon himself to make changes, for what eventuated was a building which Frances, when she saw the finished structure, considered looked more like a palace than a convent. One glance at it was enough: she sat down behind a hedge and wept bitterly; she refused to set foot inside the building. A little later it was sold at a heavy loss, though the Sisters used it as a novitiate from 1878 to 1881. By way of saving the Motherhouse at Aachen from possible confiscation, she made a pretended sale of it to a Herr Schmidt. During these troubled times she received no postulants there, and when novices were professed it was done in such secrecy that they had to forego the wreaths ordinarily worn on such occasions. On February 22nd, 1876, Frances indicates another plan for survival: "Here in Prussia we are no longer permitted to receive postulants, and of late we have sent all applicants to America. Eventually we shall have to go there ourselves. In the end, it is all the same where one goes: God, and employment in our vocation, are to be found everywhere. Should your branch house be the first to be closed, come home to the Motherhouse, if so it must be."

This might be the place to give some account of the development of the novitiate. As has been already indicated, for a long while no such institution existed for the Sisters of the Poor of St. Francis, though its lack was largely compensated for by the brilliant example of Frances herself and that of some very holy members of the community, particularly Sisters Ursula, Felicitas, Andre, and Hedwig, in all that concerned conventual discipline.

In 1865, however, a novice mistress was appointed in the person of Sister Bernardine, and under her a novitiate was established in 1868 at the Annastift in Düsseldorf. Later the troubles of the *Kulturkampf* necessitated its removal to Belgium where Frances decided to build on a hill called Andrimont near Verviers. It was about this time that Sister Bernardine was replaced by Sister Alcantara, and a year later by Sister Constantia, though she, since she was engrossed in other duties was novice mistress in no more than name.

The establishment of the novitiate in 1868 was due to Archbishop Melchers who, on a visitation, warned Frances that its absence might militate against the approbation of the Constitutions in Rome. Yet political difficulties soon afterwards made a canonical novitiate in Germany out of the question. Such few young women who were admitted to the Congregation had to be sent to the various branch houses, to be instructed there as well as possible by the local Superior. But these postulants and novices could not wear a distinctive dress and were ostensibly merely servants in the house — the only means of escaping the surveillance of the Prussian government. The last formal investiture had to be held in the Ursuline convent at Seroulle in Belgium. No retreat preceeded it, and there had been, indeed, no novitiate for these last groups except that of devoted charity and hard work.*

* The subsequent story of the novitiate of the Sisters of the Poor of St. Francis may be relegated to a footnote, as it falls outside Frances's own

The case of the twins, Sisters Ascelina and Humbelina Haltermann, who celebrated the golden jubilee of their profession at Hartwell, Cincinnati in 1928, illustrates the careful subterfuges that had to be used. They were admitted as postulants on October 15th, 1874, but were obliged to wait nearly two years before they were given the habit. Then on August 4th, 1876, Frances sent six postulants by rail, going herself with another six in a small wagon, each postulant carrying in a parcel under her arm the habit she was to be given. That same evening they returned to Aachen.

Even so, the matter had not quite ended. Lest there be governmental spies on the watch they did not dare show themselves in the chapel the next morning, but remained in the choir loft, and it was there that the Chaplain went to give them Holy Communion. Immediately afterwards they were dispersed among the branch houses, with the exception of

life. After the death of Sister Constantia in 1877, the office of novice mistress was vacant for three years. The 28 postulants who entered at Andrimont in 1878 remained without a Mistress, and their novitiate virtually consisted of three instructions given them by Sister Felicitas, the Superior of the Motherhouse at Aachen. But in 1880 Sister Mira was appointed. And when in 1881 Andrimont was sold to the Vincentian Fathers, the novices and postulants were dispersed — some of them to the Motherhouse, some to Theux, and a few among the branch houses in Germany. When in 1882 50 postulants were given the habit (in two separate groups), none of them could wear the religious habit, their sole mark of distinction being a black bonnet and a rosary at their waist. Yet they had the privileges of novices and assisted at the various community exercises.

In 1884 Sister Veronica was placed in charge of the novitiate, and she did her best to restore a regular mode of religious training. As a providential assistance instructions arrived from Rome, transmitted by Archbishop Melchers, which fixed the period of the novitiate to a standard two years, the first of which was to be spent under the direction of the Mistress, with the second devoted to the learning of the charitable activities proper to the Congregation. When in 1885 Sister Veronica became ill, Sister Mira was recalled from America and put in charge. Under her direction, and that of Mother Willeyka, the novitiate was removed to the Motherhouse on Elisabethstrasse, until it was transferred in 1893 to the new building at Lindenplatz. Later that year Sister Mira returned to the United States and was succeeded by Sister Johanna. Under her the program became fixed, and she held her office until 1920, when she was permitted to join the Recluses. Sister Beata, the next in office, saw the novitiate grow rapidly in numbers.

Sister Humbelina, who remained at Aachen. But in October, Frances became so worried that she went to Mainz where Sister Ascelina was, and told her that she and her twin had better go to the United States lest their investiture be discovered. They were permitted to go home for three days to see their parents at Borken, and when they returned, just before the time set for their departure, Frances told them, after she had given them her blessing: "I am coming soon to America. Should I die before that time I shall be in heaven, but I shall always remain with you." Ten days after their arrival in New York Frances was dead.

Whatever her difficulties Frances had no intention of running away; she first meant to try what a calm firmness would effect — that and the aid she knew the Empress would give if she could. On July 22nd, 1875, she wrote to the Superior at Coblenz: "In order not to incur suspicion of assenting to the law regarding convents, which would be a betrayal of Holy Church and an enslavement of the Congregation, the enclosed declaration * is to be made in my name. I think you in Coblenz will not be molested, in deference to Her Majesty, the Empress."

Frances sent a comprehensive declaration to the government on the 30th of the same month. She had been asked to reply to a number of questions about the Motherhouse and the branch houses. To those relating to external matters she had no objection to returning an answer, but to the questions relating to the religious life of the Sisters she replied: "The statement demanded of me is without doubt intended to serve as the state's supervision of our Congregation. It contains questions that seem to imply that the state will not permit a free disposition of our means of support and the unrestrained disposal of the members of our Congregation, and that consequently their employments will be interfered with, if not entirely suppressed, whereby especially the ecclesiastical char-

---

* It no doubt was a list of the Sisters at Coblenz and a statement regarding the nature of their work.

acter of the Congregation would suffer. As long as this my view of the statement does not prove to be a misconception, I regret to decline having it made."

This letter brought no less a person than Dr. Falk, the minister responsible for the oppressive laws, to Aachen to try and break her down. As he must have been aware that Frances had the backing of the Empress, he had to treat her as a special case. He strengthened himself by calling on her with Herr von Leipziger, chairman of the board of administration, and Herr Stoeveken, another member of the board. Dr. Falk told Frances that only on condition that the destitute children she sheltered be sent away would the Congregation be protected against expulsion. It may be that he wished to obtain no more than a "token" submission, for enquiries would have told him that this work had been undertaken — as in the United States after the Civil War — only because of an emergency. But Frances cannily refrained from saying so, and answered: "Doctor, if this is absolutely necessary I will prepare for it. But you must give me a longer period of time, as in the same house there are aged, infirm and destitute persons for all of whom I shall first have to find a suitable home. I cannot turn them out in the street."

Dr. Falk agreed that this stipulation was reasonable, but then turned to the solicitation of alms, a cardinal point of procedure. "This begging must stop!" he told Frances emphatically. To which she answered: "The proceeds of our collections are used for the poor and sick, and the prohibition of begging would greatly injure them. Indeed, I do not know how we could support them otherwise." When Dr. Falk was stubborn, Frances told him: "All right: if you make our work of charity impossible in Germany, we shall emigrate to America or some other foreign country."

This took the Minister aback, for he knew that the people of Germany would suffer a great deal if nursing orders should be lost to them. The recently passed laws had specifically exempted them, although restrictions had been imposed.

Rather aghast he asked, "Could you reconcile leaving Germany with your conscience?"

Frances had her answer ready: "Yes, I can, for we are religious first of all, and only after that nurses, and if the state interferes with our interior religious life we shall give up the service of the sick here and go to some other country." She did not bother to explain to Dr. Falk that it was a matter of indifference to her where charity was exercised; she had to keep German interests in play.

At this point Herr von Leipziger interposed, saying: "But Mother Frances, you ought to yield a little and submit." He got the reply: "No, in this matter I would lay my own head on the block, and so would every other Sister, rather than yield an inch." When he got this answer Dr. Falk was angry, as his personal visit had been in his eyes an honor to Mother Frances. As he perceived that he could accomplish nothing, he left soon afterwards. He saw from Frances's flashing eyes and the set of her mouth that she meant all she had said. He also knew that he had received a moral defeat. He was not going to press his point as there was a danger of Frances and the Sisters going elsewhere.

The trio of officials went on next to St. Vincent's Hospital, which was under the charge of the Sisters of Charity. There the Superior, a simple, very warm-hearted old lady, greeted Dr. Falk most cordially, taking his hand in both of hers and saying, "You will let us stay here, won't you?" To this question the Minister — whose anger had somewhat subsided, and had been replaced by humor — answered: "*I* am unable to do anything; you will have to settle that point with Mother Frances." Upon this Herren von Leipziger and Stoeveken explained that these Sisters were in no way subject to Mother Frances. So Dr. Falk replied: "Well, that changes the case completely; so don't worry." He already knew that many religious orders had left Germany, and he feared a general exodus. Probably, too, he and Bismarck had by now perceived that they had misjudged the hold of the Catholic

Church over its adherents and were looking for a graceful way of relaxing their persecution.

Frances had, however, been definitely told by Dr. Falk that the begging of the Sisters would not be countenanced. So on September 1st, she wrote a long letter to the Empress, as one who "but a short time ago showed love and sympathy for the poor children of St. Francis and their unworthy representative." She went on to say that she felt it her duty, after replying to some of the questions contained on the official form, to refuse to reply to those that concerned the religious life. She added that, should her view of the matter be erroneous, she was willing to give the requested answers. She did not mention to Augusta the possibility of going into voluntary exile, lest that should seem a threat. Instead she likened herself to a "child making a mother's heart the depository of her little troubles." She was sure that the Empress would do all that lay in her power to secure a mitigation of the enforcement of the laws.

The Empress in fact did not personally have much power, but she was able to consult those in administrative positions, so that on September 12th, she got her intimate friend the Countess Hacke to write to Frances saying: "New orders concerning the investigations to be made have been given to the authorities. You will receive them in a few days. According to these there is at present no question of restricting or subordinating the Orders relative to their temporal administration, and concerning governmental supervision no determination has been arrived at so far. The removal of Sisters from one house to another is not subject to approval; a monthly notice of the changes is sufficient. As these concessions were obtained principally at the instance of the Empress, Her Majesty hopes that you, dear Mother Superior, will readily yield to the authorities, as they will not insist on anything except what the law compels them to demand."

This was very kind of the Empress, yet one suspects that in making some concessions professedly in deference to Augusta,

Dr. Falk had also been actuated by what had happened in July during his interview with Frances. She was able to write to the Countess a few days later that Herr von Leipziger had paid her another visit to inform her that she might send out or recall Sisters as she wished, and she gladly undertook to comply with the regulations concerning this. She had to say, however: "Although I could not accede as he wished to other requests of the official, I nevertheless hope to God that the matter will be settled according to her Majesty's desire. Affairs have already improved so much that the continuation of our branch houses is assured, for which we cannot sufficiently thank her Majesty. I think we shall also succeed in retaining the Motherhouse without injury to its internal organization."

Something certainly had been gained — enough to make it possible for the Sisters to remain in Germany, though not by any means all that they wished for. Frances, when she petitioned Herr Leipziger for permission to receive new members, was refused. Moreover, the activities of the Sisters were restricted in various ways. The seven Sisters who worked in the prison were told that they would have to withdraw. And in November notice was served that Dr. Falk had really meant what he had said about the collections: they were to cease, cease absolutely, which was a very heavy blow to endure. Early in the new year the charity kitchens were also closed, because they could not be maintained after begging was prohibited. And the asylum the Sisters had maintained for a small group of fallen women was constituted a state institution, although the Sisters were left in charge. As for the training homes for domestic servants, they also had to be given up; but again there was a subterfuge: some Catholic lay women were officially put in charge, but the Sisters were permitted to remain, on condition that they had no authority and lived in a different part of the house — presumably so as not to contaminate the girls whom they had been trying to educate in virtue and domestic science. Yet Falk and Leipziger probably thought they had made generous concessions and may actually have gone as far as they could. The application of the May Laws varied from place to place, much being left to the discretion of local officials. Though Frances was hampered in her activities, these were not entirely disrupted. Even Dr. Falk was restrained to some extent by his knowledge that she was a friend of Augusta's — by that fact and Frances's own threats that if things were made too hard for her, she would transplant all the Sisters to the United States.

Frances certainly was more fortunate than Clara Fey, though as Clara's was an educational work it of course fell more directly under the operation of the new laws. At Clara's request Frances went early in 1876 to Berlin to interview the Empress. Clara could not make this journey herself on account of the state of her health; moreover she counted upon Frances's being able to accomplish more than she could with her friend Augusta. But this time, though the Empress was most sympathetic, there was little or nothing she could do, as the primary object of the May Laws had been to suppress all Catholic schools by imposing upon them conditions that no Catholic school could accept. Clara Fey and her Congregation therefore had to migrate to Holland.

A factor that should be borne in mind in all this is that the Rhineland — though it was mainly Catholic in population (at least nominally) — was one of the strongholds of the so-called Liberalism that had entered into a kind of alliance on some questions with the Independent Conservative Party of Bismarck, as against the ultra-Conservative landowners of Eastern Prussia. In their dislike of the *Junkers* the Liberals forgot all else. From this they too easily passed to an acceptance of the Bismarckian centralization, and in some cases were so worked upon as to become anticlerical. So fierce was the mood of the hour that Frances, when writing to her American Vicar on October 26, 1873, says: "You can scarcely imagine, dear Sister, with what scorn and hatred people sometimes regard one or other of the Sisters; in the trains, in the cities, and even in the open country one can observe it. Here in Aachen just recently in broad daylight a Sister was struck over the head with an umbrella; that happened to Sister Ludovica; two ribs of the umbrella were bent."

The disturbances of the time made impossible an important part of the normal government of the Congregation. Writing to the Sisters in the United States in 1873, Frances announced that the general chapter had been postponed until Pentecost of the following year. She added: "Who knows what will happen before Pentecost? Perhaps we may even have to leave for America, and a meeting there would proceed in an entirely different manner." As we are aware, Frances did manage to hang on, but she had to postpone the chapter again to 1875, and as in that year the situation was no better, it was feared that the journeying of a number of Sisters to Aachen might provoke some incident, so the plan was devised of having all those eligible to vote — whether in the German branch houses or the United States — send in their ballots in sealed envelopes. These were to be opened in the presence of the Commissary of the archdiocese, his assistant, Frances, and her councillors.

The postponement of the election had meant that Frances had to serve as Superior General for two years beyond her canonical term. She thought that quite enough, so that when she was elected again, she said: "I cannot and I dare not accept. The term is six years and I shall not live so long. Moreover, I must now consult the welfare of my soul and prepare for death. The Most Reverend Archbishop is aware of this, for I made a general confession to him before the election." Neither the remonstrances of the Commissary nor the tears of the Sisters would move her; she remained firm in her decision.

Some of the Sisters went to her privately with their appeals. Old Sister Josepha, who was very dear to Frances because of her goodness and simplicity, begged, "Oh, Mother, do receive us again for your children!" When Frances still refused, Josepha said, "How can you say that; in these troubled times you are like a soldier deserting during the time of war." To which Frances smilingly answered, "But I do not desert you; I am with you."

What did shake her was when a Sister Clara who was sick in bed, but apparently not seriously ill, conjured her to accept election and told her, "I have offered myself in sacrifice for the Congregation." When the next morning Sister Clara died, Frances wept bitterly but still would not yield. The Archbishop of Cologne had to write to her saying that she must not decline office: "This is my conviction, and the declaration of my will. What would you say of a shepherd who left his flock in the hour of attack?" Then she gave way, but was consoled when a little while afterwards she dreamed that her Assistant, Sister Joanna, appeared to her saying, "Mother, do not refuse to take the cross upon your shoulders; it is not for long." This coincided with Frances's own presentiment, and her presentiment may have been the origin of the dream, which turned out to be prophetic, though in 1875 she was only fifty-six and, since the cure of her asthma at Lourdes, had been in better health than she had known for five years.

She was, however, worn down by the Kulturkampf, for though she had complete confidence in God as to the outcome — and, one might add, confidence also in Catholic fidelity — she was obliged to have a good many dealings with such people as Dr. Falk and Herr von Leipziger, and her interviews with these gentlemen were often painful and exhausting. It may be that she could not have maintained her ground in Germany — as the Sisters were now forbidden to beg — had it not been for some financial help she received from the United States. Thus on March 10th, 1873, Frances wrote to Sister Vincentia, her Vicar there: "May the good Lord reward you and all the dear Sisters there a thousandfold." Shortly before her death Frances wrote what might be taken as the watchword of the Congregation: "America for Europe, Europe for America; every individual for the individual and all for all."

Though no new ground could be broken in Germany during the period of the Kulturkampf, or any new members received into the Congregation, in the United States the Sisters steadily widened their work. Thus at the end of 1876 there were 113 in perpetual vows, 75 in temporary vows, and 46 novices. A real, if unspectacular advance is indicated.

A pretty incident occurred at the end of 1875 when seven Sisters were about to leave Germany for the United States. Frances, as usual, loaded them all at parting with gifts, and at the last minute she said to Sister Emilie, their leader: "I should like to give you something more to take to America, but I don't know what. Look around and see if you can find anything." Sister Emilie's eye fell on a copper holy-water font that hung beside the door of Frances's office, so she asked for that. The band could hardly have reached Cincinnati when Frances was dead. The font still hangs at the convent entrance to the chapel of the Provincial house at Hartwell.

25

★

The Last Gift

FRANCES SCHERVIER had never been very robust and she had
had several serious illnesses, though all of them, with the
exception of asthma, were of the kind that could be cured
and from which she fairly quickly recovered. The somewhat
nervous state into which she fell when she was in her early
twenties completely passed, to be replaced by a remarkably
serene balance. While her tense condition may have revealed
a physical weakness, the result of a mind too highly charged
working upon her body, it disappeared, whereas the physical
weakness in part remained. Yet with all this there went, except at such rare occasions as she collapsed under her load, a
great deal of vital and intellectual energy. She had been
cured in 1870 of her asthma at Lourdes, and what a burden
was then taken off her shoulders can be estimated properly
only by those who suffer from this disease. The portress at
the Motherhouse used to relate how, from her little room beside the entrance door, she could hear Reverend Mother
wheezing at the other end of the corridor.

But though Frances was cured at the Grotto of Our Lady
she remained sure, though she was then only fifty, that she
did not have long to live. Father Jeiler suggests that this
presentiment may have been caused by the death of two
priests who had been close friends and who had helped her

greatly when, in the face of much opposition, she was in process of founding her Congregation. One of these was the Commissary of the archdiocese of Cologne, Canon Dilschneider, who died of apoplexy on October 9th, 1872. The other was Canon Kloth who died, simply of old age, on July 18th, 1876. But Canon Kloth has to be ruled out in this connection, as Frances's presentiment of approaching death, as we have seen, filled her mind long before his own end. She did indeed write, with the slow dissolution of the Canon before her eyes, on June 27th, 1876: "To see one dying, teaches one how to die . . . Man has nothing to do in this world but prepare for a good death." But death was nothing new to her. Of her own family only she and her eldest brother Henry were now left, and in a community such as hers death was a frequent visitor.

She had tried to refuse office in 1875 because she would not live out her term of six years, and during that year and the one that followed she seems to have been constantly preoccupied with thoughts of death. During the autumn of the year in which she died she said to a Sister, while standing at a window watching the leaves falling from the trees: "Behold the image of life! Only a little while longer, and we too shall go the way of all perishable things. So many around us have fallen off that we are like a leafless tree." Though the sentiment is one that must sometimes have occurred to everybody, with Frances it was not an idle fancy, but a settled conviction. Yet she went on with her work as though sure of another twenty years of useful life.

Looking back upon that time the Sisters saw, or thought that they saw, many manifestations of her presentiment about death. Thus when in early November, 1876, she visited Enghein, in Belgium, where she had established a branch house and had had a novitiate built at Verviers, when it was suggested that she call upon the then celebrated ecstatic Louise Lateau, through whose village they were passing, she said, "No, first I must visit and console my banished children;

they are dearer to me than Louise Lateau." That was taken to mean that she could not afford to spend any time except on essentials. Yet she did visit Mademoiselle Lateau the next day and was impressed, but when she returned to Enghein she showed some compunction, for she told the Sisters, "To spend only half a day with you seemed rather short, when you have made so many sacrifices." Upon parting from them she wept so bitterly that all were moved to tears; they could see that Frances believed she would never see any of them again. And indeed five weeks later she was dead.

Too much, however, might be made of such details. What would be better to stress is that Frances was more kindly than ever, and even playful, during these last months. Nevertheless, a presentiment was read in retrospect into almost everything she said. Thus on November 19th, when she received the profession of 23 novices, she remarked afterwards in the chapter room, "Thanks be to God that you are so far!" It was something that she could have said at any of the professions at which she had presided, and which she probably had said before. This time it was taken to mean "Thank God I've lived long enough to see you in your vows!" But as she may have noticed shadows cross the young faces, she said brightly, to cheer up those whom she feared she had depressed, "Have I nothing for my children?" She had: there was a plate of apples upstairs; she asked the novice mistress to bring them down. As there were not enough apples to go around, they had to be cut in half. She jested in pious style: "Eat, Sisters; the Spouse in the Canticle of Canticles ate apples too!" Half an apple was left over and she was urged to eat this, but she refused, saying to the novice mistress, "No, you must eat it; I am too old."

Old she was not, only in late middle age. But undoubtedly she felt worn by the anxieties she had had to undergo during the Kulturkampf, and though she had won some concessions from Dr. Falk, she could not be sure that the persecution might not be intensified. The tone of her letters during this period shows that she was often depressed. But heavily as the cross of office weighed on her, she accepted it bravely and gladly. The very last entry in her notebook reads: "Whenever during meditation I ask our Lord what He desires of me, I seem to receive the response, 'Love, love.' This is in accord with my inclination since childhood." She could be sure by now that, when she died, there were several Sisters well capable of taking her place in the Congregation she had founded so securely. Her work had been done; she desired only to be with God.

Quite suddenly she came down with a hernia she was not aware that she had. It had undoubtedly been caused by Frances's having lifted weights beyond her strength. As the protrusion, perhaps very slight at first, had gradually enlarged, strangulation had occurred before it was discovered. An immediate operation was necessary.

It was on November 30th, 1876, the Feastday of St. Andrew, that Frances discovered how ill she was. She had been at Mass as usual in the morning and afterwards had helped the Sisters in their duties until the midday dinner. But in the course of the afternoon she was attacked with pains in the stomach and vomiting. She consented to go to bed, but believed that this was an onset of indigestion. Not until a Sister insisted on examining her was an alarming rupture discovered.

Dr. Schervier, Frances's cousin, who had so often given his services to the Sisters (and never with any fee) was summoned, and he called in another doctor named Trost for consultation. Not until the evening of the following day did they reach the decision that only an operation could save her life. Her confessor, the Franciscan Father Bonaventure Wessendorf, said afterwards: "Some time before she had told me that she would not dread fire but the knife; nevertheless she was resolved to it even before the physicians had decided upon its necessity." The operation was then performed, in the Motherhouse, not in a hospital, by the two physicians, in the room dedicated to St. Francis. This took place on December 3rd between 6 and 7 in the evening and in the presence of several of the Sisters.

Just before undergoing the knife she said to the doctors: "I have but one desire — if it is God's holy will — that I shall not die during the operation. Should death come shortly afterwards, I am wholly resigned." When the doctors assured her that she would not die while she was unconscious, she was completely resigned to what had to be done.

The operation, though apparently successful, did not remove the danger. The next day she received Extreme Unction, and Frances said to the priest administering it, "Remember me when I shall be no more." Yet there seemed to be a very fair chance for her recovery, as the drainage from the incision was good. It was observed that every time that she had to be examined, she would first look up at the crucifix beside her bed, then close her eyes and keep them closed, lying perfectly still, until all was over. Then she would open her eyes again, and her first words were those of thanks to the doctors.

A letter to Sister Vincentia, the American Vicar, written by Sister Baptista at the request of Sister Fulgentia on December 6th, says: "The condition of our dear Reverend Mother is satisfactory. Her days and nights are fair, and this the doctors think encouraging, although she is by no means out of danger . . . She occupies St. Francis's Room and is nursed there by Sisters Fulgentia, Agnes and Severina. The doctors say that Mother must have been suffering from the hernia a long time, though she probably had not known about it or felt it, and hence said nothing."

About the eighth day after the operation the Sisters' anxiety was increased when they noticed how Frances was growing more languid and weaker. Yet they continued to hope, believing that this was due to her having taken so little nourishment, and thousands of devoted friends, not only in Aachen, but all through the Rhineland, were praying for the recovery of their stricken benefactress. When, however, on December 13th, about midnight the weakness suddenly became much more pronounced, the watchers, Sisters Anna and Severina, were greatly alarmed. Frances herself was aware of the change, for a little later she asked, "Will there be time enough to give the Sisters my blessing after five o'clock?" A little later she said again: "I can remain with you no longer; bid the Sisters farewell in my name." The Superior of the house and another Sister were at once summoned, and they with the chaplain and the nurses recited the prayers for the dying around the bed. Dr. Schervier had been sent for and when he arrived at 2.30 he found his cousin's life ebbing fast. The chaplain, wishing to know whether Frances was still conscious, said in a loud voice, "Praised be Jesus and Mary, now and for all eternity!" to which she responded, faintly but quite distinctly, "Amen!" One of the Sisters present then urged her to bless all the members of the Congregation, wherever they were, and to this she said, "Yes." Sister Fulgentia then asked her to pardon them all and once more there came the single word "Yes." With the uttering of these monosyllables she had exhausted herself. From then on she sank slowly and gently, like a fire that is going out. About 4 in the morning she ceased to breathe. It was Thursday, December 14, 1876.

During this last illness Frances never once expressed a wish of any kind. Her serenity and peace, though remarkable, were what might have been expected of her, but those who saw her during those two weeks thought it a little strange that she seemed to have no concern about the affairs of the Congregation. She asked no questions, and she gave no orders; the explanation is that from the beginning she believed that she was going to die and so could look upon her work as accomplished. She had resigned everything to God, willing to live if He chose, but not expecting to live. When a priest who visited her suggested that she pray with St. Martin, "Lord, if I am still necessary to Thy flock, I shall not refuse the labor," she could not quite agree, saying, "As I am quite easy about myself, so I am quite easy about the Congregation." She told some of the Sisters, "If I do leave you, I shall nevertheless remain with you. Struggle as I have struggled, then we shall all meet above." When Bishop Laurent called to see her, she confided, "Formerly I used to fear death, but now I am perfectly resigned. If I have to go to purgatory, I shall not mind it; I have deserved it."

When she had consented to the operation, Frances had felt that she was, in effect, resigning her office, which was why she took no further interest in the direction of affairs. But she by no means gave up her interest in the poor whom she had spent her life to help and save. She inquired what was being done for some needy families she had befriended and was satisfied only when told that they were being looked after. Her thoughts ran on a little further: "What," she asked, "would become of these poor people if they should one day be in my present condition, and had nobody to come to their aid?"

To anybody who did her the smallest of services she was all gratitude, especially to Dr. Schervier, who was doing his best to draw her back from the edge of the grave. "Dear doctor," she said to him, "I ought to be completely forgetful of myself when I think of all the trouble I am causing you." All those around her had anguish in their hearts at not being able to do more. But for Frances Schervier death came in its mildest, even its tenderest form. She was suffering no pain, though previously she had suffered a good deal. Gently and quietly, without convulsion, conscious almost to the last moment, she slipped away.

Her body lay in state in the chapter room from the Thursday on which she died until Monday, December 18th, when it was buried, and there could have been very few people in Aachen who did not go to see one whom they had long venerated as a saint, to pray for her, and to pray to her. It was a veritable pilgrimage, and nothing of the sort had been seen in the city before, as it overflowed with the many visitors from other places, especially those where Frances had branch houses. The intense grief of all, clergy and Sisters and lay folk alike, was plainly evident, as they filed by her coffin and gazed sadly on the worn features, so sweetly serene under the wreath of flowers that had been placed on her head. Many there could remember her radiant happiness on a day many years before, when she had worn another wreath of flowers on the joyous occasion of receiving her habit as a Sister of the Poor of St. Francis. So large were the crowds that a system had to be devised, with a queue forming at the convent entrance and leaving by a rear door. People brought rosaries and crucifixes with which they touched her. At first the folding doors of the chapter room were left open, but as the throngs increased these had to be closed, and nobody except relatives and close friends and the clergy and the Sisters could see her except through the glass.

The funeral cortege resembled a triumphal procession. A band of children led the way, followed by a group of singers. After them walked various religious societies, the members of the Third Order of St. Francis, and, behind the hearse, almost every priest of the city and representatives of the clergy of Cologne. Then came the members of Frances's own Congregation and those of the Poor Child Jesus, relatives and friends, government officials and the Mayor of Aachen. Seventy wreaths and four palms were carried by children, and on the coffin lay a cross of white immortelles embedded in moss, sent by the Empress Augusta and placed there in her name by Canon Count von Spee.

Some of the prominent men of the city had wished the requiem to be in the Aachenerdom, for they said that Mother Frances belonged not only to her own congregation but to all Aachen. This plan was abandoned in favor of a series of requiems, each in a different church. As the procession went on its way every bell in the city tolled her passing. On the day following her funeral a member of the body of aldermen, as they sat in session, rose and delivered an oration upon her. He said truly: "She had made it the object of her life to minister to the poor, to live with the poor, to devote herself to the poor." He moved that the council vote their condolences by standing. This motion was seconded by the Burgomaster.

Frances Schervier's body was first buried, in accordance with the law, in the general cemetery. But as the Sisters dearly wished to have the mortal remains of their Foundress at the Motherhouse they petitioned the government in 1877, through Mother Fulgentia, Frances's first successor as Superior General, but the petition was refused, though the Empress used all her influence to have it granted. However a number of important people continued to work to have this brought about, so that on May 26, 1880, permission for the translation was at last granted, on condition that everything be done privately with no public demonstration.

On July 13th, under the direction of the architect and the supervision of the police, a vault nine feet deep was begun in front of the altar in the Sisters' chapel and beneath the sanctuary, but took longer to excavate than was expected, as some of the massive stones of the ancient city walls were struck against. By the 22nd, however, the vault was ready.

The exhumation of the coffin and its removal to the Motherhouse took place that night. Everything was done with such secrecy that even the driver of the truck which was to carry the coffin did not have any idea as to what purpose he had been engaged. A few Alexian and Franciscan Brothers did what was necessary, and close on to three in the morning of the 23rd Dr. Schervier arrived. The Sisters had been up half an hour waiting for the body of their beloved Foundress to arrive. They received it in silence and with mingled emotions, with grief of their loss renewed, and with joy that they had her remains among them at last. The coffin was carried to the chapter room, and there, surrounded by candles and flowers, it reposed until the hour of entombment. For this service invitations had been sent to Father Fey, to the Provincial of the Franciscans, and the Superior General of the Franciscan Brothers, as well as a number of relatives and friends, among them Henry Schervier, the sole surviving member of Frances's immediate family. At eight the remains were consigned to the vault with the customary rites. There was one departure from the usual: Mother Fulgentia, acting on a sudden impulse, picked up a basket of roses and, signing to the Sisters to approach, gave each a few petals to strew on the coffin. The relatives and friends of Frances did the same, and the Chief of Police, who was present in his official capacity to see that there was no demonstration, reached across three other people, to get some petals to strew. The vault was then closed with a slab, inscribed with Frances's name and the dates of her birth and death and the translation. A tablet was set in the wall above her.

The matter was not yet quite disposed of. When in 1893 the Motherhouse was transferred to the Lindenplatz, a petition was addressed to the new Emperor, William II, and on August 22nd of that year his permission to make another translation reached the Sisters. It prescribed that a hermetically sealed vault be provided, that the translation be carried out between nine in the evening and five in the morning, and that there be no exposition of the body or any religious ceremonies. This time the burial was at the Epistle side of the altar, near the choir of the Recluses.

A third time the body of Frances was transferred. For when in 1938 the provinces had been constituted and the original Motherhouse of St. Clare had been made the Generalate of the Congregation, Mother Rufina, who then held office, obtained permission from the Sacred Congregation of Religious in Rome and from the civil authorities, to make another translation, though the Holy See ordinarily does not allow the tomb of one whose cause for beatification has been introduced to be opened. This took place on March 31, 1939, the Feast of the Seven Dolors, and in the presence of Auxiliary Bishop Huenermann. Above the vault in which she now reposes and where she is likely to remain until the beatification, which now seems probable, is what looks like an undecorated sarcophagus which is set on a base three feet high. It is in a kind of mortuary chapel and on the further wall is a painting which is a reproduction, with some modification, of the photograph taken in New York in 1863. Everything is very simple and in excellent artistic taste.

The cause for beatification of Frances Schervier opened with the Ordinary — otherwise the Episcopal and Informative — Process in her own diocese, that of Cologne. The hearings were held at Aachen, beginning on October 24th, 1913, in the presence of Archbishop Felix von Hartmann and the Postulator, Monsignor Felix Fels. Other sessions of this Process were conducted in Columbus, Ohio, in 1919, in Cincinnati the following year, and in New York in 1921. The Ordinary Process was concluded in Cologne on May 30, 1923, after which the documents in the case were sent to Rome. A decree of approval of the writings of Frances Schervier was published there on February 28, 1928.

A further step was taken when the petitioners requested Very Reverend Antonius Maria Santarelli of the Order of St. Francis, Postulator General, to handle the case. Another Franciscan, Father Fortunatus Scipioni, succeeded him in this office. In 1934 a Vice-Postulator was appointed for Germany, Father Benno Paffrath, O.F.M., and after his death in 1948 he was succeeded by Father Peter Lohe, O.F.M.; and in 1940 Father Roland Burke of the Friars Minor was appointed Vice-Postulator for the United States.

In 1934 the Apostolic Process was introduced with a decree signed on May 8th by Pope Pius XI. On January 12, 1935, a decree of "reputation for sanctity" (*in genere*) was issued by the Sacred Congregation of Rites. The Apostolic Process in Aachen continued from July, 1935, to July, 1937, including sessions at Bleyerheide, in the diocese of Roermond in Holland, the place where Frances had once thought of transferring her activities.

At this date steps are under way for the consideration of the following points: did this Servant of God practice virtue in the highest degree and was this virtue signalized by miracles? Should the decision regarding Frances Schervier's virtues and miracles be favorable, then the *Decretum de Tuto*, the Papal declaration that sets the matter beyond doubt may be looked for. It is the essential preliminary to beatification.

As to the many remarkable occurrences which are constantly being reported as due to the intercession of Frances Schervier, nothing shall be said here, not even of those cases cited by Jeiler or by her biographers. Whether or not these were actually miracles is something for the Holy See to determine. Similarly, whether or not the unquestionable virtues of Frances Schervier reach the heroic degree called sanctity is a matter to be left to the Congregation of Rites in Rome. The purpose of this biography will have been sufficiently achieved if it has told the story of one who, at the very least, must be described as an extraordinary woman.

BIBLIOGRAPHICAL NOTE

THE PRIMARY, but by no means definitive, biography of Frances Schervier is the one by the Franciscan Father Ignatius Jeiler which was published in German in 1893. The English translation, by Bonaventure Hammer, O.S.F., was published at St. Louis in 1895. Jeiler freely used the two fragmentary autobiographies Frances wrote and almost always quotes her very words. He also drew upon her notebook, her letters, and the Annals of the Congregation at Aachen. I have drawn upon all these sources at second hand, but it is so obvious that Father Jeiler was a perfectly honest man and a scholar that I feel little disadvantage at not having seen the originals.

There are other published biographies of Frances Schervier, all of them based on Father Jeiler's work. Among these are *Im Rufe der Heiligkeit* [in the odor of sanctity], by Wendelin Meyer, O.F.M. (Paderborn, 1925), and *Mutter Franziska Schervier* [Mother Frances Schervier], by Bruno Gossens, O.M.Cap. (Munich, 1932). I have been supplied with an English translation (in manuscript) supposedly by Father Ferdinand Gruen, O.F.M., of the first of these. This same translator's name appears on the title page of an English condensation of Gossens' book, published in New York in 1935. In 1946 were published a brief biography of Frances Schervier and a kind of anthology of her writings, arranged in calendar style, both by Sister M. Pauline of the Sisters of the Poor of St. Francis. *Mother Frances Schervier* (1945), by the Most Reverend Amleto Giovanni Cicognani, and *Mother Frances Schervier* (1946), by the Most Reverend John T. McNicholas, O.P., are two pamphlets. These four items, the brief biography, the anthology, and the two pamphlets, were brought out privately by the Congregation and did not circulate much beyond it.

To complete my list of printed sources, I should mention Anna Shannon McAllister's *In Winter We Flourish: Life and Letters of Sarah Peter* (New York, 1939) and the earlier work by Mrs. Peter's daughter-in-law, Margaret R. King, *Memoirs of the Life of Mrs. Sarah Peter* (Cincinnati, 2 vols., 1889). There are also *The Life of Mother Clara Fey* (London, 1923), compounded of two separate works in German by Ignaz Watterott, O.M.I., and Otto Pfulff, S.J., and John H. Lamott's *History of the Archdiocese of Cincinnati* (New York and Cincinnati, 1921). All these, of course, like Baedeker's *The Rhine* (Coblenz, London, and Edinburgh, 1864) and like the biographical, historical, and topographical material I found in *The Catholic Encyclopedia* and *The Encyclopaedia Britannica*, are of only secondary importance and vary considerably in usefulness. Also in this category is Monsignor G. H. Doane's *To and From the Passion Play of 1871* (Boston, 1872), which contains a chapter on Aachen and its famous relics, religious and otherwise.

By far the most valuable of the manuscript sources available to me were the four volumes, running to about 1,300 closely written pages, that compromise the American Annals of the Congregation, which are kept at Cincinnati. The first two of these, put together in 1896, were translated from German documents which include many letters written by Frances herself. The second two volumes, covering the years 1867 to 1876, are in the script of Sister M. Pauline, the author of the two works already cited. Sister Pauline has also translated for me over a hundred other letters written by Frances — most of them to the Sisters in America, but some to friends and relatives in Germany. She, in conjunction with Sister M. Paula, the Provincial Secretary at Cincinnati, has been most helpful, supplying me with detailed information, all very clear and to the point, in answer to my innumerable questions. Father Roland Burke, O.F.M., the Vice Postulator of the cause of Frances Schervier has given me a full account of the process to date.

Sister Pauline has also made a translation of those passages from the Annals of the Motherhouse which were not drawn upon by Jeiler, but unfortunately carried this down only to 1866. It did not, however, matter a great deal, for the American Annals contain many facts about the Kulturkampf that were not to be found in Jeiler and provided a better account than he did of Frances Schervier's last illness.

I have been furnished with a careful transcript made by Sister John M. Berchmans, the Secretary General of the Congregation, of the Statutes of 1851, and I had before me also a manuscript copy of the Constitutions of 1865, as revised by Cardinal von Geissel, the Archbishop of Cologne. The *Rule of the Third Order of Our Holy Father St. Francis, together with the Constitutions of the Congregation of the Sisters of the Poor of St. Francis*, which bears no date, is a translation of the German Constitutions which received the imprimatur of the Archbishop of Cologne in 1912. Another volume, published in Cincinnati in 1933 with the imprimatur of its Archbishop, was used by the Sisters from January 3, 1934 to June 1, 1943; it bears the title of *The Rule of the Third Order Regular of the Seraphic Father Saint Francis and the Constitutions of the Congregation of the Sisters of the Poor of St. Francis*. It was superseded by a book of the same title approved by the Sacred Congregation for Religious on July 2, 1940.

To these should be added *The Franciscan Message in Authentic Texts* (St. Louis, 1936), which contains, among other items, the Rule of the Friars Minor and the encyclical letter of Pope Leo XIII, *Auspicato*, of September, 1882, on St. Francis and the Third Order. I have also been given printed copies of the decrees issued by the Holy See in May, 1934, concerning the Process at Cologne, and rather lengthy statements regarding the cause made by the Postulator, Dr. Felix Fels and by Father Antonius M. Santarelli, O.F.M., Postulator General. These, however, do not contain much, if anything, that is not already in Jeiler and are, like Meyer's book, a consideration of Frances Schervier's virtues. Father Jeiler's book is, in short, the basis of everything. It has very solid merits, but it is a bit stolid and (in places) incomplete. It is for this reason that I have been asked to produce a new biography for the English-speaking world.

It would be hardly possible (and certainly unnecessary) to list all the documents with which I have been supplied. But mention should be given to the mimeographed *Bulletin* and *Diary* sent to the United States during 1947–49 from some of the Sisters at the Generalate in Rome. These cast many indirect lights on the subject. I have been given excerpts from Dr. Josef Gerard Rey's *Die Familie Schervier und deren Sippen* [the Schervier family and its relatives] a book sumptuously published at Aachen in 1936. It is by a second cousin of Frances Schervier and begins a series designed to deal with the ecclesiastical history of that city.

That we have any autobiographical writings from the pen of Frances Schervier is due to an accident, or rather to a pious trick, of which I cannot say that I quite approve, serviceable though it has been to me. Frances, under obedience to her confessor, who was instigated by her friend Father Lambert Bethmann, told in the first person, but most reluctantly, the story of her interior life from childhood to early womanhood. When this confessor died she begged his successor so pitifully to return her manuscript that he did not have the heart to refuse. But first he had a copy of it made, so that she died in the belief that everything had been destroyed. She wrote this some time after 1858 (the year in which she first met Father Bethmann) and set aside for her task two hours every Saturday, on which day she had a Mass said that she might tell nothing but the strictest truth. After the death of Cardinal von Geissel in 1866, his successor, Archbishop Melchers (who became a Cardinal in his turn), gave her another obedience — that of telling how her Congregation came to be founded. She handed her manuscript to a Sister to be copied for the Archbishop, but was so abashed that for several weeks she avoided that Sister or, when she had to meet her, cast down her eyes. This second fragment was, however, in the third person. Without these writings we would know hardly anything about Frances's early life.

I have seen some of Frances Schervier's letters in her own handwriting, but I could not read much in them because the script, though beautiful and flowing, was, partly for that reason, all the more difficult for me, as it resembled no German script that I have seen. But I might as well confess that, though I did once have a reading knowledge of German — acquired for my Ph.D. degree — what little I once knew has long since evaporated. This means that several of the Sisters at Cincinnati have had an extra burden thrown on their shoulders. I can only hope that I have made a not too inadequate use of what they have so bountifully provided.

Since I have American readers mainly in mind, I have emphasized the activities of Frances and her Sisters in the United States. My aim has been to produce a not too long biography, so I have freely used the principle of selection, one which must always operate if one's work is not to become unwieldy and amorphous. Yet I think that I have truly depicted this very remarkable woman — or at least that I have done my best to do so — and that her character and the nature of her work have emerged in the pages preceding. This bibliographical note is offered only to authenticate what I have written.